A
LITERARY
HISTORY
OF
SOUTHERN
CALIFORNIA

CHRONICLES OF CALIFORNIA

California Pictorial: A History in Contemporary
Pictures, 1786 to 1859, with Descriptive Notes on
Pictures and Artists *by Jeanne Van Nostrand and
Edith M. Coulter*

Gold is the Cornerstone *by John Walton Caughey*

Land in California: The Story of the Mission Lands,
Ranchos, Squatters, Mining Claims, Railroad Grants,
Land Scrip, Homesteads *by W. W. Robinson*

A Self-governing Dominion: California, 1849–1860
by William Henry Ellison

Chronicles of California

A LITERARY HISTORY OF SOUTHERN CALIFORNIA

FRANKLIN WALKER

Berkeley and Los Angeles, 1950
UNIVERSITY OF CALIFORNIA PRESS

UNIVERSITY OF CALIFORNIA PRESS
BERKELEY AND LOS ANGELES, CALIFORNIA

CAMBRIDGE UNIVERSITY PRESS
LONDON, ENGLAND

PRINTED IN THE UNITED STATES OF AMERICA
BY THE VAIL-BALLOU PRESS, INC., BINGHAMTON, N.Y.

To

Imogene Bishop Walker

Acknowledgments

My primary indebtedness in preparing this book is to the Henry E. Huntington Library for providing me with a grant out of the fund given by the Rockefeller Foundation for the study of the Southwest. Individuals who have aided me have been numerous; among them I am particularly indebted for information and advice to Mr. Gregg J. Layne, Mr. Frederick Webb Hodge, Mrs. Charles Francis Saunders, Mr. Fulmer Mood, Mr. Howard Swan, Mr. Lawrence C. Powell, Mr. Lee Shippey, Mr. George R. Stewart, Mr. James D. Hart, Mr. James Clark, and Mr. W. W. Robinson.

I also wish to thank Mr. John W. Caughey and Mr. Robert G. Cleland for reading the work in manuscript and making many helpful suggestions, Mrs. Harriet Letroadec for countless favors in preparing the book for the press, and Mrs. Imogene Bishop Walker for very extensive help in revising the study.

The Huntington Library has granted permission to draw on the manuscript sources cited in the bibliography for information and to quote from letters by Helen Hunt Jackson and Charles D. Willard. Acknowledgments are here made to the following individuals and publishers for permission to make short quotations from material on which they hold the copyright: Charles Scribner's Sons for John C. Van Dyke's *The Desert* and *The Letters of Henry James,* edited by Percy Lubbock; Harper and Brothers for Zane Grey's *The Rainbow Trail* and Mary Austin's *Lost Borders;* The Macmillan Company for William E. Smythe's *The Conquest of Arid America;* Appleton-Century-Crofts for Harold Bell Wright's *The Winning of Barbara Worth;* Houghton Mifflin Company for Mary Austin's *Earth Horizon, The Land of Little Rain, The Flock,* and *The Lands of the Sun,* and for Margaret Collier Graham's *Stories of the Foot-hills* and *The Wizard's Daughter;* the executors of the Mary Austin estate for Mary Austin's *The Ford;* Juanita Miller for *The Poetical Works of Joaquin Miller; The American Magazine* for "Breaking Through," by Zane Grey; L. C. Page and Company for George Wharton James's *California;* Myron Brinig for *The Flutter of an Eyelid;* Wallace Hebberd for William Lewis Manly's *Death Valley in '49;* The Huntington Library for Glenn S. Dumke's *The Boom of the Eighties in Southern California* and Robert G. Cleland's *The Cattle on a Thousand Hills;* J. B. Lippincott for John Vance Cheney's *At the Silver Gate;* Margaret M. McHale for John Steven McGroarty's *Just California;* Carey McWilliams for his *Southern California Country;* Prentice-Hall for John W. Caughey's *California; The Sunset Magazine* for "The Red Car of Empire," by Rufus Steele; Jacob Zeitlin for Phil Townsend Hanna's *Libros Californianos;* Horace A. Vachell for *Fellow-Travellers* and *The Model of Christian Gay;* and Peter B. Kyne for *The Long Chance.*

FRANKLIN WALKER

Mills College
Oakland, California

Contents

Illustrations

Prologue

SOUTHERN CALIFORNIA has come to be accepted as a specific American phenomenon, a clearly defined region that, in the popular imagination, has its distinctive stereotypes and curious folkways. This land stretches from the hill at San Simeon on which William Randolph Hearst perches in his baroque castle, like another Saint Simeon Stylites on his pillar, to the little Mexican border town of Tijuana where tourists gape at colored peasant-ware and lose money at roulette. In the other direction it reaches from the beaches of Santa Catalina Island, where vacationists gaze through glass-bottomed boats at green anemones and purple sea urchins, to the fantastic dunes bordering the Yuma Desert which have been pictured as the Sahara in *Beau Geste* and countless other cinema epics.

To the reader of detective novels, Southern California's capital is Los Angeles, peopled with slick lawyers at odds with the D.A.'s office. To the student, its heart is the Huntington Library with its wealth of manuscripts and rare books. To the sociologist, its focal point is the Negro quarter on lower Central Avenue, or the cantaloupe farms of Imperial Valley. To the health seeker, its haven is the hill country back of Santa Barbara, the beach at Coronado, or the sparkling desert at Palm Springs. And to the movie-goer, its lodestone and symbol is Hollywood. The attitude toward the region ranges all the way from that of the scoffers like Myron Brinig, who described Los Angeles as "a middle-aged obese woman from somewhere in the Middle West, lying naked in the sun. As she sips from a glass of buttermilk and bites off chunks of hamburger sandwich, she reads Tagore to the music of Carrie Jacobs Bond," to that of the idolators like Hubert Howe Bancroft, who wrote of California in glowing terms: "A winterless earth's end perpetually refreshed by ocean, a land surpassed neither by the island grotto of Calypso, the Elysian fields of Homer, nor the island Valley of Avalon seen by King Arthur in his dying thought."

The purpose of this book is to study the development of Southern California by examining the literature dealing with the region. The term "region" is not here used arbitrarily; geographers and physical anthropologists have long since concluded that Southern California constitutes a physiographic and climatic area distinct in its characteristics. The heart of the region is an "island in the land" lying south of the Tehachapi Mountains and west of the Peninsula Range, a plain between the mountains and the sea, a reclaimed semidesert which is now rapidly becoming one vast metropolitan community under the hegemony of Los Angeles. Southern California also includes the back country of the mountains and desert which ring the Los Angeles plain from Point Arguello to the undeveloped wastes of Baja California. To the northwest the region extends to the southern end of the Santa Lucias, where the folded valleys shift in direction from north-south to east-west. In the northeast the desert thrusts far up into Nevada and Utah, back of the Sierra Nevada, with the once-fertile Owens Valley lying between Mount Whitney, the highest, and Death Valley, the lowest spot in the United States. Owens Valley debouches into the vast and sterile Mojave Desert, south of which the bastion continues with the other deserts of the Colorado River basin, with Coachella and Imperial valleys lying as isolated garden spots in a general wasteland that swings west through Mexico to the breakers of the Pacific.

The land area which lies within these boundaries contains more than sixty thousand square miles, a terrain bigger than England and almost equal to the combined New England states. Although much of it is wasteland—either as mountains or as desert—and all of it except the steep mountain slopes receives so little rainfall that it is classified as arid or semiarid, this region has come to support a surprisingly large population. The southern part of the state long lagged behind the north, but during the boom of the 'eighties and thereafter settlers arrived in such numbers that by 1925 the majority of Californians were living in the south. It is anticipated that the 1950 census will reveal that almost six of the estimated ten million Californians will be found in the area under discussion. This is a population nearly as great as that of Sweden and considerably greater than the populations of either Scotland, Ireland, or Norway. Whether there will in time develop among these people a civilization which, as one critic has grandiloquently prophesied, will make it "the most splendid center of genuine culture and enlightenment on this continent" is a matter for endless conjecture and debate. It is certain, however, that, as time goes on, knowledge of the roots of culture in this area will become increasingly important. Most of these roots, of course, lie elsewhere than in Southern California. The people of the region have almost all come from across the mountains and the desert—or the ocean—and have brought their own bits of America or Europe or Asia with them. Thus, a study of the literature of Southern California is to a very large extent a study of transplantation. The problem is to find out how outsiders viewed the society during its development and how newcomers looked upon it after they had joined it. Naturally, both views changed as time brought new patterns.

Because Southern California was almost as empty as a tennis ball until seventy years ago, few of its writers were native-born or even reached California before they were adults. Nor is there any ground for assuming that they changed fundamentally after their arrival. Thus, Ella Sterling Cummins' definition, "A California writer is one who was born in California—or else one who was reborn in California," is essentially misleading. Better is the comment quoted by David Starr Jordan: "A Western man is an Eastern man who has had some additional experiences." The writers discussed in this volume are the ones who had something interesting or significant to say about Southern California, whether they visited for only a month or were born in Riverside and buried at Forest Lawn. That they were, with few exceptions, indifferent craftsmen does not detract seriously from the value of their writings as examples of the cultural trends in the region.

In examining the writings of Americans from the time that they first reached Southern California, when it was held by the Spaniards, it soon becomes clear that a number of indigenous themes emerged. One of these, developing in three phases, was the contrast between the Spanish and the Yankee ways of doing things. This contrast was particularly apparent in the southern part of California, for during the preconquest days this area contained the majority of the Spanish and Mexican Californians, the richest of the ranch properties, and, with the exception of Mission San Carlos at Carmel, the most important and opulent of the Franciscan missions. It is here also that is revealed most clearly the tale of the later displacement of the Spanish Californian in the period when his way of life was viewed with contempt, and it is here, finally, that the story of the creation of a largely synthetic Spanish past after the hidalgo had gone and the greaser had been segregated is seen in its most graphic form. Another subject resulted from the fact that the most numerous and important of the mission Indian groups lived in the south; the tale of their mistreatment and neglect merges rather strangely into the growing interest in the Southwestern pueblo and nomadic

Indians, who were extolled with increasing enthusiasm by Southern California explorers and writers as the area grew more sophisticated. The theme of aridity and its conquest also plays a very prominent part in the literature of Southern California; this subject ranges from the fanciful attempts to create a new Mediterranean culture to the drama of reclaiming and holding the desert. Finally, this is the region of the United States which, because of its late and almost explosive development and the nature of its immigrants, has frequently shown the traits of the nation as a whole, magnified to a degree both spectacular and disturbing. "It is as if you tipped the United States up so all the commonplace people slid down here into Southern California," once remarked Frank Lloyd Wright. The dreams, hopes, prejudices, and fears of the Indiana farmer or the Pennsylvania schoolteacher or the Chicago carpenter transplanted to Southern California were frequently expressed with an emphasis that dramatically illustrated the thinking of the nation as a whole.

These local themes were all well established before World War I and were amplified rather than displaced during the resurgence of American letters in the 'twenties. Such isolation, in fact and in spirit, as the region had known during its youth rapidly disappeared with the increase in speed and ease of communication and the growing nationalization of our culture; yet the older, basic themes lingered on. These were the products of the century-long experience of American settlers, from fur trader to real-estate agent, in a land uniquely qualified to develop unusual cultural traits.

I

Gringo Views of Hidalgo Culture

THREE ANIMALS brought Americans to that stretch of coast known as California, held thinly by the Spaniards in the first half of the nineteenth century. First, the sea otter brought American sailors looking for valuable pelts. After the precious sea otters began to thin out, the visitors turned their attention to hides for the New England shoemakers and tallow for the South American ports, both obtained from the long-horned cattle of the missions. Finally, across the great American desert came the mountain men, looking for beaver, after these valuable animals had become scarce in the Rockies. Ironically, the precursor of these various men of adventure and enterprise was a dead Bostonian, named John Graham, who was unloaded from a Spanish ship in Monterey in 1791 for burial ashore.

The first American ship to anchor in California waters, appropriately named the *Otter,* put in at Monterey in 1796 to take on wood and water and took advantage of the opportunity surreptitiously to disembark ten men and a woman, fugitive convicts from Botany Bay. After this propitious beginning, Yankee visits became more frequent, because the shipmasters soon discovered that, since California was far from Mexico City and still farther from Madrid, business could be carried on with the Californians in spite of Spanish laws forbidding such trade. Since there was a keen demand for Yankee goods in a land with no manufacturers and few artisans, the Americans had little trouble in trading their goods for sea otter pelts. As one skin was worth more than a hundred dollars in barter for oriental silks, teas, and spices in Canton, the triangle trade developed into a most lucrative one for the Yankee skippers.

The Indians, Kanakas, and Aleuts, who hunted the beautiful sea otter with spear and kayak from the Farallones to Magdalena Bay, traded their furs to the Spanish Californians, who frequently sold them to whatever ship came into their harbors, principally the ports of San Francisco, Monterey, and San Diego. Thus it was that the earliest extensive American account of California was written by a Yankee sea captain who, in 1803, fought his way out of San Diego Bay after being apprehended in an attempt to smuggle otter skins out of the country. Captain William Shaler of the *Lelia Byrd* might have succeeded in bribing the commandant at San Diego if the *Alexander,* another New England ship, had not been caught a short while before with a valuable otter-skin cargo, obtained *sans* bribe. As it was, instead of getting his pelts, Shaler had to send his partner, Richard Cleveland, to rescue at gun's point his second mate and two of his men who had gone ashore; he then took his ship out of the narrow Silver Gate, his six starboard three-pounders exchanging shots with the eight nine-pounders of the defending batteries on Point Loma. No serious damage was done by either side, however.

After many other adventures, Shaler returned to the East Coast, where his "Journal of a Voyage from China to the Northwestern Coast of America" was published in 1808 in the *American Register* of Philadelphia. Terse and restricted in imaginative quality, the narrative, which roams from Nootka to Guatemala to Canton, still gives the "feel" of the Yankee skipper of his day. California was but one port of call in a game in which the American skipper was proud to circumvent alien customs regulations wherever he went. The author's attitude toward the Spaniards in California was hostile and contemptuous. They were unprogressive, having neither artisans nor physicians. They had failed to settle more than a narrow strip of coast, and they had no adequate fortifications to defend it from a more enterprising government. The land would fare better if it were held by progressive Americans.

A more detailed account of the visit of the *Lelia Byrd* was to appear many years later, when Shaler's partner, the supercargo of the vessel, Richard J. Cleveland, published his *A Narrative of Voyages and Commercial Enterprises* in 1842. Said to have been an answer to Dana's comments on the rigors of a sailor's life in *Two Years Before the Mast,* the book tells, with infectious enthusiasm, of sailing the seven seas. Cleveland obviously loved to smuggle in the Spanish colonies, feeling that he was helping the benighted colonials, who were being mistreated by their central government. And his spirited account of how he snooped around the battery at San Diego to judge its effectiveness adds a fillip to the tale of the *Lelia Byrd*'s escape.

Shaler and Cleveland were an enterprising pair, and their friendship was most singular. When they bought the *Lelia Byrd* in Hamburg, they tossed coins to see who would be captain and who supercargo, and, in defiance of maritime practice, they sailed the ship on absolutely equal footing. After they had retired from the sea, Shaler was appointed American consul at Havana, and Cleveland accompanied him as his assistant; the two remained partners, however, no matter how the relationship appeared from the outside. But Shaler died of cholera in Havana and left his friend to live twenty-seven years without his companion.

∽∽∽∽

Many other Yankee captains visited the California coast in search not only of otter but also of seal furs, which paid less per skin but earned more in gross revenue, but none left accounts as interesting as those of Shaler and Cleveland. In the meantime, Spanish control of California was superseded by Mexican, the Mexican government placed fewer restrictions on trade in California, and the cattle industry increased in volume. In 1822 the trade for hides and tallow, which flourished for the following two decades, was inaugurated. Since, however, the classic description of this trade, Dana's *Two Years Before the Mast,* did not appear until 1840 and dealt with California in the mid-thirties, our attention shifts for the moment from the sea to the land approach. For in November, 1826, with the arrival of Jedediah Smith and his band of lusty trappers at San Gabriel, a new chapter of the American invasion began.

Jedediah Smith's party of eighteen gaunt and hardy trappers was the vanguard of a gringo invasion of California soil that was as inevitable as it was exciting. For years the mountain men had trapped the Rocky Mountain lakes and rivers and had long since reached the Pacific in the Northwest. Then, as beaver became scarce in the land from Bent's Fort to Pierre's Hole, the trappers turned their activities more and more to the Southwest, where they had earlier been checked by the hostility of the Spaniards. By this time, New Mexico and California having passed into Mexican hands, the strict rules prohibiting trade and hunting by foreigners had been gradually relaxed, either in law or in fact. Consequently, by the mid-twenties the Gila and Colorado basins were thoroughly scoured for beaver. When these were depleted, there were still the rivers and lakes of California to be exploited. In addition, there was the possibility of establishing on the California coast a place of deposit like Astoria, so that skins would not have to be carried overland all the way back to St. Louis. Thus, the mountain men who entered California were driven on by three urges—their traditional interest in exploration, their search for beaver, and their need for easier access to the market.

In spite of the fact that these men numbered in the thousands, there is a dearth of full-bodied autobiographies and memoirs by them. As H. H. Bancroft commented in 1885 in his *History of California,*

It is well, however, to understand at the outset, that respecting the movements of the trappers no record of even tolerable completeness exists or could be expected to exist. After 1826 an army of hunters, increasing from hundreds to thousands, frequented the fur-producing streams of the interior, and even the valleys of California, flitting hither and thither, individuals and parties large or small according to the disposition of the natives, wandering without other motive than the hope of more abundant game, well acquainted with the country, as is the wont of trappers, but making no maps and keeping no diaries. Occasionally they came in contact with civilization east or west, and left a trace in the archives; sometimes a famous trapper and Indian-fighter was lucky enough to fall in with a writer to put his fame and life in print; some of them lived later among the border settlers, and their tales of wild adventure, passing not without modification through many hands, found their way into newspaper print. Some of them still live to relate their memories to me and others, sometimes truly and accurately, sometimes confusedly, and sometimes falsely, as is the custom of trappers like other men.

Consequently, the records that remain are important, and of these the better have special value in the literature of exploration. Pattie's *Narrative* is not only the first but is in some respects the best.

A little more than a year after Jedediah Smith's arrival, the second party of trappers, made up of Sylvester Pattie, his son, James Ohio Pattie, and six others, reached the coast in what is now Baja California and made their way north to San Diego. Misfortune had been principally responsible for their arrival on California soil; while trapping the lower Colorado they had lost their horses to hostile Indians. Hearing that there were Spanish settlements near the mouth of the river, they had floated down the river in improvised canoes but, in inhospitable marshes near the Gulf of California, they had been checked by the tidal bore. After caching their pelts, they had stumbled blindly over the deserts and mountains, hoping for succor; doubtless in addition to other motives was a desire to reach better beaver land and ports where Yankee skippers would buy their furs clandestinely. Their hopes were short-lived, however, for they met with constant hostility from the Californians and on their arrival in San Diego were thrown in jail, where Sylvester subsequently died. James, after six years of picaresque adventures in New Mexico and Spanish California, returned to the States. In New Orleans he met and was befriended by the Honorable J. S. Johnston, United States Senator from Louisiana. He journeyed with Johnston by steamer to Cincinnati, and from him received a letter of introduction to Timothy Flint, who was known for his interest in obtaining trappers' narratives. With Flint, Pattie collaborated in writing a book about his experiences; the story included a vigorous account of Southern California, made forceful by an undying hatred of all things Spanish.

Pattie's book, which appeared six years before Irving's *Bonneville,* thirteen years before Gregg's *Commerce of the Prairies,* and sixteen years before Ruxton's *Adventures in Mexico and the Rocky Mountains,* was titled, grandiloquently, *The Personal Narrative of James O. Pattie, of Kentucky, During an Expedition from St. Louis, through the Vast Regions between That Place and the Pacific Ocean, and Thence Back through the City of Mexico to Vera Cruz, During Journeyings of Six Years; in Which He and His Father, Who Accompanied Him, Suffered Unheard of Hardships and Dangers, Had Various Conflicts with the Indians, and Were Made Captives, in Which Captivity His Father Died; Together with a Description of the Country, and the Various Nations through Which They Passed. Edited by Timothy Flint.* This was the first book of literary merit to deal with the trade to New Mexico, the pursuit of beaver in the Southwest, and the advent of Americans by land in California. Although its accuracy has

been questioned and its spirit criticized, it remains the epic
of the mountain men, perhaps more truly representing their
attitudes, their experiences, and their adventures than any
other book which has appeared on the subject.

The reason that Pattie's *Narrative* turned out so well
possibly was that, for once, the man with the right experiences
met the man with the adequate talent and the two worked
well together. Moreover, both were well qualified for the
task, Pattie even by virtue of his family background. His
grandfather had fought under Benjamin Logan in Kentucky
and under George Rogers Clark in Ohio and had taught
school in Kentucky before becoming a judge; and his father,
Sylvester, had attained some local fame for his bravery in
heading the rangers which held Cap-au-Gris in the Black
Hawk War. According to Flint, the reason for Sylvester Pattie's taking to the Santa Fe trail in 1824 was that, saddened
by the death of his wife, he was without heart for living longer
in a settled community. Leaving seven of his children with
relatives, he set out with his son James, who was fresh from
school, for a new life in the Indian country. And James himself was educated enough to keep a record and understand
much of what he saw. He was intelligent and soon after reaching New Mexico learned Spanish so well that he was later employed by Governor Echeandía of California as both translator and interpreter. He was young enough to love and resent
with passion. And he was lucky enough to be one of the first
Americans to reach Santa Fe, the Gila, and California.

Timothy Flint, his "editor," was a man who had spent most
of his adult life in trying to understand the life of the Ohio,
the Mississippi, and the Missouri valleys, which meant the
West to him; he had roamed extensively in this land and had
listened avidly to the stories of those who had gone beyond
the settlements. He had established one of the first significant
literary journals and had written some of the first novels dealing with the country west of the Alleghenies. Although hard
backwoods conditions and constant personal misfortune had

somewhat dimmed the enthusiasm of this disciple of Chateaubriand, he felt to his death that the opening of the West was a fit subject for an epic, and there is no doubt that he considered Pattie a worthy follower of Daniel Boone, quite able to play a part in an epic; indeed, he called him the Achilles of the West.

Flint accepted young Pattie's account as essentially accurate, stating clearly his reasons for doing so in his preface:

> For, in the literal truth of the facts, incredible as some of them may appear, my grounds of conviction are my acquaintance with the Author, the impossibility of inventing a narrative like the following, the respectability of his relations, the standing which his father sustained, the confidence reposed in him by the Hon. J. S. Johnston, the very respectable senator in congress from Louisiana, who introduced him to me, the concurrent testimony of persons now in this city, who saw him at different points in New Mexico, and the reports, which reached the United States, during the expedition of many of the incidents here recorded.

It is, of course, impossible at this remove to tell how much of Pattie's narrative is based on an actual journal, how much on Pattie's recollections dictated to Flint after his return to Cincinnati, and how much is the result of "editorial additions" by Flint. There is some internal evidence to suggest that a journal was used; and Pattie appears to have been available during the writing, either in Cincinnati or in the near-by Augusta College, which he apparently entered at this time. Timothy Flint minimized his own additions to the story:

> My influence on the narrative regards orthography, and punctuation and the occasional interposition of a topographical illustration, which my acquaintance with the accounts of travellers in New Mexico, and published views of the country have enabled me to furnish. The reader will award me the confidence of acting in good faith, in regard to drawing nothing from my own thoughts. I have found more call to suppress, than to add, to soften, than to show in stronger relief many of the incidents. Circumstances of suffering, which in many narratives have been given in downright

plainness of detail, I have been impelled to leave to the reader's imagination, as too revolting to be recorded.

Although we may take the Reverend Timothy Flint at his word, we may also assume that he interpreted his editorial duties in a liberal fashion. The author of several western novels, which, he was proud to say, were "free from the inculcation of a single sentiment, that had not in my view the purest moral tendency," he assumed a responsibility to his public to present the rough, hard life of the Kentucky hunters in chaste phrases. Nevertheless, for his facts he apparently felt bound to the truth, and certainly did not think that he was producing a book which one California pioneer has asserted was as far from the events as Defoe's *Robinson Crusoe* was from Selkirk's journal. Probably his spirit and talent were most apparent in his emphasizing views which agreed with those of Pattie about the character of mountain men and their mission, and in exaggerating romantic elements such as the rescue of an Indian child from an enemy tribe, the romance with the daughter of New Mexico's former governor, and the frequent bear hunts. His additions to topographical descriptions may have been generous in some parts of the *Narrative,* particularly those which deal with New Mexico. One can be fairly certain that the descriptions of the Gila basin, the Grand Canyon country, and the lower Colorado are Pattie's, since no other sources, with the possible exception of Lieutenant R. W. H. Hardy's account of sailing up the mouth of the Colorado, are likely to have fallen into Flint's hands. And there is little question that the California topographical detail was provided by the subject of the adventures.

Convinced that the conquering of a frontier brought out all that was noble in the pioneer's character, Flint would probably have been surprised at Jedediah Smith's advice to J. J. Warner when the latter asked his opinion about going into the mountains for health. Smith told Warner that "the

chances were greatly in favor of finding death rather than
health, and that if he escaped the former and found the latter
the probabilities were that he would be ruined for anything
else in life but such things as would be agreeable to the pas-
sions of a semi-savage." Certainly, as the document was "softened" at Flint's hands, Pattie's *Narrative* emerged as the work
of a man of sentiment rather than that of a man of brutality.
However, although we are told that young Pattie was almost
stirred to tears at the shooting—through necessity—of his
horse, his civilized traits were modified when he indulged in
a feast of fat puppies, took an Indian scalp, or joined in a
retributive raid on a group of Indians that had not harmed
his party. He was not quite of the breed represented by Pegleg
Smith, who boasted of inviting a group of Apaches to dinner
and murdering them in cold blood—"none of them fellows
ever returned home to tell of that event; we fixed them all"—
but it is obvious he looked upon a dead Indian as a good Indian. And, to the Spanish Californians, he was undoubtedly
an uncouth barbarian. Their view of the mountain men cor-
responded with the remarks of Yankee skipper Cunningham,
who said of Jed Smith's party: "Does it not seem incredible
that a party of fourteen men, depending entirely upon their
rifles and traps for subsistence, will explore this vast continent, and call themselves happy when they can obtain the
tail of a beaver to dine upon?"

However, Flint's injection of sentiment and romance into
the *Narrative* does no more than counteract the opposite interpretation of the mountain man as a brute. Men like Jed
Smith and Jim Beckwourth and James Ohio Pattie were, like
other men, of mixed stamps and moved by varied emotions.
Less defensible, but certainly as typical of the times, was
Flint's bowdlerizing of Pattie's sex life among the Indians
and Mexicans. Surely, one agrees with Lewis R. Freeman
that Pattie's eagerness to offer his shirt to naked women—
whether they were Pimas or the daughter of New Mexico's
governor—sounds a little silly. And one may be sure that,

when Pattie said that Jacova, his New Mexico sweetheart, insisted on his sleeping at her house, or that a night was passed with the Indians "to the satisfaction of both parties," he did not forget that some pleasant fornication took place, even if Flint glossed the situations over and hurried on to other subjects. But the editor was hardy enough to report, with little mincing of terms, the episode in which Pattie and his companions, crazed with thirst, resorted to drinking their own urine. He even takes some pleasure in the Dutchman's remark: "Vell, mine poys, dis vater of mine ish more hotter as hell, und as dick as boudden, und more zalter as de zeas. I can't drink him. For God's sake, gif me some of yours, dat is more tinner!"

Probably the point on which Flint and Pattie most fully agreed was in their attitude toward the Mexicans and Spaniards as colonists. Flint, in traveling in the area beyond the Mississippi, had viewed earlier Spanish endeavors to settle the land with a wholly unsympathetic eye. Pattie felt that he had been treated badly by the Mexicans in New Mexico, who had on several occasions confiscated his furs. He felt bitter toward the Mexicans in California who, instead of succoring him and his companions from their thirst and starvation, had clamped them into a flea-infested San Diego jail over the door of which was inscribed the words, *Destinacion de la Cattivo;* had fed them dried beans, corn, and rancid tallow, food which reminded Pattie of a mess for diseased cows they used to make in Kentucky; and had kept his sick and disheartened father in solitary captivity until his untimely death. According to young Pattie, who worshiped his father, the only communication he received from the dying man was one that the older Pattie had written surreptitiously in his own blood.

Among the experiences Pattie had in California was the practicing of medicine in a limited field, an activity for which he was no more ill-trained than Joe Meek, the mountain man who turned doctor for a period after the toe he had replaced

on a Mexican remained firmly attached to the patient, and
was only a little less well equipped in that particular branch
of science than John Marsh, who almost a decade later, set
up as a physician in Los Angeles on the basis of a Harvard
liberal arts diploma. Having with him vaccine that his father
had brought from the mining country in New Mexico, Pattie
was commissioned by Echeandía, the Mexican governor, to
attempt to prevent a threatened smallpox epidemic by vac-
cinating the Mexicans and Indians. The task was a sizable
one; in going from mission to mission he vaccinated twenty-
two thousand persons, according to his account, which makes
clear also that he felt the Mexicans quite uninformed in
medicine. Pattie was not alone in gaining some measure of
security in an unfriendly country through the use of vaccine;
the *Autobiography of Kit Carson* tells of a trapper who saved
his life among the Sioux by using the vaccine he had carried
into the mountains.

The vaccination tour, during which Pattie visited practically all the places held by the Mexicans in Southern California, took him from the little village of San Diego, then
the capital of California because Governor Echeandía liked
its climate, to San Luis Rey, San Juan Capistrano, San Gabriel, the missions at and near Santa Barbara, and eventually
to San Francisco. His description of Los Angeles is typical of
his informal sketches:

My next advance was to a small town, inhabited by Spaniards,
called the town of The Angels. The houses have flat roofs, covered
with bituminous pitch, brought from a place within four miles of
the town, where this article boils up from the earth. As the liquid
rises, hollow bubbles like a shell of a large size, are formed. When
they burst, the noise is heard distinctly in the town. The material
is obtained by breaking off portions, that have become hard, with
an axe, or something of the kind. The large pieces thus separated,
are laid on the roof, previously covered with the earth, through
which the pitch cannot penetrate, when it is rendered liquid again
by the heat of the sun. In this place I vaccinated 2,500 persons.

In spite of the fact that Pattie had been commissioned by
the governor, he was refused pay when the task was completed, except on the conditions that he become a citizen and
adopt the Catholic religion. He proudly refused to com-
ply with such demands, although there is evidence that Sylvester Pattie had embraced Catholicism on his deathbed,
perhaps to gain a Christian burial (there is no admission of
this in the *Narrative,* and one assumes that the son was very
unhappy about his father's conversion). Although all his companions but two, who had returned to the States overland,
had married Mexicans, turned Catholic, and become known
as "el bueno mozo," "Miguel, el platera," and so forth, young
Pattie was of another mind. Such sacrifice of ideals did not
suit him, and his arrogant answer must have made Timothy
Flint thrill with pride and pleasure as he wrote it down:

> Upon this the priest's tone became loud and angry as he said,
> "then you regard my proposing that you should become a Catholic,
> as the expression of an unjust and whimsical desire!" I told him
> "yes, that I did; and that I would not change my present opinions
> for all the money his mission was worth; and moreover, that before
> I would consent to be adopted into the society and companionship
> of such a band of murderers and robbers, as I deemed were to be
> found along this coast, for the pitiful amount of one thousand head
> of cattle, I would suffer death."

As a matter of accuracy it must be noted, however, that
Pattie felt kindly toward many of the individual padres he
met on his tour.

Much more violent was his dislike of the government of
California; a number of circumstances combined to incense
him against this Mexican regime. He was unfortunate in
reaching San Diego in the administration of the weak and
vacillating Governor Echeandía, described by H. H. Bancroft as "fickle and infirm of purpose," who habitually sub-
stituted whim and tyranny for strength. During the entire
two years he spent in California he was at outs with this
government and frequently reiterated the idea that if he

could get Echeandía within the sights of his rifle he would indulge in a little of the direct action for which the trappers prided themselves. As a consequence of his attitude toward the authorities, he connived with Captain Bradshaw of the *Franklin,* who fought his way out of San Diego harbor after being accused of smuggling; he joined up with the smuggler Lang to hunt sea otter at Ensenada; and at first he favored the revolt of Joaquín Solís, thinking that a change in government might bring more advantages to the outlanders. His description of the revolt is that of an *opéra bouffe,* typical of the American's idea of Mexican scraps. The cannon balls at Santa Barbara were so ineffective that men stopped them with their arms and legs, and the fort at Monterey was recaptured by soldiers too drunk to fight. But if Pattie hated the governor, he felt a strong friendship for Sergeant Pico—apparently Pío Pico, later governor of California—and his lovely sister, who befriended him in his hour of trial.

James Pattie's attitude toward the ideals and institutions of Catholic California, far from being that of a unique individual suffering unique experiences, was the same as that of many of the other trappers, who refused to settle in the country and were glad to shake its dust from their feet. Although they frequently spoke well of individual priests such as Father Sánchez and Father Peyri, they were invariably annoyed by the hampering effects of military government in the country, particularly the emphasis on passports and restriction of movement, and they said much about cruelty and inefficiency of both priest and soldier. Zenas Leonard did not like to see Mexicans capture steers for slaughter by cutting their tendons, and Jedediah Smith was disturbed by the deliberate starvation of horses to cut down overproduction on the range. Rogers, Smith's clerk, who was even annoyed when a forward Mexican girl asked him "to make her a blanco Pickinina," told with obvious repugnance of the practice followed at Mission San Gabriel of setting out bear traps to catch backsliding Indians. Jedediah Smith felt that the

Mojave ambush which nearly wiped out his party on his return trip in 1827 was instigated by Governor Echeandía, and Ewing Young and Kit Carson accused the Mexicans of trying to get their men drunk in Los Angeles so that they could break up the party and jail them. Joseph Reddeford Walker refused as firmly as Pattie, but doubtless more gracefully, to give up his religion and citizenship in return for Mexican land and bounty, stating clearly that he preferred American institutions.

Pattie's estimate of California at the time of his departure in 1830 is sober but strongly worded:

The period of my departure from this coast was now close at hand, and my thoughts naturally took a retrospect of the whole time, I had spent upon it. The misery and suffering of various kinds, that I had endured in some portions of it, had not been able to prevent me from feeling, and acknowledging, that this country is more calculated to charm the eye, than any one I have ever seen. Those, who traverse it, if they have any capability whatever of perceiving, and admiring the beautiful and sublime in scenery, must be constantly excited to wonder and praise. It is no less remarkable for uniting the advantages of healthfulness, a good soil, a temperate climate, and yet one of exceeding mildness, a happy mixture of level and elevated ground, and vicinity to the sea. Its inhabitants are equally calculated to excite dislike, and even the stronger feelings of disgust and hatred.

What more obvious conclusion could be drawn than that this fair land should be inhabited by good, free republicans, who enjoyed the "priceless blessings of liberty"?

Thus, both seafaring Yankees and Kentucky hunters felt that a good country was in bad hands, although their reasons for reaching this conclusion differed. To the trapper, used to roaming a vast land directed by no orders but his own, the restrictions of a feudal Spanish or Mexican system were repellent. He accordingly felt quite free to break the law, and his grievance was that of one who possessed and cherished almost unlimited liberty and resented infringement of it. The

Yankee skipper and his supercargo also felt free to smuggle in Spanish-speaking countries, but, in addition, they compared the poorly developed California littoral with the farms they had seen back home and asked why this potentially rich farmland was not in the hands of the men who would use it properly. Thus, each group expressed one of the tenets which were to rationalize the expansive urge known as manifest destiny. The trappers adhered to the concept of the extension of the area of freedom in the world. The Yankees asked that the land be used by people who carried out the intentions of the Creator, which they firmly believed to be that wheat and fruit should be grown where cattle then roamed —cattle that were to be slaughtered solely for hides and tallow. The point of view of the Kentucky trapper was expressed by James Ohio Pattie; the objections of the Yankee, already voiced by William Shaler, were summed up by Richard Henry Dana, Jr., another young man who did not curb his tongue.

∽∽∽∽

Richard Henry Dana, Jr., reached California on the *Pilgrim,* sailing out of Boston, on January 14, 1835, seven years after Pattie and his companions had stumbled into a San Diego jail and a little less than four years after Pattie's *Narrative* was published. The resemblances between Pattie and Dana were slight: they were about the same age when they came to California (Dana was nineteen), they spent about the same length of time in the Mexican province, and each had been affected deeply by the death of his mother when he was a youth. Pattie, however, drew strength from a father who sought forgetfulness in action; Dana had long been under the shadow of a father who was a neurotic recluse. Pattie departed from the hearth to accompany his father into the wilderness; Dana, in a sense, fled from his father, whose timidity in the face of life's problems was reflected in his hope that his son would die early to escape misery: "I'm afraid he is too sensitive for his own happiness." Pattie went into the fur trade in search of action and fortune; Dana sailed to California before the mast to improve his health and to escape from the confining heritage of Calvinism and genteel conservatism.

The Danas of Cambridge were of the Brahmin caste, long important in New England affairs. Richard Henry Dana, Jr., was the fourth of his line and the thirteenth in his branch of the family to go to Harvard. Living on a scant inheritance, his father, who had been one of the founders of the *North American Review,* was a dilettante poet and critic. Hampered by the twin curses of his ancestry, pride and procrastination, he had talked much but had produced little; as James Russell Lowell said of him, "Yet he spends his whole life, like the man in the fable, In learning to swim on his library table." Such a man wasn't at all certain how to care for a motherless boy. Accordingly, he sent him to a number of private schools, even placing him for a while under Emerson's tutelage, and then entered him in Harvard College. Unhappy at home, where dilettantism and Calvinism both disturbed him (he was taught that babies were God's little enemies), the boy found little pleasure in school, where corporal punishment was a prominent feature of life and the boys sometimes objected to his weak efforts at playing ball with them. ("They don't chuse me in the game.") Nor did Harvard bring happiness, pleasing him, apparently, little more than it did his classmate, Henry Thoreau; the most pleasant event associated with his early years there was his half-year rustication for taking a harmless part in a student "rebellion."

Dana had hardly returned, reluctantly, to Harvard when he was stricken with a bad case of measles. The illness left him weak, with eyes so sensitive that he could not endure even ordinary daylight. Because further study was out of the question, he went home to his melancholy father. The almost automatic recourse in such a difficulty in Dana's circle was to go abroad on the Grand Tour, but the family competence would not allow that luxury. Instead, young Dana looked for a job on a sailing vessel, reasoning wisely that hard work, plain diet, and open-air life would, by effecting a gradual change in his whole physical system, ultimately restore his eyesight. After turning down an opportunity to loaf as a companion to Nathaniel Bowditch's nephew on a trip to India, he got a job as an able-bodied sailor on a ship bound for California.

Dana's action was not unprecedented, for the sea had been the refuge of New England boys ever since the days of the colonies, and many sons of well-to-do families had shipped before the mast. In fact, one of his companions on the *Pilgrim,* Ben Stimson, was a boy of good family out for the experience. Such lads were sufficiently numerous that Melville even took a jibe at them in *Moby Dick:*

> For nowadays, the whale-fishery furnishes an asylum for many romantic, melancholy, and absent-minded young men, disgusted with the carking cares of the earth, and seeking sentiment in tar and blubber. Childe Harold not infrequently perches himself on the mast head of some luckless and disappointed whaleship and in moody phrase ejaculates:
>
>> Roll on, thou deep and dark ocean, roll!
>> Ten thousand blubber hunters sweep over thee
>> in vain.

Fortunately, Dana chose for his adventure not a whaling ship but a small trading brig, the *Pilgrim,* which sailed from Boston on August 14, 1834, with the short, blond, broad-shouldered Harvard refugee fully disguised in duck trousers, checked shirt, and sailor's tarpaulin hat. The exciting voyage round Cape Horn gave the boy just that "course in natural life" which he had wanted; he needed toughening if he was to deal successfully with practical life, and he got it, from the time he fought through seasickness to his near fall from the fore topgallant yard. The toughening was not, however, such as to prevent him from developing a bitter loathing for his skipper, Captain Frank Thompson, the "regular-built down-east johnny-cake" who was perhaps no more of a martinent than his fellows; but the boy who had already taken the responsibility of seeing that one of his schoolmasters was dismissed for whipping him excessively was not likely to feel any cordiality for a captain in the absolute despotism of ship life. It has been suggested that Dana was flogged when he was aboard the *Pilgrim;* he certainly saw others flogged, and in later life he did much to correct the abuses suffered by sailors.

It is not our concern, however, to examine Dana's accounts of cruelty to seamen, or his vivid, memorable description of sailing the rough oceans in a ship no bigger than many a present-day fishing smack. Rather, it is the reaction of the boy, already well on his way to becoming a man, who sailed into Santa Barbara 150 days out of Boston, which claims our attention. For the account which Dana was to write of the many months he spent in curing and loading hides was to be the most influential report of California life to appear before the American conquest.

At the time Dana had his experiences in California the Boston hide trade was at its height. It had been inaugurated in this area by Bryant and Sturgis, the company for which he was working, in 1822, the year in which California trade restrictions had been modified as the result of Mexico's independence from Spain. At first hard pressed by the British firm, McCulloch, Hartnell, and Company, which had cornered the mission trade, Bryant and Sturgis eventually became the most successful, though not by any means the only, trader on the Coast. The *Brookline,* the *California,* the *Pilgrim,* the *Alert,* and other ships of the firm brought everything that could be imagined, "from Chinese fireworks to English cartwheels," including lumber, shoes made at Lynn from California hides, and even raisins. Arrangements for disposal of these goods were made by the supercargoes, or business agents, who represented the company in California.

For Bryant and Sturgis these were William Gale, or "cuatros ojos," the pioneer otter hunter turned trader; Alfred Robinson, and Henry Mellus, who came out before the mast with Dana, became a clerk after reaching the Coast, and settled down in Los Angeles. After paying heavy duties, often amounting to 100 per cent, on the Boston goods, the supercargoes exchanged them with the presidio merchants, the mission padres, and the rancheros, for cowhides, the California bank notes, which eventually supplied much of the leather used in the Massachusetts shoe industry. Although the secularization of the missions in 1833 cut down the trade, the largest single cargo of hides to be taken from the Pacific Coast was carried in the *Alert* in 1836, when Dana returned to Boston.

The principal source of wealth in California in the 'twenties and 'thirties was the open-range cattle industry, in which stock could be grown profitably with a market averaging about $2.00 per head. Until 1833 most of the cattle belonged to the missions; after the missions were secularized the industry rapidly passed into the hands of the rancheros, who operated somewhat less profitably than the mission fathers had done. When the cattle were slaughtered at the annual *matanzas*, the marketable products were the hides (uncured), horns, and tallow. The last was sometimes converted into soap; but more frequently, after being tried out, it was shipped to South American ports. Some of the meat was dried for *carne seca*, but most of it went to waste, because refrigeration was not available.

The hides, usually hard, unwieldy, dirty, and sometimes garnished with bits of decaying flesh, were delivered by the *vaqueros* to the beaches. At the anchorages along the coast, such as San Pedro and San Juan Capistrano, Dana and his fellow seamen had the task of picking them up and carrying them through the surf to the ship's boats. After the hides were transported to the central storage and curing depot, "Hide Park" at San Diego, they soaked, softened, and salted them, and eventually stowed them in the hold for the voyage home. Naturally, seamen hated these jobs. Dana, who was less inured to such tasks than his fellows, referred to his work as "the vulgar, wearisome toil of uninteresting, forced manual labor." "They [the hides] brought us out here, they kept us here, and it was only by getting them that we could escape from the coast and return to home and civilized life."

In evaluating Dana's picture of California, it is well to remember that his contact with the country, although far more intimate and genuine than that of the ordinary traveler, was limited by the trade in which he took part. Of the sixteen months he was in California, from January 14, 1835, to May 8, 1836, he spent six at San Diego, curing and stowing hides, and ten sailing up and down the coast, picking up the hides. In the course of the latter task, he took two runs on the brig *Pilgrim*, which had been sent out as a sort of tender for the *Alert*, and three on the ship *Alert*, each time stopping at San Pedro and Santa Barbara and twice loading hides near San Juan Capistrano from the cliffs of what is now known as Dana's Point in commemoration of his activity. On only two of the five trips did Dana go beyond Southern California: the *Pilgrim* sailed to Monterey for an accounting with the customs authorities after first putting in at Santa Barbara on the trip out; and the *Alert* made one trip as far north as San Francisco, where Dana spent the Christmas of 1835.

Always under strict ship discipline, except during his stay at the hide houses in San Diego, Dana worked hard in the surf or on the ship all days except Sunday, when he frequently used shore leave to visit a town or explore along the beach. Thus, he came to know Santa Barbara and San Diego well; he visited the secularized missions, already starting to decay, at those spots, and he was very familiar with the rocks at San Pedro and San Juan Capistrano. But he was never able to visit Los Angeles, known to him as "the Pueblo," nor did he ever penetrate more than five miles from the beach. His remaining contacts were limited to his opportunity to see Californians who came to the ships to buy goods or take passage from one coastal point to another. As one of the crew of the captain's gig after he joined the *Alert,* he helped carry native passengers and visitors through the surf. Further, he sometimes acted as interpreter for Captain Thompson. Thus, he felt that he had made the acquaintance "of about half of California." His really close contacts, however, were with sailors and workers on the beach, such as the Kanakas.

Although Dana was clearly eager for rugged experience, his aristocratic background, bookish training, and aloof temperament all left their marks on his reaction to sailing before the mast and laboring on the California shore. It was a point of pride with him that, although of good birth and education, he maintained the view of the common sailor on his trip. And certainly he pluckily carried out the responsibilities of his job and even at times faced danger unnecessarily, as in the famous episode in which he rescued the hides from the face of the cliff near San Juan Capistrano. Much of the charm of his narrative results from his convincing the reader that he took his hazing with the rest, never reminding his fellows that he was there on "an enforced holiday," that his service before the mast was merely a "parenthesis" in his life. He had resources at his disposal, however, when it came to forcing Thompson and Robinson to send him home on the *Alert;* at this critical moment, the captain and the supercargo, both somewhat at odds with the Boston firm for which they worked, could hardly have overlooked the fact that the Danas were an influential family at the home port of Bryant, Sturgis and Company. For that matter, the junior partner of the firm made a point of greeting Dana when the *Alert* returned to Boston. Moreover, we have Dana's testimony that his position was understood in California. Of the commandant of San Francisco, Mariano Guadalupe Vallejo, who "knew my story," he wrote that that personage sometimes stopped to chat with him, a common sailor, concerning California politics. And it is to a Dana of Boston that Captain Faucon, newly

arrived on the *Alert,* passed the remark in Latin: "Tityre, tu
patulae recubans sub tegmine fagi."

As a sailor Dana amused himself during watches by a regular routine of drawing on his memory, passing from the mul-
tiplication tables through "the kings of England in their order" to the Kanaka numerals. When the watch was long, he
went on to the ten commandments, the thirty-ninth chapter
of Job, Cowper's "Castaway," and Goethe's "Der Erlkönig."
As a worker at the hide-curing depot at San Diego, where he
soon grew tired of the limited pleasures in the sleepy village
(although he did once give his handkerchief to a black-eyed
señorita), he sought for reading material with the diligence
of a pack rat. He mentions that he found at least eighteen
books in sea chests and odd corners; Godwin's *Mandeville*
and Scott's *Pirate* and *Woodstock* he viewed as treasures. In
addition, he studied German from a Lutheran prayer book,
picked up Spanish as rapidly as he could (he appears to have
learned by ear, for his Spanish is notably misspelled in the
first edition of *Two Years Before the Mast*), and even tried
to learn as much Hawaiian as possible from Hope and his
other Kanaka friends on the beach at San Diego. His Spanish, as has been pointed out, stood him in good stead in in-
terpreting for the captain and in talking to passengers such as
Vallejo and Bandini.

What his biographer calls that "certain formality which
did not encourage intimacy," so marked in his later life, did
not prevent his making close friends of his sailor companions,
although it may have deterred him from increasing his contacts with people outside his immediate assumed economic
class, such as trappers, ship agents, and California citizens.
He found in his companions men of pluck, merit, and shrewd
native intelligence and left unforgettable portraits of some of
them, such as the English sailor, who was almost a prototype
for Billy Budd, and Hope, the Kanaka, a true "noble savage."
Other figures did not fit so easily into his essentially romantic concept of human nature; he had but a low opinion of

Captain Frank Thompson, clearly disliked Alfred Robinson, spoke with contempt of "rangers" such as Russell, was disgusted with the "big, vulgar shop-keeper" Fitch, a noted San Diego merchant, and even looked upon Don Juan Bandini as an example of decayed gentility, an attractive but futile figure. Just as Juan Fernández struck him as the most romantic spot he had ever visited because he associated it with the adventures of Robinson Crusoe, Dead Man's Island became a truly poetic spot in San Pedro harbor merely because it suggested mystery, and San Juan Capistrano was to him "the only romantic spot in California" because he remembered adventure set against bold scenery there. So, too, he found sailors and Kanakas with unusual backgrounds more interesting than the dull fellows concerned with the hide trade. He remembered himself later as "a boy who could not be prudential, and who caught at every chance for adventure." And yet the adventure, if there was such, of Spanish-Mexican life on the Pacific littoral touched him not at all; whether he was alienated by Catholic customs, whether he found the *mañana* atmosphere too disturbing for his Yankee soul, or whether he merely showed a natural reaction of a boy away from home in a fairly barren land, homesick for Cambridge and culture, he looked upon California as "that hated coast" and was very happy to leave it.

It was not only a hated coast, but a "half-civilized coast." Dana's first impression of California was "very disagreeable," and it remained so, except for occasional experiences or scenes which pleased him, such as the view of Monterey in early spring, or San Diego Bay on a lazy summer's day. The Californians, among whom he found very few of pure Castilian blood, appeared to him "to be a people on whom the curse had fallen, and stripped them of everything but their pride, their manners, and their voices." They were an "idle, thriftless people," who could make nothing for themselves, who were more interested in fandangos and cockfights than in industry. Perhaps there was a little envy here, for Dana and his companions had few holidays: "Yankees can't afford the time to be Catholics," he once wrote.

According to Dana there was no justice in the country, the trade had been taken over by industrious outsiders like Richardson and Stearns because the natives were lazy and not resourceful, and the living standard was notably low—even ladies who wore fine dresses lived in huts with dirt floors. Revolutions were common, and secularization of the missions had been effected only to distribute the spoils. "In their domestic relations, these people are no better than in their public. The men are thriftless, proud, and extravagant, and very much given to gaming; and the women have but little education." "The fondness for dress among the women is excessive and is often the ruin of many of them. A present of a fine mantle, or of a necklace or pair of ear-rings, gains the favor of the greater part of them," the young Puritan sniffed.

In his conclusion as to what should be done about the country, Dana agreed with Pattie. This was a fair country, being wasted by an inefficient and corrupt people. Certainly, such is not the way of God nor of progress.

Such are the people who inhabit a country embracing four or five hundred miles of sea-coast, with several good harbors; with fine forests in the north; the waters filled with fish, and the plains covered with thousands of herds of cattle; blessed with a climate, than which there can be no better in the world; free from all manner of diseases, whether epidemic or endemic; and with a soil in which corn yields from seventy to eighty fold. In the hands of an enterprising people, what a country this might be! we are ready to say. Yet how long would a people remain so, in such a country? The Americans (as those from the United States are called) and Englishmen, who are fast filling up the principal towns, and getting the trade into their hands, are indeed more industrious and effective than the Spaniards; yet their children are brought up Spaniards, in every respect, and if the "California fever" (laziness) spares the first generation, it always attacks the second.

Soon after his return to the East Coast, Dana set about writing an account of his experiences at sea and in California. The result of his work, *Two Years Before the Mast*, was brought out by Harper and Brothers in 1840. The story, accurate in almost every detail, reveals a very observant mind and an imaginative grasp of the materials; and the picture of California it contains is vivid, honest, and remarkably consistent. The book captured the imagination and the sympathy of a world-wide public and gave to it knowledge of California shortly before that faraway land was to become American territory and the site of the gold rush.

◇◇◇◇

Six years after the publication of Dana's book came Alfred Robinson's *Life in California*. This was the Alfred Robinson, the Bryant and Sturgis agent, whose personality and activities, particularly his marriage to Doña Ana María de la Guerra, Dana had described with malicious zest in *Two Years Before the Mast*. He was, moreover, one of the Americans who had joined the Catholic Church, having left their consciences behind at Cape Horn, as Dana expressed it. Robinson had been rechristened José María Alfredo in 1833 and had become a California citizen.

It is possible that Dana's dislike was at least in part justified, for Robinson had a personal reserve which kept him from being highly popular on the Coast. And no doubt it was natural for sailors who hated hide droghing to carry on a feud with any or all supercargoes. However, one cannot help but sympathize with Robinson's discouragement with ships and sailors from Boston at the time when Dana arrived on the *Pilgrim*. He, like Dana, wanted to go home to Boston, but his company would not let him. He had been so ill that he had had trouble keeping up with his work. He was homesick, and the owners had failed to see that the letters for him were put on the *Pilgrim*. He felt that he had represented the company well in California, but he had just been notified that his commission was to be cut, with the result that he would make much less money. The *Alert* had brought out, not the clerk he had requested, but a Mr. Park who was to act as his partner or companion. He didn't like Mr. Park, and he didn't want a partner; "People seem to suppose they have come here to do just as they like," he wrote of him. Times were hard because of the secularizing of the missions, and Robinson had trouble getting enough hides to fill the *Alert*. Furthermore, he was heavily in debt because Bryant and Sturgis had failed to send the cash necessary to pay the duties on the goods aboard the *Pilgrim* and the *Alert*. And finally, just at a time when the company was shorthanded on the Coast, Dana and one of his companions insisted on returning to Boston on the *Alert* rather than wait another year to go back on the *Pilgrim*. Robinson was probably a bit fed up with gentlemen's sons who were ready to exert pressure from home to get their way.

Considering Dana's treatment of Robinson in his book, it is not surprising that when Dana visited in Santa Barbara after returning to California in 'fifty-nine he hesitated to call on the former supercargo. Robinson, however, was very cordial, an attitude which, according to Dana, "gave him, as between us, rather the advantage in *status*." He might also have added that in his account of events during hide-droghing days in *Life in California*, Robinson had made no attempt to get even for the unkind treatment Dana had accorded him. But if retaliation of a personal nature was not Robinson's objective in writing the book, there is probably some truth in the theory, advanced by Theodore Hittell, that one of his reasons for writing it was to answer certain criticisms that Dana had made of Californians, particularly of California women. Certainly, Robinson spoke more kindly of the Californians than did Dana, and particularly he praised the virtues of the women of the country: "perhaps there are few places in the world where, in proportion to the number of inhabitants, can be found more chastity, industrious habits, and correct de-

portment, than among the women of this place." But his love
for the Mexican Californians was no greater than might be
expected from the son-in-law of a *gachupin,* or Spanish loyal-
ist, Don José de la Guerra, who had escaped execution by a
hair's breadth in San Blas in 1810 and had been refused his seat
in the Mexican Congress in 1828 because of his disaffection toward the Mexican cause. In fact, Robinson ended his book
with an even more open plea than Dana's for American occupation of California: "in this age of 'Annexation' why not
extend the 'area of freedom' by the annexation of California?"

Robinson's account of California life treats its subject
graphically and sympathetically, telling of the experiences
which the supercargo underwent in trading on the Coast and
marrying into one of its leading families. A Boston boy of
Scottish ancestry, Robinson had made three trips to the West
Indies by the time he came of age. Soon afterward he came
out to California as clerk for William Gale on the *Brookline,* in 1829. With Gale he traveled from one end of the
chain of Franciscan missions to the other, learning the business of supercargo, which he was to take over on Gale's departure. Thus, he saw the missions in their prime. One of
the principal differences between his account of California
and that in *Two Years Before the Mast* is that he gives vivid
glimpses of life under the padres, whereas Dana, who arrived
shortly after secularization, limns a disintegrating mission
life, in which padre and Indian are at their worst. Robinson, in discussing secularization, pictures the country in a
sad state of anarchy and looks back to the days when he rode
from mission to mission and received high hospitality and
marketed rich bounties of hides and tallow.

Although Robinson became a Catholic and married the
daughter of the *síndico* of the missions, the official responsible for handling their revenues and effects, he wrote about
the padres with a Yankee humor that is frequently delightful. Occasionally he shows a marked dislike for one of the

padres—Father Ybarra at San Fernando, for instance, whom
he calls *cochino,* or "hog." More kindly is his portrait of
Father Uría at San Buenaventura: "At dinner the fare was
sumptuous, and I was much amused at the eccentricity of the
old Padre, who kept constantly annoying four large cats, his
daily companions; or with a long stick thumped upon the
heads of his Indian boys, and seemed delighted thus to gratify
his singular propensities." And there is the padre at San Diego
who kept his eye on a large fly during his prayer, "and pro-
nouncing the word Amen! Jesus! he brought his cane down on
the poor fly and crushed it, and then turned around to renew
the conversation, as though nothing had transpired." Finally
there is an episode which sounds as if it came direct from Field-
ing's *Joseph Andrews,* concerning two padres who indulged in
a water fight after a wedding:

Padre Antonio, urgent to follow up the attack, pursued him;
when Menendez, seeing no means of escape, seized from beneath
the bed an article, oftener used than mentioned, and let it fly,
contents and all, full into the face of Padre Antonio, who had just
appeared at the door. The consequences were, the loss of two of the
poor friar's front teeth, and a conclusion of the *fun.*

From his accounts of California fleas and the hilarious
episode in which Señor Lugo accidentally blew himself up
with a trick *cigarro* prepared for Robinson, to the graphic
pictures of mission churches and gardens and the realistic accounts of plots and revolutions, Robinson demonstrates his
keen ability as an observer and writer. That he was by no
means a mere chronicler of business affairs is indicated not
only by his *Life in California* but by his versatility in the
arts; he carried a sketchbook as well as a notebook with him
and made some of the first pictures of California missions.
And, late in life, years after he had returned to California
(after taking his wife to Boston for a course in New England
indoctrination), he wrote another book, *California: An Historical Poem* (1889), which contains somewhat better verse

than the usual product of the enthusiastic layman. Among other things, it comments on the fate of the Indians:

> For culture must enforce its way
> With onward march from day to day
> Where rudeness lies;
> And so the Red Man, here to-day,
> To modern progress must give way,
> Though thus he *dies!*

Robinson's interest in the California Indians was one of long standing. Nearly a half century earlier he had translated a Spanish account of Mission Indian life, called "Chinigchinich." This account, consisting of observations made by Father Gerónimo Boscana when he was in charge of Mission San Juan Capistrano, had, after Boscana's death, fallen into the hands of Robinson's father-in-law, José de la Guerra, when the latter was serving as syndic for the mission system. Robinson translated the treatise; wrote a preface, "Life in California," three times as long as the translation; and published the whole under the title of the preface. "Chinigchinich" remains perhaps the best contemporary account of the mission Indian, giving a detailed and at times graphic picture of the lives of the neophytes under the rule of the padres. Robinson's purpose in translating and illustrating Boscana was the same as his purpose in writing his account of life in California—to tell the truth as accurately as he could. Because he did so with both grace and imagination his book is one of the most reliable and interesting documents dealing with Spanish California.

∽∽∽∽

Mexican California was thus graphically described, by the young trapper, James Ohio Pattie; by the sturdy boy before the mast, Richard Henry Dana; and by the Yankee trader turned Californian, Alfred Robinson. There are, of course, many other accounts from which the historian builds his

mature estimate of this bit of Mexico, or to which the lover
of old journals turns for picturesque detail or amusing incident. Certainly, such a reader will not neglect the memoirs
of William Heath Davis, *Seventy-five Years in California,* in
which that son of a Yankee merchant in the Hawaiian trade
tells of his early visits to California from the Sandwich
Islands, or of the open smuggling by the island traders, or of
the many incidents of ranch life which he saw after he settled in California in 1838. Episodic and discursive, light-
hearted and amiable, it supplements the more effective contemporaneous accounts found in Pattie, Dana, and Robinson.
Nor will the browsing reader neglect those two surveys of
California, the rich plum of the Pacific, made by representatives of two countries which lost out in the scramble for the
prize—Alexander Forbes, the English merchant at Tepic,
who, in his vivid and charming *California* (1839) did his best
to persuade the English to act while there was yet time; and
Eugène Duflot de Mofras, sent by the French government in
the early 'forties to report on the economic wealth of the disputed Pacific Coast, who wrote perhaps the most detailed and
accurate account of California resources of the period in his
*Exploration du territoire de l'Orégon, des Californies, et de
la mer Vermeille . . . 1840, 1841, et 1842,* published in
Paris by the French government in 1844. These, with earlier
accounts by visitors like Charles Wilkes, J. F. Galaup de La
Pérouse, and George Simpson, and countless other sources
make up the historical account. But the portrait of a lone-
some coast as seen by the American visitor received most
clearly the stamp of literature, gift of the informed imagination, in the accounts discussed above.

II

The Cow Counties

DURING the two decades following the occupation of California by the Americans in 1846, Southern California was known somewhat contemptuously as the "cow counties." Apparently it was being by-passed by the prominent events of history and culture. Its comparatively undramatic activities offered no serious competition to the lure of the gold rush, which had put San Francisco and the mining country on the lips of the world. Those who cared at all about its existence knew it simply as a land where Spanish Californian customs still survived, where unsettled conditions fostered an excessive amount of lawlessness, and where cattle were grown for the San Francisco meat market.

Yet much was happening in the cow counties that rivaled the events of the north in providing saga material which might have been used by romantically inclined writers. Most of the violent and picturesque episodes of the American conquest of California in 1846, for instance, took place in the south. Whereas northern California gave up quietly after the orderly arrival of Commodore Sloat at Monterey, there was a different picture in the south. Here took place the pitched battle of San Pascual, won by the Mexicans, and here the Los

Angeles plain saw various skirmishings, with the capture, surrender, and recapture of the Southern California capital by the American forces. Here, also, the course of empire which had captured Texas and California for the United States played itself out in the Pacific Southwest, with the southern counties offering traverse to a series of filibusters, such as Raousset-Boulbon and Crabb, and haven to William Walker, the gray-eyed man of destiny, when his short-lived twin republics of Baja California and Sonora collapsed and his men retreated to safety across the Tia Juana River.

During the 'fifties, Southern California, harboring bandits and criminals from the mines and from across the border, was a land of ferment, in comparison with which San Francisco and the gold country, even though lawlessness was prevalent, were tame. An aroused Mexican population, disheartened by the inequalities of the new American laws and encouraged by the absence of strong government, gave more than tacit support to such bandits as Juan Flores, Tiburcio Vásquez, and Joaquín Murieta. And the concomitant outbreaks of lynch law were only too frequent. To further one lynching in Los Angeles, the mayor of the pueblo, Yale-trained Stephen C. Foster, resigned in order to lead the mob. And legend has it that the Los Angeles *Southern Californian* published an account of the hanging two hours before it took place, in order to catch the deadline for the steamer edition. Here, truly, was the land of a corpse for breakfast and a hanging for lunch.

Fit subjects for a healthy school of "Westerns" were present long before the day of Owen Wister, in the activities of the great cattle ranches, where cattle ranged on a thousand hills, the bulls ran uncastrated, and the *vaqueros* developed the handling of the lariat to a fine art. And more than a decade before the great cattle drives from Texas to the Kansas railhead were started, huge herds were driven from Southern California to the mining country, and more than forty thousand head a year were brought across the deserts of the Southwest by hardy and skillful drovers. But the cowboy of the "Western," although he inherited the lasso from the *vaquero,* was to be a later product, created by the American; and his domain was to lie outside Southern California, although eventually his celluloid descendants and his chroniclers in the pulp magazines were frequently to call Hollywood their home.

The approaches to California by the southern desert trails offered to writers as good subjects as the more widely publicized northern routes. From ten thousand to fifteen thousand of the 'forty-niners, for instance, came across the desert and rounded the southern end of the Sierra, crossing into the San Joaquin by way of Walker Pass or Tehachapi Pass, or entering the Los Angeles plain through the Cajon or across the burning sands from Fort Yuma. This was an approach to the gold fields over the desert, where, "even the coyotes carried canteens," where the mirage disappointed the thirsty traveler and gave rise to many a myth, and where Apaches plundered and murdered the stragglers. This was the desert from which marauding Mojaves and renegade whites like Pegleg Smith emerged to steal whole herds of horses from the defenseless rancheros. This was the desert which was crossed by the first transcontinental stage line, the heroic Butterfield Overland Mail, which tried the hardiest soul but brought him through, hungry and bleary-eyed, in record time. Opened in 1858, the Butterfield line was far more significant than the later short-lived Pony Express, which was more spectacular than effective.

Raw material for many a romance or local-color sketch abounded in the cow counties, which might, had not the Civil War come along, have set up the new territory of Colorado, approved by the California legislature but never accepted by the national Congress. There were also the community ventures which might well have supplied themes for the adventurous historian. San Bernardino, nestling near the Cajon and San Gorgonio passes, suddenly became the choice of Brigham Young for a second Salt Lake City, a forward point to hold open a Mormon corridor to the sea. And Anaheim, settled in 1857 by a group of San Francisco Germans, all artisans except one, a poet, was one of the most interesting and for a while one of the most successful socialistic experiments in America. El Monte, tough squatter town of rough Texans, exhibited community spirit of a different sort; always ready to take over the Old Pueblo in interracial squabbles, it attempted to do so at least once.

Even the sleepy villages of San Diego, Santa Barbara, and San Luis Obispo held their treasures for the romancer, for they not only reflected an attractive though senescent hidalgo culture, but they epitomized the conflict between the older Spanish Californian and the insistent Yankee, who was to displace him almost completely by the end of the period. In these towns and in the Old Pueblo, men were more conscious than anywhere else of the disintegration of the *ranchero* culture, of the boom prices for cattle, of the heyday of fine clothes and rich trappings, of disputed land grants, exorbitant interest rates, squatter invasions, floods and droughts, and the conquest of one type of agriculture by others, which marked the complete defeat of the Spanish Californian. Nowhere else in the West was the conflict spelled out in such large letters and nowhere were the consequences more sweeping. Here in Southern California was fought one of the final battles between the peoples that had been at each other's throats even before the bold followers of Queen Elizabeth had challenged the Spanish Armada.

But though the subjects were at hand, the writers had not yet arrived. The southern counties were still too sparsely settled, in spite of the increase in population from six thousand in 1850 to nearly fifty thousand in 1870, to produce or support a school of writers. The spirit of the times did not, however, go unrecorded. True belles lettres might still be wanting, but there were other media of expression—the emigrant's diary, the soldier's record, the journalist's chronicle, the traveler's account, and the evanescent and varied forms of folklore. These were both important and interesting; later they were to be used as bases for literary expression in its more conventional forms.

≈≈≈≈

The isolation of the little communities in the southern part of California in the days of the American conquest and the gold rush is vividly portrayed in contemporaneous accounts by men who made their way through bandit-infested hills or across parching deserts to the watered oases at the foot of mountains or beside the treeless bays. There were three major land approaches by which these men came: the two desert routes—one from Salt Lake down the east side of the Sierra, the other from the east along the Gila River—and the one from the northern part of California by way of the Salinas Valley and the coast. The San Joaquin Valley, although actually traversed by Frémont and his men in the winter of 1843–44, was but an unsettled wilderness, carrying little of the immigrant traffic.

The route from San Francisco, following the line of missions dotting the littoral, was a rugged one, not to be made into a stage road until the mid-fifties. One gets a taste of the difficulties encountered, from *What I Saw in California,* written by Edward Bryant, who was with Frémont on his 1846 expedition to California when, with his California Battalion of some four hundred men, he moved down the state to help relieve Southern California after it had been retaken by the Mexicans. By 1849 conditions were apparently even worse; the trail was no better, and in addition the area between Monterey and Santa Barbara had became a badman's land, a region where ne'er-do-wells of all races hid in the hills to rob travelers. J. Ross Browne, the engaging and efficient wanderer from Dublin who had already anticipated Melville's *Moby Dick* in his *Etchings of a Whaling Cruise,* and Mark Twain's *Innocents Abroad* in his *Yusef,* followed the route in carrying out an assignment to set up a string of post offices along the road from San Francisco to Los Angeles. His story of the trip, published as "A Dangerous Journey" in his *Crusoe's Island,* constitutes as engaging a bit of writing as is to be found in the works of that talented narrator.

Browne's trouble, on his solitary trip, started with his inability to handle his mule, with which he was clearly not *en rapport.* (Here also he anticipates Mark Twain's feud with horseflesh.) When he was not falling off his mule he was chasing him across the landscape in order to get on and fall off again. Browne on foot had many adventures. First, he barely escaped a charge of wild cattle, only to view, from his perch in the only tree in sight, a fight to the death between a bull and a bear. Then he fell in with a group of American desperadoes, who abstained from killing him only because he persuaded them that he was returning later with a large sum of money. After escaping through the connivance of a tenderhearted member of the group, he crawled into an adobe hut near San Miguel, where, groping in the darkness, he found his arms around a corpse. Daylight revealed the mutilated bodies of a woman and two children, killed by the desperadoes from whom he had escaped, and mangled by wild animals. His attempt to get help from an indolent "son of the hidalgos" he found near by failed, except for the recapture of his mule. The Californian politely refused to accept his watch, explaining, first, that he was a member of the *gente de razon* and therefore could not take a reward and, second, that it was unsafe in such a country to own a watch, as one might then be killed for his possessions. Browne eventually reached San Luis Obispo, where he attended a *baille* and saw the belle of the dance—a half-breed murderer, child-killer, and adulterer —stab one of her lovers, a Texas "ranger" who had been the sympathetic member of the party of desperadoes who had caused Browne so much trouble. Later, the murderess, who was so disconsolate that she would not leave her victim's grave, was torn to pieces by the wolves.

Although Browne exaggerated with the license of a professional humorist, there is unquestionably a solid core of truth in his bizarre recital. Stripped of its exaggerations and viewed soberly, it gives a good account of the dangers of the overland route from the north.

Of the approach along the Gila, over the Colorado Desert, and thence across the Laguna Mountains to San Diego, or by way of Warner's Ranch to Los Angeles, accounts vary in detail but not in substance. One of the most graphic is that written by Major William S. Emory, topographical engineer with Colonel Stephen W. Kearny's "Army of the West," who, in his *Notes of a Military Reconnaissance,* tells of the torturing march of the ragged band of about a hundred men from Santa Fe to the crossing of the Colorado near Yuma, the struggle across the desert, and the rough welcome that was accorded the dispirited troops at San Pascual. Bayard Taylor, noted journalist and poet, also gives an account of the difficulties of the route, the more impressive because it is by implication, in his description of the appearance of the men who had just come across it at the height of the rush in 'forty-nine. These he saw when his ship, en route to San Francisco, put in at San Diego and picked up a number of men still hungering for the gold fields in spite of the hardships they had undergone. He pictures them, in *El Dorado,* as "men, lank and brown 'as is the ribbed sea-sand'—men with long hair and beards, and faces from which the rigid expression of suffering was scarcely relaxed." They muttered about "a country of burning salt plains and shifting hills of sand, whose only signs of human visitation are the bones of animals and men scattered along the trails that cross it." And they told him that, strung out over the desert, were ten thousand of their fellows, searching for forage, struggling through long *jornadas,* banding together for fear of the Apaches and Maricopas and Yumas, plodding on through the dunes of the Colorado sink.

The third route, that from Salt Lake City, crossed the desert of which Frémont wrote in his graphic report of his expedition of 1843–1844:

"There," said our guide, stretching out his hand towards it [the desert], "there are the great *llanos* (plains), *no hay agua; no hay zacate—nada:* there is neither water nor grass—nothing; every animal that goes upon them dies." It was indeed dismal to look upon . . . a vast desert plain spread before us, from which the boldest traveller turned away in despair.

But this vast desert plain had been crossed by many a bold trapper, and it was to be crossed again by tens of thousands of emigrants in search of gold or farming land. Most of those who passed this way did so with no greater loss than the emigrants of the central route suffered, although the hazards of starvation, thirst, sickness, and Indian forays are not to be minimized. Like the Sierra crossing, however, this route is remembered in folklore and letters for the disastrous exception. The incident in the southern approach to California which most closely parallels the famous Donner-party tragedy in the north involved a group of men and women who also started at the wrong time and took the wrong cutoff; but instead of being snowed in, high in the Sierras, they wandered into a waterless hellhole below sea level. The story is vividly told by one of their survivors, William Lewis Manly, in his *Death Valley in '49*.

Too late in 1849 to be sure of a safe crossing over the central Sierra, a party of gold seekers with some hundred wagons decided to enter California by the trail which led from Salt Lake City to Los Angeles. Apparently the first party to attempt this route with wagons, the group, organized under the name of the Sand Walking Company, laid its plans carefully and would doubtless have arrived safely in Los Angeles had not a majority, eager to get to the gold fields as soon as possible, turned off on what they thought was a good cutoff. A misinterpretation of Frémont's *Report,* which by that time had become a Bible for those moving over the western trails, was to a considerable degree responsible for the tragic error. In that account Frémont had told of an easy way east round the southern end of the Sierra Nevada by way of the Tehachapi Pass and across the Mojave Desert to the Old Spanish Trail leading toward Salt Lake. Such a route, followed in reverse, spelled to the emigrants a quick way to the mining country. Accordingly, they left the well-marked trail to seek the cutoff, but they left it at the wrong point, near Mountain Meadows in southwest Utah.

From there they wandered west across a barren, rugged country. Remembering Frémont's description of a green land beyond a high chain of mountains running north and south, they pushed across the Amargosa Range, breaking into small groups as their position became more desperate, each pushing ahead for its own salvation. In time, group by group, they stumbled into the desert sink which they were to christen Death Valley, a name singularly appropriate because its cruel nature meant even greater disaster to them than had the Valley of the Shadow of Death to the persevering Christian in his journey to the Celestial City. No earlier traveler had left a record that would have told them that safety lay in following the valley south into the Mojave; they had only that alluring description by Frémont, which they again remembered as they saw the Panamints before them. Hence, they sought again to move across the mountains and desperately scrambled over cruel, dry spurs only to find more than a hundred miles of a second desert to cross. Their hopes had seemed quite logical: "Some who had read Frémont's travels said that the range immediately west of us must be the one he described, on the west side of which was a beautiful country, of rich soil and having plenty of cattle, and horses, and containing some settlers, but on the east all was barren, dry, rocky desert as far as could be seen."

Some of the members of the disintegrated Sand Walking Company died in the valley and in the desert beyond the Panamints, of thirst, hunger, and exhaustion. Others, like the J. W. Brier family, stumbled on and eventually got out by twos and threes, no one knows quite how. The members of the largest group, who called themselves the Jayhawkers, struggled out round the northern side of Telescope Peak and eventually reached the Mariposa mines, with only a few fatalities. The most memorable group was known as the Bennett-Arcane party, made up of the Bennett and Arcane families, including four small children, together with Lewis Manly and John Rogers. Volunteering to try to get through to civilization while the rest of the party stayed near Furnace Creek in Death Valley, Manly and Rogers crossed the Panamints; traversed the Mojave; found blessed water, food, and help on Rancho San Francisquito, not far north of Mission San Fernando; and, hardly waiting to catch their breaths, returned to the families stranded in the desert and led them safely back to Los Angeles. That was all, except for the perseverance, hardships, doubts, struggles, and gruesomely humorous events that attended their heroic venture.

The dramatic story of the Death Valley party of 'forty-nine was of the sort which is not allowed to die. Almost immediately there began to appear in local papers scattered accounts written by one or another survivor. Twenty years after the event the surviving Jayhawkers were holding annual get-togethers to swap experiences, meetings which continued annually until only one man was still living. And thirty years after the fateful trek, a play called "Argonauts of Death Valley," which pictured prominently the roles of Mrs. Brier and her husband and children, was presented in the California towns. Then, in 1894, Lewis Manly published his memoirs in San Jose, where he had long made his home. Much earlier he had written a shorter version, based on a daily record he had kept from Salt Lake to Los Angeles, but it had been lost in a fire which destroyed his family home in Wisconsin. Now, in his seventies and crippled by a severe accident, he set about doing what he considered his duty, an admittedly "unpleasant work." He felt that, even at his age, every point of that terrible journey of nearly a half century earlier had remained indelibly fixed upon his memory. Aided by extensive correspondence with remaining survivors, he built up his saga.

Later research has borne out the accuracy of his story; the spirit and vivid imagination of his book speak for themselves.

The twenty-nine-year-old Manly, at the time of his experiences in Death Valley, was amply qualified to be a hero. He had learned resourcefulness and piety from his parents in Vermont, and he had lived under pioneer conditions in Michigan and Wisconsin when they were still territories. He had, moreover, intellectual resources gained in country schools; he consoled himself in the desert with snatches of poetry and comparisons of the wanderings of the Israelites with his own experiences. And that he had sufficient courage is proved by his acts. He, along with that sturdy Tennessean, John Rogers, stayed with the women and children when other single men thought only of their own survival. They hesitated not a moment to return with the pitiful supplies at their disposal, even though they had gone through soul struggles and nightmares as they had pushed across the desert, where sometimes they did not have the saliva to swallow their dried meat, and where a handful of evanescent ice or a raw and unsalted gob of meat cut from a starved ox kept them alive for a few more miles. In a land where "at night no stars forgot to shine" they struggled on, thinking sardonically of the gameless wilderness, "a grand, but worthless landscape" where "a vest pocketful of powder and shot would last a good hunter till he starved to death." The reader will agree most heartily with Mrs. Bennett, who exclaimed when Manly and Rogers returned, "Such boys should never die!"

Manly's honest memory and his ability to re-create a scene make it possible for the reader to follow every step of the way, experiencing the range of despair, faith, and ecstasy on arrival. He tells of a world in which sight of an occasional solitary Indian merely accentuated the loneliness of the travelers. When they came across an Indian squaw, frightened to see a white man in the desert,

She instantly caught her infant off its little pallet made of a small piece of wood covered by a rabbit skin, and putting the baby under one arm, and giving a small jerk to the little girl that was crying at the top of her voice, she bounded off and fairly flew up the gentle slope toward the summit, the girl following very close. The woman's long black hair stood out as she rushed along, looking over her shoulder every instant as if she expected to be slain.

It is also a strangely timeless world, as Manly felt when he looked down a hole in a rock and saw there, curled up, an Indian perhaps centuries old, "Adam's brother," looking like a dried venison ham.

The experiences of the Death Valley sufferers, like so many others on the frontier, brought out the fact that some men are heroic, some weak, and some base under intense and extended trial, and that frequently the animals put the men to shame. Good faith and true sacrifice were the rule in the Bennett-Arcane party, but discord among the larger Jayhawker group, an all-male aggregation in which too often no man was willing to give his friend a hand, was apparent even before they went their own way. Manly's admiration for Mrs. Juliette Brier, that heroine who weighed less than one hundred pounds yet brought a sick husband and three small children through alive, is only matched by his puzzlement over the Reverend James Brier, whose enthusiasm for the short cut was partly responsible for the party's predicament, who was calmly discussing his theories of education with his two small boys when Manly and Rogers came upon their camp in the Panamints, and years later was still to insist that roses would grow where only "the cabbage tree," as Manly called the Joshua tree, was then found. Even more unusual but decidedly more heroic in Manly's eyes were Old Crump, the tough old ox that carried four children on his back the entire way, and the faithful dog Cuff, which did his daily turn as watchman for the families and survived the alkali sands that had killed so many dogs moving west. Most wonderful and endeared of all, however, was the little donkey that Manly had obtained from the Mexicans near San Fernando. This "little black, one-eyed lady" survived the three horses, which died in the desert; she foraged successfully where no forage was visible, lived for days without water, and perked the company up whenever it felt low. She blithely hauled along the meat from a slaughtered ox, calmly ignoring in her donkey fashion the fact that the ox had been much bigger than she. "The little mule was the liveliest, sharpest witted animal of the whole."

The gayest event in the days of horror was the wild ride made by Mrs. Arcane on a frightened ox. Wearing the finery that she had determined to take through to California, with ribbons streaming out over the crystal salt, the lady dashed on oxback over Devil's Sink. It is good to know that everyone in the party could still break down with laughter. The most desperate moment was perhaps that in which the body of Captain Culverwell was discovered—he who had once thought of staying with the Bennett-Arcane party but had lost faith that the boys would return and had gone on his way alone. Manly and Rogers found him a few miles below the Death Valley camp: "stretched out upon the sand . . . dying all alone, with no one to transmit his last words to family or friends. Not a morsel to eat, and the little canteen by his side empty. A sad and lonely death indeed."

Strong is the gratitude that Manly expresses toward the good Spanish Californians who came to his aid in the country over the mountain. "We were glad of the good feeling," he writes, for he had been haunted by the stories he had heard, mindful of the tradition of earlier travelers; "if what we had read about them in books was true, we were in a set of land pirates, and blood thirsty men whom we might have occasion to beware of." Rather, they killed fat young heifers and sent oranges to the children, crying in pity for the "pobre niños." And in the end, the Indian guide's description to Frémont of the land over the mountains, "where the country is so beautiful that it is considered a paradise," was more than borne out; the motif of the tale is thirst for water and greenness, the ecstasy comes with the crossing into the San Fernando Valley:

O! if some poet of wildest imagination could only place himself in the position of those poor tired travellers to whom water in
thick muddy pools had been a blessing, who had eagerly drunk the
fluid even when so salt and bitter as to be repulsive, and now saw
the clear, pure liquid, distilled from the crystal snow, abundant,
free, filled with life and health . . . with the gentle accompaniment of rustling trees—a soft singing hush, telling of rest, and
peace, and happiness!

∽∽∽∽

On May 30, 1855, the *Southern Californian* made a not un-
typical comment on affairs in the cow counties:

The past week or two has been tolerable good for killing. Two
poor redskins have passed from among us to the happy hunting
grounds; two of the "light-haired" race have paid the penalty for
their misdeeds in the Monte; three others have expiated their of-
fences against the sacredness of horseflesh at the Tejon; the bones
of two human beings [have been] found near Santa Barbara, and
one unfortunate being has been hurried to destruction by his own
hand—delightful isn't it?

This state of affairs and the bantering attitude toward it
were accepted as the keynote of the times. Such a society
needed a chronicler who had seen the violence first hand and
who had a sense of humor in telling about it. Major Horace
Bell, who sometimes wrote under the nom de plume of Don
Guillamo Embustero y Mentiroso, was the man for the job.
He not only had seen the life but had so thoroughly taken
part in it that one of his contemporaries called him a "black-
mailer, murderer, thief, house-burner, snake-hunter, and de-
famer of the dead." He, however, labeled himself a truthful
historian who delighted in "taking the ludicrous side of the
horrible history of pioneer times." Experience, taste, and
talent all combined in producing an unusual record in *The
Reminiscences of a Ranger*.

Although Bell never pretended to give an entirely accurate
picture of his life, choosing to write with the flair for hyper-

bole of the frontier journalist, his autobiographical comments, supplemented by obituary notices and a scurrilous *Life of Horace Bell* published by an anonymous enemy in the 'eighties, provide a reasonably reliable account of his adventures. Born in 1830 on the Indiana side of the Ohio River some forty miles below Louisville, Kentucky, Bell crossed the country with thousands of others to hunt for gold in 1850. How much mining he did in the two and a half years he spent in the Hangtown, Shasta, and Klamath regions is not clear; his detractor says that Bell's father sent him west "where the young hoodlum might find a society more congenial to his rough character," and that after he reached California he became a capper for the gamblers. Bell says nothing of helping the gamblers, but he does insist that the gold-rush gambler was "a man of integrity—a dignitary." At any rate, he shared the fate of the average miner in that he stayed "broke." Late in 1852 he turned up in Los Angeles, where his uncle, Alexander Bell, a pioneer of 1842, was well established in business and owned the largest building in town.

Bell was in Los Angeles for most of the next four years, after which he, with many another adventurer, joined William Walker and went to Nicaragua. There is no record, however, to support his detractor's statement that he finally left Los Angeles by order of the vigilantes. It is not clear what his occupation was during these early days in the Old Pueblo. He may have helped his uncle or he may have sponged off him; he may have worked as a waiter or assistant in one of the hotels or saloons—perhaps even acted as a capper at the Bella Union, "begging his half dollar for breakfast from the first miner to arrive in the morning." One doubts, however, that, as his enemy asserted, he "became a drunken debauchee and frequently found his way into the chain-gang." Always given to dressing in a spectacular manner, having a histrionic soul, he may have continued appearing in the garb attributed to him in the mining regions: "He wore long hair down to his shoulders, a wide-brimmed Spanish hat known as a sombrero, a dirty red shirt, breeches supported by a belt and tucked inside the long leggins of his boots, while two or three Colt's revolvers and a Bowie knife or two were in his belt."

One point, however, is certain, that he was one of an irregular body of volunteer police known as the Los Angeles Rangers, formed in 1853 to combat lawlessness, particularly by such bands as those of Jack Powers and the putative Joaquín Murieta. The Rangers included a number of Southern California's most respected citizens, such as Stephen Foster, Benjamin Hayes, and Phineas Banning, but, like other ranger outfits, it may have had some ne'er-do-wells in its ranks. According to Bell, the Rangers did not do much but ride madly from ranch to ranch and fortify themselves with *aguardiente*. They apparently got no direct grants from the state legislature as did Harry Love's vigilante group up in the San Joaquin Valley, which, assured of a reward for Joaquín's capture, came back with a head purportedly his but so impaired by time and heat that many doubted that it was the head of the near-mythical bandit.

After sharing William Walker's disastrous experiences in Nicaragua, Bell probably returned to California for a short period and then moved to his father's home in Harrison County, Indiana. According to the anonymous *Life*, he there shared in a sort of guerilla war that was going on between Indiana and Kentucky settlers over slave smuggling, at one time escaping from the jail in Brandenburg, Kentucky, with the aid of seventy-five Northern invaders. Late in 1858, it is said, he was involved in a knifing scrape in which he wounded his sweetheart in an altercation and hastened his mother's death by throwing her violently on the floor when she attempted to intervene. His next appearance was in Vera Cruz, where (Bell states) he served under Juárez during his fight with Miramón. From there he went to Tehuantepec. Eventually he returned to the United States, to serve with the Northern troops in the Civil War, at Shiloh and Antietam and in

Louisiana as a scout under Generals Banks and Canby. War Department records show that he was a Union spy in the New Orleans area but assign him no rank.

In July, 1866, he returned to Los Angeles as Major Horace Bell, and there, according to his reminiscences in the posthumous *On the Old West Coast,* continued to fight the war almost singlehanded for a number of years. He was certainly one of the few Angeleños to serve on the Northern side, and there is every reason to believe that he met many enemies in the unregenerated secessionist community on his return. Other factors may have contributed to his unpopularity, however: there may have been lingering feuds from his former stay; his temper and unquestioned bravery may have made him additional enemies; and his activities as lawyer for the unpopular and dispossessed, and his behavior as editor of *The Porcupine,* a prickly reform sheet which threatened to "clean up" the town, may have contributed to his reputation. At any rate, after his return he was mightily hated by certain parts of the community in Los Angeles, and according to tradition he was involved in a good many acts of violence. Handsomely dressed in black, his six-foot-two figure was well known on the streets and in the courts; like Ambrose Bierce, he had something of the theatrical about him, although he did not have the range of intellectual interests that the San Francisco gadfly possessed.

Bell's *The Reminiscences of a Ranger* appeared in 1881, the first clothbound book to be printed, bound, and published in the city of Los Angeles. The destruction of most of the copies in a fire made it a rare item for many years, but since its republication in 1927 it has been easily available. The book has rightly been accepted as a chronicle which catches the spirit of the early 'fifties in Southern California. Although it admittedly contains many exaggerations, it is based essentially on fact. In addition, it has a tang that seems particularly suited to the subject.

Bell's flair for humorous rhetoric was partly a result of his work as a journalist (its spirit is similar to that of many an editorial issued by the frontier newspapers), and partly a product of his activities as a lawyer of the old flamboyant school that always put on a show when the time arrived to appeal to the jury. His style of writing is at the same time a continuation and a parody of old-style legal oratory. As a result, Bell is frequently trying, often monotonous, and always difficult to read in long sections. But he can also be very good. Take for example his definition of a "gringo":

> *Gringo,* in its literal signification, means *ignoramus.* For instance: an American who has not yet learned to eat chili peppers stewed in grease, throw the lasso, contemplate the beauties of nature from the sunny side of an adobe wall, make a first-class cigar out of a corn husk, wear open-legged pantaloons, with bell bottoms, dance on one leg, and live on one meal a week. Now the reader knows what a terrible thing it was in early days to be a *gringo.*

Or his explanation of the creed of filibustering:

> "First, that the earth is the Lord's, and the fullness thereof, and we are the Lord's people; second, that all Spanish-American governments are worthless, and should be reconstructed, and that such is our mission; that the people of Lower California and Sonora are, or should be, dissatisfied with Mexican rule, and are, or should be, ripe for rebellion, and if not in terror of the Mexican central despotism would cry out for American aid to shake off their galling chains; the Sonoreños ought to rise, proclaim their independence, and cry for help from the generous Filibuster, who stood ready to help the down-trodden Mexican and to feather his own nest in particular." We were, therefore, determined to succor the oppressed people of Lower California and Sonora, who were silently praying that we might come and relieve them from their cruel yoke, and their surplus supply of horses and such like, and possess the lands of the country and receive the thanks of a grateful people after we had won their liberties and relieved them of their property.

From such a writer, one is not surprised to hear that when a man was shot an "individual was accidentally perforated,"

or that Los Angeles was "a place where every man carried
his code strapped to his posterior." "Was not California then
the double-distilled quintessence of chivalry?" We are assured
that "Indians did the labor and the white man spent the
money in those happy days," and that an American back-
woodsman was a man who always killed an Indian before he
skinned him. Nigger Alley and the old Plaza were inhabited
by desperadoes and native damsels "of lascivious mien and
voluptuous proportions." Los Angeles was a town in which
extraordinary things were always happening:

> The two dignitaries were quietly supping together in one of the
> back rooms of the *Montgomery,* when the pioneer legal representa-
> tive of the Government emptied a plate of soup full in the face of
> the Land Office man, who, not in the least disturbed in his cool
> equanimity, quietly proceeded to lay the attorney across the table
> and deliberately bite off about an inch of that great Federal nose.

The Reminiscences of a Ranger tells of a hard society in
which the drabness of life and the constant materialism are
relieved but not brightened by excitement. Bell's description of activity in Nigger Alley, the lowest section of the
frontier city, gives a taste of it: "Americans, Spaniards, Indians and foreigners, rushing and crowding along from one
gambling house to another, from table to table, all chinking
the everlasting eight square $50 pieces up and down in their
palms." The arrival of "a small army of fair and frail sisters
from San Francisco" in 1853, the first large group of prosti-
tutes, did nothing to raise the tone of the place. "We had
thieves and cutthroats of all nations under the sun, but up
to November, '53, the *monde* and the *demimonde* was
represented by ladies to the manor born." Under the circumstances it is not surprising that most of Bell's principal characters were rascals. There was the famous Peter Biggs, the
Negro barber and pimp who was known as "the black
Democrat" and died with a carving knife in his ribs; Doña
Ramona, a member of the demimonde referred to locally as

Mrs. Frémont because she was said to have "cast the sunshine of her maiden affection on the conquering hero"; and the "divinely sharp practitioner" who posed as a minister, obtained a big collection from the repentant Angeleños, invested the *pious fund* in a stock of *aguardiente,* red shirts, and striped calico, and went to Colorado to gamble and trade with the Indians. There was the openly corrupt city government and the occasional honest marshal who was assassinated while doing his duty. There were the men like Bill, "the patron saint of Los Cuervos," and Aleck Bell, who told tall tales, and there were the practical jokers like John Raines, who staged a mock revolution, much to the discomfiture of the mayor.

Although Bell avowed that, as "this truthful historian," he would prefer to deal with the great legal battles of early Los Angeles, he devoted most of his pages to violence. Filibusters, bandits, lynching parties, and Rangers throng his pages. Although he indicates that in several cases the wrong man was hanged, he accepts the local code in the matter. "The failure to get up a first-class lynching cast a gloom over the city, from which it did not recover for near a month, at the expiration of which time they started in one Sunday morning, two men being assassinated and three hung before the bull-fighting commenced in the afternoon." Although the Rangers were organized to pursue Joaquín, Bell apparently knew little about that bandit, but he gives interesting sketches of a number of other desperadoes. Among these were Crooked Nose Smith, "a very prince of a desperado"; Ricardo Urives, who "could stand more shooting and stabbing than the average bull or grizzly bear"; and Jack Powers, that "first-class sport" from Santa Barbara who, "under favorable circumstances might have obtained the most honorable distinction" but was eventually chopped up and fed to the pigs in Sonora. Another, unique by virtue of her sex, was an unnamed female brigand, "as pretty a little brunette woman as ever excited the lustful desires of a Mormon missionary," who was captured and sent back, with her companions, to San Luis Obispo, where the gang had operated. The Angeleños regretted that it was not their turn to mete out justice, but they admitted that "it was not their hang." Yet another was Manuel Vergara, who brutally murdered a local merchant and escaped the Rangers. And there was Senati, who shot down the city marshal and later was killed, along with four of his fellows, by Moreno, who then collected the reward. Not until Moreno had been sentenced to San Quentin for another offence was it discovered that the murdered men were members of his own gang.

Bell's most attractive side is found in his defense of minorities, both in his later days as a lawyer and a journalist in Los Angeles and in his accounts in his reminiscences. He spoke well of the Mormons in spite of the fact that they were in disrepute. He spared no words in describing the mistreatment of the Indians, the forced laborers of the period. He was also constantly sympathetic toward the Spanish Californians, whom he saw disintegrate under the predatory tactics of the *gringos*. But his fondness for them did not extend to a defense of the mission system, which, of course, had been done away with prior to his arrival, but about which he had heard a great deal. He felt that the Indian's soul had been saved at the expense of his body and spoke of "a certain devout friar, who earned a crown immortal by his success in capturing converts with the lasso and converting them with the lash." His attitude toward the mission system, typical of that of the newly arrived Americans, was well expressed in a half dozen lines by Albert Fenner Kercheval, a Los Angeles truck gardener whose poems Bell quoted at length in *The Reminiscences of a Ranger:*

> They brought up proud sinners with sharp, sudden pulls,
> And lassoed their converts like broncos and bulls,
> Or gathered confessions from red, rosy lips,
> To hoard as the treasure the honey bee sips,

With hands that were ready and hearts that were bold:
How I envy those clean-shaven Padres of old!

But to Bell, "the California Spaniard was in the olden time an over average Christian and good fellow, full of jovial good humor, hospitable to a fault, patriotic, liberty-loving." He always insisted that "the Mexicans are a gentle people, and have more virtue than the *barbaros del Norte*—which means us blue-blooded Americans—ever gave them credit for." He summed up his attitude when he wrote:

The gringo nation is great, the affirmative of which this military scribe is free to maintain on horseback or on foot, with spear of pen, because he belongs to that immaculate race himself; but there is an old adage which is as truthful as the writer thereof, and that is, that "the gringo spoils all other peoples with whom he is brought in contact."

∽∽∽∽

Other, less bombastic chroniclers drew essentially the same picture as Bell of the violent and disordered society in which the gambler played a more prominent part than the minister, in which most of the former Californians disintegrated and a few turned bandits, and in which earthquakes, droughts, and bitter feeling over the Civil War augmented the sense of isolation of the southern counties. They did not approach the theme with the boisterousness of the Ranger-filibuster-editor of *The Porcupine,* and they added descriptions of typical everyday life of a more peaceful nature. In 1860, for instance, the sober and industrious William H. Brewer, at thirty-two the principal assistant to Josiah Dwight Whitney, who was about to embark on his famous geological survey of California, noted in his diary that conditions in Los Angeles were very unsettled:

We all continually wear arms—each wears both bowie knife and pistol (navy revolver), while we have always for game or otherwise, a Sharp's rifle, Sharp's carbine, and two double-barreled shot-guns. Fifty or sixty murders per year have been so common here in Los

Angeles . . . as I write this there are at least six heavy loaded revolvers in the tent, besides bowie knives and other arms.

Just a few days earlier, riding to Don Benito Wilson's
ranch in what is now Pasadena, Brewer had been escorted by
a minister carrying a rifle. But his honest, meticulous account,
published under the title, *Up and Down California in 1860–
1864,* includes, in addition to comments on firearms, remarks
on the sweetness of the padres' bells at San Gabriel, the many
ingenious uses for rawhide that the Californians had developed, the absence of any bridges in Southern California,
the prettiness of the half-breed women, and the sleepiness of
Santa Barbara, which resembled a prehistoric ruin with its
crumbling adobes. In San Luis Obispo he spoke of court's
being dismissed because both the judge and the district attor-
ney were drunk. At Los Angeles he wrote mostly about the
downpouring rain, which made life in a tent camp a miserable
business.

Brewer was in fact describing the rains which were to pre-
cede the disastrous droughts of 'sixty-three and 'sixty-four.
The floods did much damage, but it was nothing in comparison to the ravages of the next two, rainless, years which
ended the cattle industry in the south. J. Ross Browne,
describing a journey to Yuma in his *Adventures in the Apache
Country,* wrote vividly of the discouraging state of affairs.
From Chino to Vallecito, along the route of the defunct Butterfield Mail, the way was punctuated with dead cattle lying
around the black, muddy pools. "Thousands drawn to the
pools by thirst were unable to extricate themselves from the
mud; and the road was sometimes blocked by the gaunt,
shrunken bodies of still living animals unable to get out of the
way." The disaster was so sweeping that it took years for Southern California to recover, and it completed the ruin of the
struggling Spanish Californians, already heavily weighted
with mortgages held at usurious interest rates.

When Stephen Powers arrived in 1868, after walking from

Raleigh, North Carolina, to Los Angeles—in order to make a "personal and ocular study of the most diverse races of the Republic"—his most vivid impression was the number of tramps he met in the region. Not even the "frowsy South" and "a continent of dust" had impressed him as adversely as did the squalor of Southern California. In his *Afoot and Alone* he told of the dirt and poverty he saw in the cow counties, of a grog shop in the wing of a mission with a door opening directly on the chapel, of men lined up to look at a girl through a crack in a cabin, of "white trash" more pitifully fed and lodged than even the wretched marginal dwellers of defeated Dixie. It was a land of disorder and distress, a land where man's ambition seemed to atrophy. Powers' sober account warrants special attention, for he was a shrewd observer and a man of culture, who had carried volumes of Longfellow and Horace with him on his 3,556 mile walk and had planned articles to be published under the recondite and odd nom de plume, Socrates Hyacinth. He was also interested in botany, agriculture, and ethnology and was well equipped to speak on those subjects. Eventually he was to write the most reliable early study of the California Indians.

The picture of Southern California given by Harris Newmark in that remarkable collection of anecdote and fact, *Sixty Years in Southern California,* is a little less disturbing, perhaps because, unlike Brewer's and Powers' accounts, it was written long after the events described. It was, moreover, written in large measure not by Newmark himself but by a paid collaborator, the scholar Perry Worden, who both verified the information supplied by Newmark and added to it by extensive research. In spite of being thus removed from the scene, this Pepys Diary of California offers evidence of days often made disheartening by violence, epidemic, and drought. To the sensitive Jewish boy from West Prussia who abandoned his brandy for an umbrella in crossing the Isthmus of Panama in 1853, the City of the Angels was a place demanding rapid readjustment on his part. After a wild ride from San Pedro on one of the famous stages, he arrived in the pueblo on a Sunday afternoon to find the city filled with drunken Indians. Soon he learned to expect two or three violent deaths each Sunday, particularly in that hellhole, Calle de los Negros. Apparently, life was the cheapest thing to be found in Los Angeles. Learning that the city council had rescinded as impractical a rule against the carrying of arms, and frightened when a normally worthy citizen drew a bead on him and demanded, "Treat or I shoot," he bought a pistol and found himself peppering the sides of buildings, like the rest of his companions. In time he even came to feel that lynchings were necessary as a desperate remedy to control a lawless community.

From Harris Newmark's reminiscences of early Los Angeles, one gets a vivid picture of two civilizations—the old, threadbare, and shabby; the young, thrashing about in its struggles to take form. There were the adobe houses, with their three-foot walls, small windows, dirt floors, and lack of any conveniences, even heat. Water for drinking, cooking, and washing was taken from the public *zanja*, where *indianos* did the family wash and the entire family bathed at irregular intervals. Those who lived away from the *zanja* bought water at fifty cents a week (for one bucket a day, except Sunday) from a peddler who dipped it up from the open ditch. As late as the 'sixties no serious attempt had been made to establish a sewer system; numerous dogs, acting as scavengers, served as a poor substitute for a garbage disposal system. Fires were heralded by a general shooting of pistols and were fought by a volunteer bucket brigade: there was not a fire engine in town. Sidewalks did not exist, and during the rainy season the streets were muddy morasses. There were no cells in the jail, and the prisoners were chained to a log. Smallpox and diphtheria were terrible plagues, and no systematic steps were taken to check them. A few enterprising citizens planted willows or pepper trees on their property, but the general appearance of the town for years was that of a mud village in a sterile plain, without a sign of a bridge to cross a creek or a river, and with no lights at night to guide the wanderer home. Nigger Alley and Sonora Town were but pronounced examples of a general squalor, relieved only when spring brought grass and flowers and longer evenings. As a rule, the dirty, tobacco-spitting population took all inconveniences in stride. The excitement and adventure that the Old Pueblo afforded did little to alleviate the drabness imposed by this low standard of living.

〜〜〜〜

As the southern communities lay sleeping in the sun in the 'fifties, with violence and intrigue in the shadows and whispers of future booms off stage, incidents were occurring which were to work their way into the folklore of the region. A shipwreck, a lynching, or a practical joke animated the gossip of the day, starting yarns that were carried from pueblo to rancho, or from the trail to the new squatter towns. But folklore material is frequently difficult to reproduce for a later generation. In many a tale the facts of the episode giving rise to it are impossible to determine because in the oral retellings the love of yarning was far stronger than the tellers' desire for truth. The two accounts of duels forced against cravens by the fabulous Colonel Macgruder, one in San Diego and one in Los Angeles, both fought with dummy bullets made of corks, are clear examples of this type of story. The facts of other episodes are well authenticated, but the tales which from oblique references in contemporary writings one knows developed from the episodes have died. Of the Mountain Meadows Massacre, for example, which deeply affected Southern California, much factual material remains, yet most of the tales which rose out of it no longer exist. But in some instances, of course, both facts and resultant fiction are known.

The Pacific Southwest's most celebrated contribution to the Indian captivity stories which form a special branch of

American literature was the kidnapping of Olive and Mary Ann Oatman in 1851 by the Apaches who attacked the Oatman family when they were near the Gila River en route to Southern California. This attack, one of the many examples of marauding Indians' molesting small emigrant parties on the southern desert route from Tucson, seemed particularly brutal because of the murder of the parents and four of the seven children. One boy escaped to El Monte; but two girls —Olive, who was thirteen, and Mary Ann, who was seven— were captured and forced to march hundreds of miles in their bare feet, and were treated as slaves by the most cruel of the Southwest Indians. Later, the girls were traded to the Mojaves, a more kindly tribe who lived some three hundred miles up the Colorado from Fort Yuma. Mary Ann died of malnutrition. Olive, adopted by a friendly chief and his tenderhearted squaw, learned to cultivate gourds and submitted to being tattooed with disfiguring lines from mouth to chin. But, as she wept constantly and as food was scarce, the Mojaves were eventually glad to exchange her for a gift of beads and blankets brought by a messenger sent out from Fort Yuma for the purpose of effecting the girl's release.

Olive Oatman was soon brought to El Monte, near Los Angeles, where she told her story in an interview which appeared in the Los Angeles *Star* on April 19, 1856—the first important personal interview to appear in a Southern California newspaper. Later, she was taken to Oregon by relatives and on the way told her story once again (she had told it many times in between) to a Reverend R. B. Stratton of Yreka, California, who wrote a sentimental book titled *The Captivity of the Oatman Girls* which appeared in San Francisco in 1857 and was reprinted in the East, selling thirty thousand copies in two years. Thus, folk throughout the country could thrill when Olive made such unlikely statements as: "Food was offered me, but how could I eat to prolong a life I now loathed?" Those close at hand shuddered as they remembered their own narrow escapes on the desert and contemplated the story she had told to the *Star* of seeing captive Cocopa Indians crucified in a native dance. Doubtless they also pondered her assurance that she was not "made a wife" by the Indians, for their theories concerning her five years among the savages pointed to other conclusions. As for Olive, she fast relearned her English (although she seemed somewhat mentally retarded), demonstrated that she could sew like a mantuamaker, and years later married and settled down to a quiet domestic life, disproving the more logical rumor that she had been placed in an insane asylum.

Again, the trials of the overland crossing were made vivid when, late in 1857, word reached Los Angeles of the Mountain Meadows Massacre, in which almost all of a party of Arkansas emigrants on their way to Los Angeles by the Salt Lake trail had been wiped out. In this notorious massacre, which took place almost at the point where the Sand Walking party had taken the ill-fated cutoff eight years before, both Indians and Mormons were involved. As a result of it one of the main routes of approach to Southern California was temporarily closed and the Mormon community of San Bernardino, twelve hundred strong, packed up and returned to Salt Lake. The Southern California papers were filled with editorials about Brigham Young and his Danites and "avenging angels," and there was much hope that the federal government would allow the Californians to organize a battalion to march to Deseret and hang the villains "upon the highest peaks of the overhanging mountains," there to "remain suspended in the frigid atmosphere of the mountain tops, as an example from ocean to ocean of retributive justice." More practical members of the community rushed to San Bernardino to buy land and equipment at bargain prices. Immediate literary response to the incident took the form of doggerel verse such as that which appeared in the *Star:*

A heart-rending *scene* to all that can *hear,*
For the maidens that died their *beaus* shall not fear,

They will come to the mountains their *love's bones* to see
That *lies* bleached on the grounds by the sad massa*cre*.

An incident which went through a good many retellings in
print and doubtless many more in oral tradition was the finding of the wild woman of San Nicolas Island. For eighteen
years, from 1835 to 1853, this Indian woman had lived alone on
a rocky island seventy miles off the Santa Barbara coast. Isaac
Sparks, of the twenty-ton *Peor es Nada* (Better than Nothing)
had left her there when he removed some eighteen natives
from the island at the request of the padres. His story was
that she had gone to search for her child and that, because of
rough weather, the rescuers were unable to wait for her return. Sparks, it seems, intended to return for her, but the
Peor es Nada was wrecked on its next voyage, and there were
no other ships on the coast large enough to make the trip.
Apparently, all during the period that the woman was isolated the folks ashore knew of her existence, although there
was some speculation that she might have starved or have
been eaten by the wild dogs "with human eyes" who were her
companions on the lonely island. Eventually, George Nidever,
a mountain man who had come west with Joseph R. Walker,
put in at San Nicolas to hunt sea-gull eggs and there saw signs
of human habitation and even caught a glimpse of a "beckon-
ing ghost." On a later trip, encouraged by the church authorities, he made a thorough search and found the woman, who
was living in a hut made of whalebones and brush. Although
she appeared old and her teeth were worn to the gums, she
was very friendly, and her first act was to offer her guest two
varieties of roasted roots. It was evident that she had been
resourceful during her stay, for she had made shagskin clothes,
baskets, water bottles, and fishhooks, had tamed some of the
dogs, and had remained healthy on seal blubber and wild
plants. Taken to Santa Barbara, she danced and chattered for
the amazed inhabitants, but, as no Indian could be found who
spoke her language, she could not tell of her experiences as

a female Robinson Crusoe. She lived for about seven weeks after leaving the island; green vegetables and fruits, which she could not resist, proved too much of a change for one accustomed to blubber and roots. Just before her death, tradition has it, she was baptized under the name Juana María Peor es Nada.

As time went on, legends developed about her. In a quarter of a century she had become young and comely, her uncouth smock had turned into an iridescent, low-necked gown of green cormorant feathers, and her return for her child had become a plunge into the dangerous surf; she was "one who voluntarily breasted the waves, and fought death, in response to the highest love of which the human heart is capable." Later, the stark footprints that Nidever had found on San Nicolas were softened to "the prints of slender, naked feet" in the California moonlight. And by the time Gertrude Atherton retold the story, in her "The Isle of Skulls," the lost woman had become a red-haired enchantress who specialized in birdcalls. Now the story takes its logical place in the folklore of a region which named one of its towns Tarzana.

There was also the legend, told by the Indians, of the days when the Mojave basin was a valley of perpetual bloom which nourished a fine civilization crowned by a magic city with turrets and hanging gardens. Of this city Father Serra is said to have caught one glimpse. Legend says it disappeared during a terrible windstorm. After days of winds from the west, from the east, from the south, and from the north, the dread *ventarron,* or whirlwind, blew "till the mountains rattled in their sockets like teeth in an ancient skull." After the *ventarron* had pushed the mountains around like a *vaquero* herding cattle, the floods came and turned the former paradise into its present desolation. Even the latecomer could believe this story, for he knew that the ordinary west wind blew through the Tehachapi so strongly that bullets from the east were blasted back clean down the pass.

Down below the Sierra Madre it was the Santa Ana wind

which caused the trouble, as it blackened the sky with dust and rolled tumbleweeds from Puente to Gospel Swamp. This wind, which blew from the desert down the Santa Ana canyon, was named after the good St. Anne, for Portolá and his men had first camped beside the little river on July 28, 1769, two days after the saint's feast day. In time, Santa Ana became the name of the river, the mountains, the town, and the wind. In later days, some inhabitants suggested the name of the wind was derived from Satan; and others, with even less knowledge of history, blamed it on the dust raised by Santa Anna's cavalry. In more recent days, an ambitious chamber of commerce has tried to persuade visitors that the wind is named after an Indian term, "santana," meaning "big wind," but no one yet has been able to find the word in any native dialect.

Thus folk etymology continued, illustrated in the place names selected. Anaheim became perhaps the earliest of many Southern California hybrids, combining the saint's name with the German word for "home," but tradition has it that it was named after the first child born in the community. Farther north, meanwhile, "Los Angeles" had become firmly established as the proper shortening of the flamboyant "El Pueblo de Nuestra Señora la Reina de Los Angeles de Porciuncula." This in time was reduced to "Pueblo de Los Angeles." For a while it had appeared that the name would be shortened to "Pueblo," but the angels won out. Anglo-Saxon settlers brought about other changes as the town shifted its character. As seemed fitting, the Street of the Virgins disappeared entirely; and, of the delightful trio of Faith, Hope, and Charity streets, only Hope was retained as appropriate by the new settlers.

Within the Old Pueblo, "Doctor" Money, the eccentric religionist, who, according to his story, had been born "with four teeth and with the likeness of the rainbow in my right eye," attempted to further the reputation he had established in Sonora in debating the fate of the world with the seven padres of Pitaquitas by publishing his *Reform of the New Testament Church* and by preparing a much more formidable volume to deal with his Kuro Siwo currents, sometimes referred to as his Zwirro-Zwirro theory. This discussed thoroughly the alarming subterranean volcanic floods that swirled beneath the earth's surface and prophesied that the crust was too thin at San Francisco long to stay intact.

Money's theories did not seem extraordinarily bizarre to the Angeleños, who gazed, openmouthed, as two camels ambled down the *calle principal* in November, 1857. They were the vanguard of Uncle Sam's camels, introduced by Jefferson Davis in an attempt to solve the transportation problem of the Southwest. Here was an animal that would get fat where a jackass would starve to death. The terror of the desert was indeed minimized by a camel that had journeyed for ten days without water and then refused to take a drink on arrival. The local papers announced the appearance of Hadji Ali (known locally as Hi-Jolly), the Syrian camel driver with his native costume decorated with jingling bells, encouraged weird and faraway associations with the Sahara and the Holy Land. Years later, after the camel experiment had failed, lonely men told tales of seeing the strange animals loom up on the desert.

The most constant subject for legend, however, was the adventurer and brigand, both Mexican and American. Paragon among the badmen about whom folk tales were told, although not as celebrated as the renegade Jack Powers or the ubiquitous Joaquín Murieta, was Don Ricardo Urives of the Rancho de los Coyotes. The current belief was that Urives, a member of a well-known Mexican family, was a bandit for the fun of it, not for gain. Many yarns were spun about the shootings and stabbings in which he had been the victim on his periodic forays on Nigger Alley in Los Angeles. Finally, a dirty little coward from the Bowery got him with a shot through the back. But even after he died, Urives put up a good fight, twitching vigorously at propitious moments. After he was dead his arm suddenly twitched and shot his murderer squarely between the eyes. Again the body twitched and shot the gringo sheriff through the leg. It kicked the padre when he came to say the last rites over the corpse. Finally, the enraged citizenry lynched the corpse for good measure and buried it with difficulty. But Urives was not to lie contented. Years later, some paisanos who had drunk too much at a *baille* went out and dug up the coffin to satisfy their curiosity. They received the shock of their lives, for there was Don Ricardo's skeleton twitching away like a gambler at a fandango.

III

Southern California Becomes American

MARK TWAIN's description, in his *Life on the Mississippi,*
of the development of culture on the frontier is particularly
appropriate to the Southern California scene between the
gold rush and the tourist rush:

How solemn and beautiful is the thought that the earliest pioneer of civilization, the van-leader of civilization, is never the steam-
boat, never the railroad, never the newspaper, never the Sabbath-
school, never the missionary—but always whisky! Such is the case.
Look history over; you will see. The missionary comes after the
whisky—I mean, he arrives after the whisky has arrived; next comes
the poor immigrant, with ax and hoe and rifle; next, the trader;
next the miscellaneous rush; next, the gambler, the desperado, the
highwayman, and all their kindred in sin of both sexes; and next,
the smart chap who has bought up an old grant that covers all the
land; this brings the lawyer tribe; the vigilance committee brings
the undertaker. All these interests bring the newspaper; the newspaper starts up politics and a railroad; all hands turn to and build
a church and a jail—and behold! civilization is established forever
in the land.

As has been pointed out, the whisky, the trader, the gambler, the desperado, the vigilance committee, and even the

shyster lawyer arrived with great dispatch; the more commendable features of a growing community, however, were much slower to appear. The cow counties in the early days seem to have been barren ground for cultural seeds, as Robert G. Cleland pointed out in *The Cattle on a Thousand Hills*, a book which gives an excellent picture of this society:

> The contrast between the civilization of today and the cultural poverty of Southern California eighty or ninety years ago is almost unbelievable. The census return of 1850 listed no newspaper, hospital, college, academy, library, public school, or Protestant church in Los Angeles County. Three Catholic churches ministered to the religious needs of a region larger than many an eastern state; two-thirds of the population could neither read nor write; and school attendance was limited to nine.

Yet, at the same time that the violence and tawdry materialism of the frontier society seemed to be its most characteristic traits, another sort of world was growing painfully but surely. The church, the school, the library, the newspaper, even the arts, were gradually making their way in spite of the more boisterous and lurid elements in the picture.

Thus, the valiant and often heartbreaking attempts of pioneer Protestant ministers, such as J. W. Brier and James Woods, to establish churches in what they discovered to be a very hostile community eventually succeeded, in spite of the fact that, as late as 1858, there was no Protestant minister in Los Angeles to perform the services for the murdered Sheriff Barton, and even by 1864 regular Protestant services had not become established in Los Angeles. But by 1870 all the major denominations had gained footholds in the city, and in 1873 the Jews, who had held services since 1854, built a synagogue. These last, as so many chroniclers have pointed out, were one of the finest elements in the population. The Catholics, of course, had never been inactive.

In the field of education also the Catholics were active, and in 1865 they opened the first college in the south, St. Vincent's (now Loyola). The small private elementary schools, which had existed before the conquest, were gradually supplemented by publicly supported institutions. The city of Los Angeles opened its first public school in 1855, and by the end of that year there were eight in Los Angeles County, with a total enrollment of 180 pupils. That progress was slow is indicated by the fact that ten years later the enrollment was only 581. By 1876 there were three grammar schools and a high school in Los Angeles. Expansion in the smaller towns in the region had about kept pace.

Occasional theatrical performances, sometimes in Spanish, were presented in Los Angeles soon after the conquest; and, according to Newmark, a regular theater was started by William Temple in 1860 with a performance by a traveling company from San Francisco. That same year, Bartholomew's Rocky Mountain Circus held forth in the plaza, people coming for miles around to see the show. The management advertised: "A strict Police is engaged for the occasion!" One wonders what animals and what performers appeared in those days of difficult transportation. That was the same summer that the bullfight was abolished and baseball was introduced to the City of the Angels.

Music made its way slowly. The Spanish guitar, standby of fandangos, was augmented by American cornets and trombones when Commodore Stockton, in the days of the occupation, won the approval of the natives by having the band play daily in the plaza. As time went on, military bands, such as those stationed at Drum Barracks (Wilmington) and Fort Tejon, were brought to Los Angeles for festive occasions. When "Round House George" opened his crude "Garden of Paradise," in 1858, he provided a balcony for "the playing of such music, perhaps discordant, as Los Angeles could then produce"; his enterprise was encouraged by the Turnverein, many of whose members took part in the biweekly musical drills put on by the German Benevolent Society. In 1868, Harris Newmark brought a piano from the East, the second

such instrument, according to his statement, to be seen in the
Los Angeles area.

It is difficult to gauge the reading habits of the mixed population of these early days. Certainly, many of the inhabitants
were illiterate, and even more were little interested in polite
reading. However, as William B. Rice pointed out in his excellent history of the Los Angeles *Star,* the news vendors
apparently found it worth while to advertise in the local
weekly such journals as the London *Quarterly Review, Yankee Notions,* and *Godey's Lady Book.* Apparently, local merchants carried a few books, and by 1859 Hellman's was advertising a special book department and circulating library.
According to Newmark, the first bookstore in the city was
founded by Broderick and Reilly in 1871. There were a number of private libraries, such as the Indian collection of Hugo
Reid, the archives on local history developed by Stephen Foster and Judge Benjamin Hayes, and the library of Henry
Mellus, who had been one of Dana's companions on the *Pilgrim* and eventually became the mayor of Los Angeles. There
appears to have been a Mechanics' Library in Los Angeles
from 1856 to 1858, and in 1859 the first move was made to
start a public library. This effort failed, however, and another
thirteen years passed before a permanent library was established.

A half dozen names are prominent among those who in one
way or another assisted in the development of these various
institutions of civilization. Stephen C. Foster was a Yale
graduate from Maine, who had experience both in practicing
medicine and in teaching before coming to Southern California as interpreter for the Mormon Battalion. Dr. John S.
Griffin, a graduate of the University of Pennsylvania who arrived as surgeon with Kearny's troops, finally settled in Los
Angeles and became a civic leader. Henry D. Barrows, "educated as a Yankee schoolmaster," quit the mines because of
ill-health and took a job with the former trapper, William
Wolfskill, as a tutor; he was prominent as a leader in moves

for adequate education in the new country and also wrote sketches of early pioneers. J. Lancaster Brent, a lawyer from the South, brought with him what Newmark describes as "a fairly representative, though inadequate library." A "highly educated French lady" named Mlle. Theresa Bry came to town and established a private school, which flourished in spite of the scandal occasioned by her marriage to an unrefined gardener, M. Henriot. And Ralph Emerson, a distant cousin of the Concord sage, lent his name to worthy civic enterprises.

When the first issue of the bilingual Los Angeles *Star* appeared on May 17, 1851, nearly five years after Stockton's entrance into Los Angeles, it seemed that another hardy perennial American institution had taken root in Southern California soil. It had indeed. The paper's struggles for survival, however, were bitter and arduous for the next twenty years. Within five years of its founding, the weekly *Star* was offered to anyone who would take it off the hands of its distressed owner for a thousand dollars below its original cost, the amount to be paid either in cash or barter. Its purchase by the energetic Henry Hamilton, an Irish emigrant who had already edited the *Calaveras Chronicle* of Mokelumne Hill, was the only thing that saved it. Hamilton did well enough until his rabid secessionist editorials resulted in its suspension by the government during the Civil War. It was revived, however, and became a daily in 1870, only to expire in a sheriff's sale for debts nine years later.

Most of the competitors which sprang up during the early life of the *Star* had even more difficulties and were of much shorter duration. The *Southern Californian,* founded in 1854 as a Democratic weekly and rival of the *Star,* survived less than two years, Andrés Pico, its backer, losing $10,000 on the venture. *El Clamor Publico,* the first all-Spanish paper and the first Republican journal in Los Angeles, lasted only four years, from 1855 to 1859, even though it had an unusually energetic and able editor in the person of Francisco

P. Ramírez. J. J. Warner's *Southern Vineyard* struggled along
for two years (1858–1860) before it succumbed to the "per-
nicious financial anemia" which eventually claimed most of
the newspaper ventures of the period. *El Amigo del Pueblo,*
a Spanish sheet founded in 1861 to continue the policy of
addressing the original Californian public, lasted hardly six
months. One competitor, however, was more successful and
outlived the *Star.* This was the Los Angeles *News,* founded
in 1860 as a semiweekly. Because it was a Republican paper it
had access to a campaign fund somewhat more affluent, with
the political shift after the Civil War, than that of the Democrats, even in rebellious Southern California, which had been a
Confederate stronghold during the War. In 1869, when the
News became Southern California's first daily, a period of
greater prosperity for the local newspapers began. The *Express* (1871), *Las Dos Republicas* (1872), the *Herald* (1873),
the *Weekly Mirror* (1873), the monthly *Rural Californian*
(1877), and the *Times* (1881) proved hardier, having a larger
and more literate public to support them.

During the difficult early period, the only journals outside
Los Angeles in the southern part of the state were the San
Diego *Herald,* which started its weekly appearance twelve
days after the first issue of the Los Angeles *Star* and later
gained great notoriety because of the association with it of
"Boston" Ames and John Phoenix; the Santa Barbara *Gazette,*
which was inaugurated with both English and Spanish pages
in 1855; the San Bernardino *Herald,* which was started by the
bibulous Ames in 1860 and barely survived his death in 1861;
and the Wilmington *Journal,* the weekly put out by the ambitious and ever-active Phineas Banning on the *Star* press during the period when Henry Hamilton's activities were under
a cloud (1864–1868).

All these sheets were nominally newspapers, but the evidence indicates that the dissemination of news was but one of
their minor activities. As John Phoenix explained in the San
Diego *Herald:*

Very little news will be found in the *Herald* this week: the fact is, there never is much news in it, and it is well that it is so; the climate here is so delightful, that residents, in the enjoyment of the *dolce far niente*, care very little about what is going on elsewhere, and residents of other places care very little about what is going on in San Diego.

The reason is not difficult to explain. Adequate coverage of local news was never attempted; it was too expensive and, after all, the inhabitants usually knew the news long before the weekly papers were out. The interview with Olive Oatman which appeared in the *Star* was by no means typical. A short news entry and a blistering editorial, if the matter was controversial, sufficed to cover most happenings. Most of the remaining space in the little four-page journals was taken up by advertisements and government notices, the latter being one of the chief sources of income. For news from outside the community, the papers were hamstrung from the start. California news of local interest could, it is true, be summarized from the San Francisco newspapers; but news from more distant points was discouragingly slow in arriving. Until the Butterfield stages began operating, Southern California received its out-of-state news only from the Eastern journals dropped off by such steamers as chose to put in at San Diego, and Los Angeles waited until chance brought the papers north. And after the stage line was started, editors were dependent on kindly stage drivers who brought an extra bundle of Eastern journals as a courtesy to friends in the cow town. In 1860 a telegraph line was strung from the plain below the Tehachapis to the Bay Region, which was soon to receive fast news by the pony express; but, because of storms and wear and tear, it provided only intermittent service, and that for only exceptionally important items. Not until the 1880's was the area to have anything resembling a regular telegraphic news dispatch service. In the meantime, rumor frequently served for fact.

Literary activities of early Southern California were almost entirely connected with the newspapers. The items which appeared in the papers were, to be sure, for the most part borrowings from Eastern journals. This practice of borrowing was so common that one is tempted to assume that, after the advertising and leaders were set up, the columns were frequently filled by drawing on Mrs. Hemans or Fanny Fern. But there were also genuinely local activities, the most ambitious of which were the attempts to give the papers a literary flavor: Ramírez added the phrase "Periodico Independiente y Literaria" to the masthead of *El Clamor Publico;* the eccentric William Money issued at least one number of a monthly magazine entitled *The Christian Church,* which was devoted to "theological disquisition"; and some sixteen-year-old members of a local debating club started a paper called *Young America,* devoted to the expression of ideas, and displaying the slogan "Our faith is *Freedom,* and our hope is *Liberty.*" More successful were the efforts of some of the editors to write well-phrased editorials, but even these were rare. Among the best editorials were those of Henry Hamilton and of "Colonel" John O. Wheeler, the latter a Ranger and practical joker who anticipated Horace Bell with his rhetorical invective in the *Southern Californian,* and later in *El Clamor Publico,* and also tried his hand at writing humorous squibs of the frontier variety. Of greater interest was the poetry of a genial young Peruvian named Manuel Clemente Rojo, who prepared the Spanish page of the early issues of the Los Angeles *Star.* Before he wandered off to Baja California to become a "sub-political chief," he contributed a number of Spanish love lyrics and religious poems to the journal. The following stanza is representative of his work.

> Gloriosa divinidad
> Yndivisa in tres personas
> Al hombre mortal perdonas,
> A pezar de su maldad;
> Yncomparable deidad

Que todos los bienes donas,
Donas luz en abundancia
Libranos de la ignorancia.

More promising, however, were the contributions of the
lay members of the community to the *Star,* which apparently
encouraged such offerings. Of the material it printed, the
most noteworthy are the letters and editorials of Judge Benjamin Hayes, the poems of Ina Coolbrith, and the articles on
Indians by Hugo Reid. Judge Hayes, a native of Baltimore
who had come to California in 1850, served competently, except for errors that resulted from his heavy drinking, as district judge for the entire southern part of the state for more
than a decade. His reputation was excellent. He occasionally
contributed editorials on local social and legal problems to
the press. It is not, however, as a writer that Hayes is chiefly
remembered, but as an avid collector of historical data who
left an entire library of clippings from the local press, classified and arranged under comprehensive topics. It later passed
into the H. H. Bancroft collection and forms one of the major
sources of information on the social history of Southern
California.

Of surer literary reputation is Ina Donna Coolbrith, the
first poet laureate of California, who spent an eventful youth
in the southern part of the state. Because her experiences
there, however, were so unfortunate, she used the region
rarely in her mature writing and consequently is too infrequently associated with it. When she arrived in Los Angeles
early in the 'fifties, she already had a secret in her background
—the fact that she was the niece of Joseph Smith, the founder
of the Mormon faith. In the days of persecutions in the
Middle West, her mother, Agnes Coolbrith, had married the
Mormon prophet's younger brother, Don Carlos Smith. Just
four months after the birth of his daughter, Smith died. The
widowed mother separated from the Mormons, in the critical
period of church schism which preceded Brigham Young's
trek to Utah, and went to St. Louis, where she met and mar-

ried William Pickett, a printer and lawyer. The family came west in 1851. When they crossed the pass discovered by Jim Beckwourth, that famous mountain scout and squaw man carried ten-year-old Josephine (Ina) D. Smith on his saddle. A few months in the mines, in Marysville, and in San Francisco apparently persuaded Pickett that better fortune awaited him in the southern part of the state.

Little Ina was an attractive and lively girl. She attended the first public school established in Los Angeles and doubtless played in the mustard fields and bathed in the *zanja*. In time she became one of the belles of the town; one of the brightest memories of her teens was that of leading the grand march, at a dance, with former Governor Pío Pico. She also began writing poetry. At eleven she wrote only private verses, but when she was fifteen years old, in 1856, some of her work was printed in the Los Angeles *Star*. Most of her poems were slight lyrics on sentimental subjects, such as "Little Elsie," "My Childhood's Home," and "One on Earth, and One in Heaven." But the stirring events of the Old Pueblo did not leave her untouched; and when, early in 1857, Sheriff Barton and three of his posse were ambushed and killed by the Daniel-Flores gang, young Ina was right in the middle of the excitement that gripped Los Angeles. Her poetry this time was a call to arms:

> Aye, *revenge on their murderers!* Is there no true *man*,
> Not one, to act as an avenger
> Of the four noble beings who lost their own lives
> In defending this people from danger?

Four years later, the *Star* commented somewhat boastfully that "Ina" had "already obtained almost a world-wide reputation." It is true that she had for some time contributed to San Francisco and Marysville papers, and doubtless her poems had been borrowed in the exchanges, but she had published little in the preceding three years, and her stay in Los Angeles was about to come to a painful end.

On April 1, 1858, she had married Robert B. Carsley, a partner in the Salamander Iron Works and the player of the bones in the first minstrel show to be held in Los Angeles. The marriage having proved unhappy, Ina had gone to live at the home of her stepfather, who by then had established a law practice in San Bernardino and had introduced the first law library to the town. Carsley, apparently a pathologically jealous man, pursued her there and in an altercation with Pickett he was injured so severely that he lost an arm. At that, the affair turned out better than the famous one in which Hilliard P. Dorsey, Register of the Land Office, was shot by an indignant father-in-law, Uncle Billy Rubottom, at Spadra, not far from San Bernardino. Rubottom felt that Dorsey had so mistreated his daughter that killing was none too good for him. But Rubottom was an El Monte man, and therefore had a code of ethics foreign to Pickett.

The prosaic result of it all was that Josephine Carsley obtained a divorce from her husband late in 1861 and shook the dust of Los Angeles from her dainty feet. She went to San Francisco to start a new life, took the name of Ina Coolbrith by combining her nickname with her mother's maiden name, and lived to be one of the leading members of the San Francisco literary school of the 'sixties. There her marital experiences in Los Angeles remained a secret, even as did her relationship with the Mormons; but she often spoke of the southern country and occasionally mentioned it in her poems, as in her "Retrospect." Her memories of the early days remained brilliantly clear, and were so unclouded by the later changes in the region that at least one Southern California historian made a point of visiting her frequently to get a detailed picture of how Los Angeles had looked before the Iowa invasion. But, although she always planned to write a book about her experiences, the earthquake and fire, procrastination, and reluctance to open up a painful subject prevented her from doing so. That she left no account is unfortunate, for her experience was both immediate and representative, and, had she written with talent unhampered by sentiment, she might have done an excellent job.

The third of the trio of important local contributors to the Los Angeles *Star* was the Scot, Hugo Reid of San Gabriel, a very extraordinary character. A man well trained by Scottish schools and two years at Cambridge University, he had come to Los Angeles first in 1832, when he was twenty-two, and had returned two years later to set up as a merchant. Soon he fell in love with and married a full-blooded Indian, the daughter of a chief and the widow of an Indian by whom she had had four children. These children, Reid, who had taught school in Hermosillo, set to work to educate properly. Coming into control of much of the property of Mission San Gabriel through his wife's connections, he was for a long time a prominent member of the community, in which he was known as Don Perfecto Reid. Even before the conquest he apparently was interested in literature, for he had some fame as a translator of English songs into Spanish, among them "Home Sweet Home."

In the early 'fifties he lost most of his property and suffered the worse misfortune of seeing his Indian wife not only grow more and more bitter about the treatment of her people but also become apparently mentally unbalanced by the death of her lovely daughter, for which she blamed the reading of white man's books rather than the smallpox. Tired and sick, Hugo Reid set about carrying out the promise he had made when he married—to tell the world something of the nature of his wife's people and the mistreatment they had received. The result was a series of twenty-two letters which appeared weekly in the *Star* in 1852. Only barely completing his series, Reid died of tuberculosis near the end of the year. The letters as well as the mixed marriage were to play their parts in the literature of the Southwest Indian, the former through direct influence, the latter in forming one of the threads of *Ramona*.

When Reid wrote his letters describing the state of his

wife's people, he knew that the Indians were already doomed.
"Death has been busy among them for years past, and very
few more are wanting to extinguish the lamp that God
lighted," he wrote. In truth, the process of decay and decline
which was to reduce the native population of Southern California from an estimated thirty thousand in 1769 to slightly
more than a thousand at the turn of the century was well on
its way. Concerning the Indians, Reid was in emphatic dis-
agreement with Father Boscana and Father Baegert, Boscana's
Jesuit predecessor in Baja California, who had called them,
among many other things, coarse, untidy, shameless, ungrate-
ful, stinking, and lazy. Reid, on the contrary, felt that they
were an able and virtuous people, who had been ruined by the
Spaniards and the Franciscan mission system. Having had the
patience to learn his wife's language (he was working on an
Indian glossary when he died), he was able to interpret some
of the customs of the peoples of Southern California, who,
far from being lowly Diggers, had developed an acorn culture
which had adequately supported a population several times
the average density of pre-Columbian Indian populations elsewhere in the United States. He pointed out that, although
they had no written tongue, they cherished many legends of
considerable dramatic interest, such as the myth about the
girl who conceived a child by lightning and the story of the
seven deceived sisters who became the Pleiades; that, although near-nakedness was customary for the women, they
often adorned themselves with boas of flowers; and that, although they had no word meaning exactly the same as the
English "love," the concept of a bad spirit or the devil had
not existed before the padres came.

Reid wrote that, when the Spaniards had first arrived, the
Indians thought they were gods, but the behavior of the soldiers in killing animals and raping squaws soon persuaded
them that the newcomers were human beings, "reasonable"
creatures of a "nasty white color, and having ugly blue eyes."
At first, they avoided contact with the new people as much as

possible; the women who had been violated were subjected to crude forms of purification, and bastards tainted with white blood were destroyed at birth. But the padres kidnapped small children, refused to return them to their mothers unless the latter agreed to be baptized, and then they baptized the men who wished to join their wives and children. The baptized Indians became pariahs among their own people, according to Reid, and thus the unbaptized Indians helped the mission fathers to exert the pressure which forced the neophytes to become slave laborers, subject always to the ten-foot lash and the bear trap used for those who tried to escape.

Although Reid spoke of Father Zalvidea with respect for his rigorous system of economic planning and with awe for his discipline ("On a breach occurring between man and wife, they were fastened by the leg, until they agreed to live again in harmony") and of Father Sánchez for his kindness and joviality (the latter once served a roast puppy to his friends as a practical joke), he did not hide his condemnation of the Spaniards and the mission system as a whole. It was with grim humor that he spoke of the Indians' refusal to eat pigs on the ground that they were transformed Spaniards. It is not surprising that for nearly a century the last ten of the twenty-two Reid letters which appeared in the *Star* (the ones which described the mission system) were not included in the reprints, and that Father Engelhardt, official Franciscan chronicler of mission affairs, referred to Reid as "that embittered Scotchman" who "lied about religious matters."

～～～～

The most famous literary event connected with early Southern California journalism took place not in Los Angeles, however, but in San Diego. It came about when "Boston" Ames, editor of the San Diego *Herald,* left his paper for a few weeks in the fall of 1853 in the hands of the first celebrated western humorist, Lieutenant George H. Derby, better known by his nom de plume, John Phoenix. The *Herald,* like

other Southern California newspapers, was but a poor affair;
its only claims to being a newspaper were that its four pages
appeared more or less regularly and that it carried leaders, a
few local news items, some exchanges, and an occasional con-
densed news story from the outside world. Approximately
two-thirds of its space was allotted to advertisements and state,
county, and city notices.

The editor, John Judson Ames, who was known as "Judge"
Ames or "Boston" Ames, was a prodigious figure. This young
man from Maine, who was more than 6 feet 6 inches tall and
weighed 250 pounds, had killed a man with his fist in a brawl,
had received a prison sentence, and had been pardoned.
Later, after editing the *Dime Catcher* in New Orleans, he had
set out for El Dorado with the equipment for publishing a
paper, an old-style Washington hand press, Hoe and Company's No. 2327. But before he got it to San Diego he had seen
it dunked in the Chagres River in crossing the Isthmus, had
rescued it from one of the fires that burned most of early San
Francisco, and had used it to print the *Placer Times and
Transcript* in the Mother Lode country. His primary reason
for coming to San Diego was the belief that the boom, the
first in Southern California, triggered off by the activities of
William Heath Davis and his friends, would develop. This
belief was nourished by the presence of the Boundary Commission, the rumors that an army depot would be established
there, and the hopes for a southern transcontinental railroad
that would have its terminus at San Diego. San Diego was then
the biggest city in the United States in area, embracing some
seventy-five square miles; and, although it had only seven
hundred citizens, the more optimistic thought that number
would increase until the population and the area were com-
mensurate. Then too, Ames may have been influenced by the
fact that it would be of obvious advantage to the Democratic
party, and particularly to Governor Bigler and Senator Gwin,
to have a Democratic journal in the only town with a harbor
in the southernmost part of the state.

"Boston" Ames fitted the pattern of the western editor to a fine degree. He lent energy to his policies by making such announcements as these: "There are several individuals in this city who don't like the *Herald*. We don't care a damn whether they like it or not"; and "A LIAR! The person who fabricated and put into circulation the report that we ever had a personal difficulty of any kind with Vic Turner, Esq., of San Francisco, is a SNEAKING, CONTEMPTIBLE VILLAIN AND LIAR!" He wrote forensic editorials supporting the Democratic party, state division, and the building of a transcontinental railroad to San Diego; he composed sentimental poems and struck off squibs marked by elephantine humor; and he served as notary public and county superintendent of schools. And he made many enemies by his feuds and his failure to pay his debts. After his divorce and remarriage his second wife's grave was desecrated before he left San Diego to try again in San Bernardino in 1860. He died the following year, just forty years old, of apoplexy, having fought the whisky bottle all his life in the glorious manner of the frontier editor. His funeral—in an era of big funerals—was an outstanding affair.

It is not surprising that such an editor occasionally left his journal in other hands while he tended the irons elsewhere. After all, San Francisco was where the political powwows were held and Barry and Patten's Saloon offered congenial company; and what did it matter if, on the coastal steamers, a man of Ames's size had to sleep on two salon tables covered with mattresses because there was no single bunk large enough for him. Thus, less than three months after he started the *Herald*, Ames notified his subscribers that they should leave contributions with "a friend" while he was away in the north, and in the winter of 1852–53 he left his press so completely unattended that a man named William N. Walton was able to steal it and publish his own paper while the owner was away. Under the circumstances, it must have been a joy to Ames that in August, 1853, when Democratic Governor Bigler was facing a stiff race with the Whigs for state control, he had so dependable a fellow as Lieutenant George H. Derby of the Topographical Engineers to take over his paper while he went north to have a good time and to get his foot a little farther into the Democratic trough. Derby had already published a few articles in the *Alta California* in San Francisco and was quite willing to try to escape from the boredom of San Diego, "this dreary and desolate little place," by writing the local newspaper. This thirty-year old wag, who had a very serious streak running right down his middle, possessed more time and energy than it took to carry out his current army assignment of damming the San Diego River, a river which he acknowledged that he damned at frequent, almost monotonously regular, intervals.

Lieutenant Derby had been sent west in 1849 and had already worked on three important military topographical surveys, one in the Sacramento Valley, one in the marshes of Tulare Lake at the south end of the San Joaquin Valley, and one at the mouth of the Colorado River. The last expedition was the first to be made in that area by Americans and placed Derby in the enviable position of the explorer who could name islands and recommend measures for navigation. Although he had found it impossible, with his equipment, to get up the river as far as Fort Yuma, he provided the War Department with an accurate description of the delta country and recommended the proper form of river boat to be used in opening up commerce in this area.

His official reports were devoid of humor, except for an occasional sly reference, but a good many anecdotes came to be associated with his explorations. One was the assertion that hens in Yuma laid hard-boiled eggs; another was the classic, repeated by Mark Twain, concerning the deceased soldier from Yuma who telegraphed back from Hell for his blankets. Derby's recommendations for the alteration of the United States cavalry uniform by the installation of hooks in the pants seats of recruits also came to be associated, in the minds of Southern Californians, with the Colorado exploration venture. Derby is said to have suggested that the hooks could be used for holding the recruit in the saddle, as points of attachment in hauling cannon up hill, and for retrieving startled neophytes in their baptism of fire. The last was to be accomplished by dextrous sergeants equipped with retrieving hooks on the ends of long poles. Legend added many other uses: the pants hooks could be employed by day to carry pots and pans during forced marches, and by night to hang the soldiers from a fence when no better place for sleeping could be found.

Under the circumstances it is a little difficult to accept the traditional view that Ames had no idea that Derby would play pranks if he was left in charge of the *Herald*. Certainly the pranks were immediately in evidence. No sooner had the steamer carrying Ames rounded Point Loma on its way to San Francisco than John Phoenix set about having the time of his life. He gleefully boasted to his readers ("Some white, some black, and some kinder speckled") that they were going to receive a new kind of newspaper: "if you don't allow that there's been no such publication, weekly or serial, since the days of the 'Bunkum Flagstaff,' I'll *crawfish*, and take to reading Johnson's Dictionary." Having no responsibility for news, he turned the journal into a hilarious joke. He even announced that one of his readers had already exploded with mirth, bursting into no less than a thousand fragments, including a tooth that was "filled by Dr. R. E. Cole, Dentist, whose advertisement may be found in another column!" He assured his readers that the *Herald* was being printed on a magnificent Power Press, manned by two tremendous Indians.

Nothing is heard but the monotonous *houp! hank!* of the Indians, as in a cloud of steam of their own manufacture they strike off the paper. Nothing can be seen without but a shower of quarters, bits, and dimes darkening the air as they are thrown from the purchasers. Fourteen bushels and three pecks of silver have been received since we commenced distribution, and the cry is still they come.

After this send-off he spent the weeks of his editorship printing burlesque news items, preposterous editorials, and doggerel poetry. He even issued an illustrated edition, "Phoenix's Pictorial," by using stock advertising cuts as pictures of San Diego life and national events. But the prank which brought his greatest fame was his changing of the paper's politics; he supported the Whig candidate for governor, William Waldo, at the very time Ames was in the north apparently trying to get campaign funds from Governor Bigler, the Democratic candidate for reëlection.

In conducting his campaign, the irrepressible graduate of West Point loose in San Diego had a field day. He announced: "The public at large . . . will understand that I stand upon 'Jos Haven's platform,' which the gentleman defined some years since to be the liberty of saying anything he pleased about anybody, without considering himself at all responsible." He proclaimed: "Old Bigler hasn't paid the people of this county anything for supporting him." And addressing Bigler he warned, "Phoenix is after you, and you'd better pray for the return of the editor *de facto* to San Diego, while yet there is time, or you're a *goner,* as far as this county is concerned." He travestied the issues by scrambling the candidates; the fight was between "Baldo and Wigler," "Wagler and Bildo," anything but Bigler and Waldo.

Whether the fact that San Diego County voted for Waldo was the result of Derby's campaign is a matter of conjecture, but there is every reason to believe that many of the local boys switched their votes to join in the fun. Actually, Derby's success did not alter the over-all results, for Bigler carried the state. But it gave rise to Phoenix' famous account of the return of the editor after the mischief had been done. Undoubtedly the cream of the jest was to imagine the huge Ames, the man who had broken another man with his fist, gaining retribution on the stubby topographical engineer. Its climax is the much-quoted account of Phoenix' strategy which so delighted General Grant: "We held 'Boston' down over the Press by our nose, (which we had inserted between his teeth for that purpose), and while our hair was employed in holding one of his hands, we held the other in our left, and with the 'sheep's foot' brandished above our head shouted to him, 'Say Waldo!' "

The friendship between Derby and Ames continued unaffected, however; John Phoenix contributed an occasional item to the *Herald* in the remaining year that he was stationed in San Diego, and Ames, when he was in the East in the winter of 1855–56, collected his friend's squibs into a book which he called *Phoenixiana.*

Although Derby was primarily a humorist, the reality beneath his joking is recognizable in his editions of the *Herald* and in his contributions to San Francisco journals during his San Diego sojourn. It is this which makes him one of the best chroniclers of life in Southern California in the 'fifties. A description such as the following, however humorous in expression, is basically factual in content: "There are seven stores or shops in the village, where anything may be obtained from a fine-tooth comb to a horse-rake, two public-houses, a Catholic church, which meets in a private residence, and a Protestant *ditto.*" Similar is his exaggerated account of a Fourth of July celebration: "The San Diego Light Infantry, in full uniform, consisting of Brown's little boy in his shirt-tail, fired a National salute with a large bunch of fire-crackers." Derby's criticism of the scene is implicit in much of his work, as in "Phoenix's Pictorial," where he represented San Diego as a ship, two houses, a mud hen, and a mortar and pestle. As an antidote for the ubiquitous fleas, he suggested applying to the sufferer a thin coat of hot tar. Visitors at his office are typified in the *yaller*-gilded Mr. Mudge of Arkansas, who squizzled watermelon seeds and juice over his shirt front as he read his "Dirge on the Death of Jeames Hambrick."

> we wraped him in a blanket good
> for coffin we had not

and there we buried him where he stood
when he was accidently shot

and as we stood around his grave
our tears the ground did blot
we prayed to god his soul to save
he was accidently shot

. . . he was accidently shot with one of the large size colt's revolver
with no stopper for the cock to rest on it was one of the old fashion
kind brass mounted and of such is the kingdom of heaven.

truly yourn
ORION W MUDGE ESQ

Even the fiestas he found shoddy rather than impressive. Of
the one at San Luis Rey he wrote:

High mass was celebrated in the old church on Thursday morning, an Indian baby was baptized, another nearly killed by being
run over by an excited individual on an excited horse, and that day
and the following were passed in witnessing the absurd efforts of
some twenty natives to annoy a number of tame bulls with the tips
of their horns cut off . . . The nights were passed in an equally
intellectual manner.

He summed up his impressions in his "Sandy-ago—A Sol-
iquy":

Oh my what a trying thing it is for a feller
To git kooped up in this ere little plais
Where the males dont run reglar no how
Nor the females nuther, cos there aint none.

. . . .

All night long in this sweet little village
You hear the soft note of the pistol
With the pleasant screak of the victim
Whose been shot prehaps in his gizzard.

. . . .

Oh its awful this here little plais is
And quick as my business is finished

I shall leave here you may depend on it
By the very first leky steambote
Or if they are all of em busted
I'll hire a mule from some feller
And just put out to Santy Clara.

～～～～

By the end of the third decade of American occupation of
Southern California the transformation of the society from
the easygoing and unprogressive Spanish Californian ways to
the more energetic and forward-looking Anglo-Saxon civilization was all but complete. Every year now saw the arrival of
thousands of new settlers—farmers, artisans, and professional
men from the East and Middle West who were eager to develop the same institutions in this sun-graced land that they
had known in the homes they had left behind them. And to
meet the needs of these newcomers who wanted to farm small
holdings or to build houses in the growing towns, the economic picture was changing rapidly; the day when the padres
of San Gabriel controlled more than a million acres was far
in the past, and the big ranchos were now on their way out,
in the process of being broken up into small tracts. The squatter sovereignty of El Monte had also come to an end, for
neither the old-timers nor the newcomers wanted any part of
the uncertain titles of the early cow-counties days. The
changed way of doing things was exemplified in the founding
of new towns: Compton and Westminster, settled by church
members eager to provide wholesome surroundings for temperate and hard-working families from back East; Santa
Monica, laid out in sites for modest, seaside villas by Senator
John P. Jones of Nevada when he broke up the ancient
Rancho San Vicente y Santa Monica; Lompoc, founded by
prohibitionists who staunchly enforced their own laws; Pasadena, planned and developed by farsighted settlers from the
Middle West who had sent as forerunners agents from Indiana to locate the most favorable tract for the establishment
of a farming community clustered around a civic center.

Just as certainly as they were abandoning the Spanish Californian economic system, the southern counties were emerging from their period of transitional lawlessness. The change of name from Nigger Alley (the old Calle de los Negros) to Los Angeles Street was symptomatic. The Chinese massacre of 'seventy-one, which came as a climax to decades of rowdyism, was probably the most violent and certainly the most disgraceful outbreak in Los Angeles history; but the newer ways were indicated by the fact that Sheriff Burns and Judge Robert M. Widney, together with a few other law-abiding citizens, were able to outface the mob and stop the disorders before Chinatown was entirely burned to the ground. And when the notorious bandit, Tiburcio Vásquez, was captured three years later, the law took its natural course without suggestion of lynching. The editor of the Los Angeles *Star,* the genial Ben C. Truman, one of the new breed of boosters, made it clear, in his account of Vásquez, that the bandit was but a sneak and a ruffian and not the kind of man to be made into a folk hero.

In Los Angeles, the cultural scene had shifted, leaving the American way of life in possesion of the stage. Although the view from the top of the mountains had not measurably altered, the life within the city had completely changed. When the German-speaking Harris Newmark came to the city in the early 'fifties he automatically set out to learn Spanish rather than English because Spanish was the standard tongue. But now the town supported a three-day drive to raise money for a local library, including five hundred dollars for a Shakespeare collection, and in celebration of the successful completion of the campaign held a grand ball at which, in the grand march, sixty-eight characters from Dickens were impersonated. The list of early Los Angeles imprints also tells the story of the change. The Old Pueblo did not even see a printing press until five years after the American occupation, and in the 'fifties and 'sixties the town's publishing output was limited to such things as political handbills, notices of court actions, theater programs, and one pamphlet by the erratic

William Money. In the early 'seventies, however, appeared the first city directory, the first local almanac, the first real-estate blurb, the first chamber of commerce publication, and the first local history. And there was even one item, prophetic of things to come, titled *The Golden Songster for the Land of Sunshine and Flowers.*

The spirit of the times was fully exemplified in 1876—the year that the last spike was driven on the first railroad connecting Los Angeles with San Francisco and the East, the year that Los Angeles sent Ben C. Truman and Henry T. Payne to the Centennial Celebration at Philadelphia to advertise Southern California with booster talks and brightly colored lantern slides, and the year that Los Angeles celebrated the first thirty years of American occupation of California and the first hundred years of American independence.

This Fourth of July celebration was in complete contrast to the local festivities accompanying that holiday in earlier days. In the mid-fifties, the features of the day had been the caballeros riding through the streets in their fanciest clothes, their bright tight-fitting jackets, their broad-brimmed sombreros, and their *calzoneras,* through which peaked their *calzoncillos;* the playing of guitars for the mantilla-adorned señoritas and señoras; and a fandango, with its graceful dancing and its fun with *cascarones.* For the rest, there were cockfights, perhaps a bullfight, and frequently a liberal amount of gunplay. In the 'sixties, Fourth of July had come to be a painful holiday because of the bitter feeling between Northern and Southern sympathizers in the Old Pueblo, and in more than one year there was no celebration at all.

Now, in 1876, the Americans had purified the holiday to their own purposes, and the older Californians, such as had survived, either dressed and acted like Americans or stood on the side lines to shout. No distinctively Mexican or Spanish Californian unit, with the exception of the Junta Patriótica de Juárez group, is listed in the account of that day's festivities found in a supplement to *An Historical Sketch of Los*

Angeles County, California, prepared "at the specific request of the President of the United States," by J. J. Warner, a former fur trader, Judge Benjamin Hayes, a district judge and collector of local news items, and Dr. J. P. Widney, one of the most enterprising of the new boosters from over the mountains. The place of honor went to the forty-two "battle scarred" American veterans of the Mexican War, headed by General George Stoneman, who had helped to bring the railroad to Los Angeles. In the parade, the grand marshal sported a red sash, a star on his left breast, and a black feather in his hat, and carried a baton. Riding in a magnificent carriage, Miss Carrie Cohn impersonated the Goddess of Liberty, attended by Miss Lulu Lehman, representing Peace, and Miss Ally Carpenter, representing Plenty. There was a float on which rode thirteen young ladies representing the thirteen original colonies, and on another twenty-five damsels portrayed the rest of the states. The fire brigades were there in their full regalia. The " '38's" had fifty men on the ropes, handsome in their red shirts; and the rival Confidence Boys, in blue with silver trimmings, were proud to have Miss Emily Smith, as America, perched on their steamer fire engine. The lodges, such as the Knights of Pythias and the Odd Fellows, were represented; the Irish Literary Society and the Irish Temperance Society had original floats of historical significance; and the commercial entries included, among others, the "inevitable forty-niners on their mules," representing the Butchers Association, and a handsome Philadelphia Brewery wagon with George and Martha Washington as riders.

The parade took its sinuous way through the streets of the town, passing under the specially constructed triple arches on Main Street, "the subjects of universal comment." A statue of Columbia surmounted the central arch, and Washington and Grant stood on the flanking columns. The buildings were adorned with bunting, flags, and pictures; Southern Pacific engines and trains were covered with decorations. The grand ceremonies were held before fifteen hundred people, "both native and foreign born," who crowded into Lehman's Round House Gardens, where statues of Adam and Eve usually drew the attention of the visitors. "With one or two exceptions, everyone was on good behaviour." The band played "Hail Columbia!" and General Phineas Banning, a featured participant in all celebrations, gave "a short speech replete with patriotic sentiments." The combined church choirs of the city sang "America." Professor Thomas A. Saxon read the Declaration of Independence, J. J. Ayers recited the original poem of the day, and James G. Eastman, the orator of the occasion, set the keynote in his magnificent address, tuned to national aspirations:

When the mournful zephyrs, passing the plain where Marathon once stood, shall find no mound to kiss; when the arch of Titus shall have been obliterated; the Colosseum crumbled into antique dust; the greatness of Athens degenerated into dim tradition; Alexander, Caesar and Napoleon forgotten; the memories of Independence Hall shall still bloom in imperishable freshness.

IV

Boom

In 1878, Benjamin Franklin Taylor, a poet and journalist from Ohio who had known hard times in his boyhood and had vividly described the cruelties of the Civil War, published a book titled *Between the Gates* in which he told of a trip he had just made to California. In a "confidential" foreword he informed the reader that "the only care-free, cloudless summer of my life, since childhood, was spent in California." The tone of the book ranged from contentment to ecstasy, the ecstasy being reached in the description of the principal town in Southern California:

Whoever asks where Los Angeles is, to him I shall say: across a desert without wearying, beyond a mountain without climbing; where heights stand away from it, where ocean winds breathe upon it, where the gold-mounted lime-hedges border it; where the flowers catch fire with beauty; among the orange groves; beside the olive trees; where the pomegranates wear calyx crowns; where the figs of Smyrna are turning; where the bananas of Honolulu are blossoming; where the chestnuts of Italy are dropping; where Sicilian lemons are ripening; where the almond trees are shining; through that Alameda of walnuts and apricots; through this avenue of willows and poplars; in vineyards six Sabbath-days' journeys across

them; in the midst of a garden of thirty-six square miles—there is
Los Angeles.

The reader long inured to Southern California publicity
might assume that Taylor was working for the Los Angeles
Chamber of Commerce or acting as a literary agent for the
Southern Pacific Railroad. Such an assumption is contrary to
the facts. Taylor was an unpaid representative of the plain
folk of America who had suddenly discovered Southern California. His enthusiasm was echoed many times by the newcomers from beyond the Rockies, who were pleased to feel
that they had found in "sub-tropical" America a place where
both their physical ills and their economic disorders would be
forgotten in a new sun-blessed land. The boom period had begun, and middle-class America was moving in. The Southern
California boom was not, of course, unique to the region, for
much of America had been settled by the spasmodic, almost
rhythmic, forward movement of the wave of land-hungry
settlers as it lapped into the valleys and over the plateaus of
western America. But the queen of the cow counties had become the center of the most spectacular tourist rush in the
country.

Had Charles Dickens visited Southern California in the
'eighties as he had toured the Middle West in the 'forties, he
would have found in a Banning on the edge of the desert or an
Azusa in a dry river bed excellent models for the Edens of
another *Martin Chuzzlewit*. He would, however, have been
mistaken if he had concluded that the growth would prove to
be ephemeral; in spite of the wild fluctuations attendant on a
boom economy, the growth of the area was in the long run
genuine enough. With the breaking up of the cattle ranches,
the introduction of a varied fruit culture, the development of
scientific irrigation methods, and the improvement of transportation, the land which the Spanish Californians had settled
so sparsely was, in the course of the next half century, to absorb a population which would number well into the millions.

Southern California had, in fact, already gone through a

period of growth and prosperity between 1868 and 1876 which had to some degree foreshadowed the much bigger and more famous boom of the 'eighties but had not been so marked by excesses. The distressing Civil War period, when Los Angeles—unlike San Francisco—was at its lowest ebb and the southern counties suffered from dissension and drought, had been followed by an era of rapidly growing population and expanding business. The foundations for the modern Los Angeles were laid at this time, as Remi A. Nadeau in his *City-Makers* has recently shown. And San Diego, hopefully nursing the dream of becoming the largest California city south of San Francisco, and thrilled at the assurance that Tom Scott's Texas Pacific would establish its West Coast terminus on San Diego Bay, moved in anticipation to New Town under the virile leadership of "Father" Alonzo E. Horton. It was at this time also that a number of new communities, such as Santa Monica, Pasadena, and Compton, were founded. With the building of local railroads from San Pedro and Santa Monica to Los Angeles, the arrival of the Southern Pacific in Southern California, and the expectation of the completion, in the near future, of a competing transcontinental line, the outlook of the local citizens became buoyantly optimistic. But the nation-wide depression of the 'seventies, the resultant failure of the Bank of California, and another severe drought put a temporary check on the era of prosperity even while the people were celebrating the national centennial. Even with this setback, however, Los Angeles grew from five thousand to eleven thousand in the 'seventies, and the southern counties doubled their population within the decade.

The second and most famous of all Southern California booms started in 1886. The arrival of the Atchison, Topeka, and Santa Fe Railway in the area broke the Southern Pacific's long monopoly of transcontinental railroad traffic and made it possible for many thousands of restless people back East to travel cheaply. When a rate war between the two railroads resulted in rates as low as five dollars from Missouri to the

West Coast, excursion trains poured tourists into the country, tourists whom the boom psychology gripped almost as they stepped from the trains. Many, hearing of exorbitant profits in Southern California real estate, bought lots purely as speculative ventures. It is variously estimated that in one year between one and two hundred million dollars was involved in real-estate transactions in Los Angeles County alone. And in the city of Los Angeles, where the first bank had been established but twenty years earlier, the transactions in one record day totaled nearly a million dollars. At the height of the frenzy, professional boomers from all over the nation descended on Southern California. Brass bands, free lunches, and extravagant ballyhoo were the order of the day, and most buyers expected to resell without ever even seeing their property. But many, even of these, remained to become permanent residents when, staying over a summer, they learned that Southern California was not, as they had assumed, merely a winter vacation spot for transients.

The most exaggerated aspects of the boom were to be found in places like San Diego, where "50,000 people tried to get rich in a week," and Santa Barbara, which grew excited in 1887 over the arrival of the coast line of the Southern Pacific from Los Angeles, although it had to wait fourteen years for its completion northward to San Francisco. Most of all they were apparent in the many suburban communities created overnight. The greatest concentration of these boom towns was along the Santa Fe right of way from Los Angeles to the San Bernardino County border; for thirty-six miles there was a new town for every mile and a half of railroad. In Los Angeles County in the two principal boom years there appeared sixty mushroom towns with more than 500,000 lots and less than 2,500 people in all of them put together. Developed according to their town plats—in the single year 1887 twenty large plat books were filed with the county recorder—they would have contained a population of two million. John W. Caughey in his *California* has pointed out how

preposterous were some of these ventures: "The site of
Ballona was swamp land; Chicago Park nestled in the rocky
wash of the San Gabriel; Carlton perched precariously on
a steep hillside east of Anaheim; Border City and Man-
chester were stranded on the far slope of the Sierra Madre,
their only real asset a noble view of the Mojave Desert."

After the inevitable crash, which came in 1888, the southern counties were spotted with ghost towns, some of them
containing a few houses, others little more than sagebrush
dotted with white stakes, with perhaps one of the many boom
hotels standing alone in its baroque grandeur. The populations of a few hundreds which had congregated at the height
of the boom and, as one local historian put it, "for a time
managed to subsist in a semi-cannibalistic way on the dupes
who came there to buy lots" were soon dispersed. Glenn S.
Dumke, who tells the whole story of the extravagant frenzy
in his excellent *Boom of the Eighties,* states that "of more
than one hundred towns platted from 1884 to 1888 in Los
Angeles County, sixty-two no longer exist except as stunted
country corners, farm acreage, or suburbs." Gladstone gave
up its boast that the popular prime minister would come
there to live, and Chicago Park was ploughed back into farms.
Lexington and Waterloo died a-borning. Gone were Alamitos
Beach, La Ballona, Cahuenga, and Morocco, as well as Hyde
Park, Raymond, Sunset, and Dundee. Kenilworth, Ivanhoe,
and Rowena were never more than paper subdivisions; and
the Scottish sounding Glen-Barham disappeared in spite of
the boast that it was "God's own arrangement for the consumptive, the dyspeptic, and the broken down."

But not all of the new towns became ghost towns. Just as
Los Angeles, Santa Barbara, and San Diego gained a permanent increment in population, villages like Pasadena, Pomona, and Santa Ana became small cities. Dozens of new
towns like Monrovia, Glendale, Burbank, Long Beach,
Elsinore, and Fullerton, like Escondido, Banning, Ontario,
Orange, and La Jolla, were here to stay. The southern coun-

ties had indeed benefited by the boom of the 'eighties, even though for a while it seemed as if more fortunes had been lost than made. Their population in 1880 was about 80,000; by 1890 it had jumped to 230,000—nearly a threefold increase. Of the 150,000 newcomers, the great majority were from the Middle West—the East North Central states, with Illinois and Ohio leading, and the West North Central states, with Missouri and Iowa in the van.

~~~~

As for the promotion literature of the early booms, it is probably not unfortunate that, as James M. Guinn put it, "The literature of the boom perished with the boom—buried in waste-baskets and cremated in kitchen stoves." Books, poems, editorials, and novels about Southern California were only part of the fuel which fed the excitement. Fit companion pieces to the brass bands, excursion trains, "gothic" railroad stations, gingerbread hotels, and upstart colleges of arts and sciences, they were for the most part concerned with depicting in glowing colors "the salubrity of our climate, the variety of our production, the fertility of our soil and the immense profits to be made from the cultivation of semi-tropical fruits." It is needless here to reprint amusing or tedious examples of this real-estate literature. Others have collected and reprinted examples of it, but have turned up nothing that outdistances the singing commercial of 1950. Typical was the lyric of a song sung lustily by San Diego boosters:

> Away to the west, where the sun goes down,
>   Where the oranges grow by the cargo,
> They've started a town, and are doing it up brown,
>   On the bay of San Diego.
>
> The railroad, they say, is coming that way,
>   And then they'll be neighbors to Chicago;
> So they built a big hotel, and built it mighty well,
>   In the town of San Diego.

Moral

Let's take an early train and haste with might and
main,
By lightning express if you say—go,
Where every man's a fortune in a lot that costs him
nought,
In the town of San Diego.

Fortunately, the Southern Californians felt that its use as
advertising copy was not the only purpose of writing. Thus,
"literature" came to be looked on as one of the social graces
of the ideal community, a necessary ingredient of the new
Utopia, and an attraction for newcomers. As one magazinist
put it, "Nature's atmosphere assures health, and social atmosphere combined with it will assure happiness." Life might
indeed be dull, they recognized, after the first excitement
wore off. And it was written of one boom town, "Matters
progressed slowly for a time, settlers came in; but it required
a great deal of nerve to keep them up to the enthusiastic point
that is necessary in pioneer life." A little culture might help.
But building a new town with rich attractions for well-bred
people was perhaps not as easy as it had seemed to Father
Horton; one could name a town Elsinore without successfully evoking the spirit of Shakespeare, call a lake the Como
of California without producing a D'Annunzio, and christen
a village Alhambra—even construct a Moorish railroad station—without attracting a Washington Irving. In San Diego,
however, rather more positive actions than merely giving
literary names to places were taken, and when, after *The
Golden Era* was enticed there in the boom period by a gift
of five thousand dollars, the boast that "San Diego will soon
be known for its literature as well as its harbor" seemed not
impossible of achievement.

The harbor had been there for a long time without helping San Diego a great deal toward its desire of becoming a
western metropolis. Since the disappointments following the
collapse of Tom Scott's railroad plans in the mid-seventies,

the fifteen hundred of the five thousand boomers who had remained had lived on "faith, hope, and climate." But San Diego stirred so mightily during the boom of the 'eighties that enough lots were laid out to take care of a population the size of London's, two colleges were started, the most romantic of the boom hotels was built across the bay on a sandspit known as Coronado, and the suburban La Jolla began to boast that it was a center of art and culture. It was at this time that, in a bold attempt to stimulate the arts, San Diego boosters persuaded Francis Shepard, the famous musical improviser, to join their community, providing him with an entire city block and money to build a house. The big mansion, named Villa Montezuma, was erected on a hill overlooking the town. Its stained glass window representing Saint Cecilia at the organ reminded people that they had corralled an artist who had played to select audiences in the principal capitals of Europe (Mallarmé said that he achieved "with musical sounds, combinations, and melodies what Poe did with the rhythm of words") and formed an impressive background for the lavish receptions that Shepard accorded visiting celebrities. Later, after the boom collapsed and the house was sold, Shepard returned to Europe where, under the name of Francis Grierson, he wrote his celebrated *The Valley of the Shadows,* which effectively described the Middle West as it was before the Civil War.

San Diego was also able to boast that, in addition to its other artistic activities, it was nurturing a true literary boom. Los Angeles had its newspapers; Santa Barbara entertained the popular novelist, E. P. Roe, who planned to write a novel dealing with the new paradise; but San Diego had two literary magazines, the only ones south of San Francisco. One was an ephemeral weekly called *The Coronado;* but the other was *The Golden Era,* the longest-lived and sturdiest of the West Coast journals, which had been favorite reading for the miners of the Mother Lode in the early days and had carried much of the early work of Bret Harte, Joaquin Miller, Mark

Twain, and others of the San Francisco school of the 'fifties and 'sixties. In March, 1887, the *Era* was moved to San Diego, where, under the editorship of Harr (James Harrison) Wagner, it appeared monthly during the boom and for some years thereafter. It had little of the vitality of its early days, but there was still some life for a final spurt. Among other contributions by local writers, Wagner published poems by his wife, "Madge Morris," articles by the ebullient Ben Truman, who was for a while editor of the San Diego *Bulletin,* and essays by the thoughtful, talented T. S. Van Dyke. His two trump cards, however, were Rose Hartwick Thorpe and Joaquin Miller.

Mrs. Thorpe was the author of "Curfew Shall Not Ring Tonight." This poem, which she wrote when she was a Michigan schoolgirl of sixteen, had been frequently reprinted and was a favorite recitation in American schoolhouses by the time she was thirty. Although it had gained for her a nationwide reputation, she always felt that her fame was somewhat accidental, and her later writing career did little to dispute her statement. Perhaps the best that can be said for it was expressed by George Wharton James: "No line she has ever written has influenced a soul for ill." But as the *Era*'s editor of a children's department, in which she liberally administered such advice as "Boys, don't use slang," she worked hard to help support her family and take care of her tubercular husband, E. C. Thorpe, who had come to Southern California for his health.

Joaquin Miller, the "Poet of the Sierras," who had returned to California in 1885 because he had grown tired of Europe and Washington and Europe and Washington had grown tired of him, arrived back in the West on the edge of a wave of real-estate speculation; he bought cheap land above Oakland, named it "The Hights," and planned to establish a literary colony. He also became the literary editor of *The Golden Era,* and when Harr Wagner brought the *Era* south Miller followed. In San Diego he gave the first public speech of his career and planned to buy land and settle there. San Diego was pleased at the prospect of securing a real live poet of international reputation who boasted he could throw a tomahawk as skillfully as he could toss off a ballad, but Miller arrived after the collapse of the boom and did not stay for long. Before returning to "The Hights," however, he wrote poems on such subjects as "The Perfumed Night" and "San Diego." The latter is certainly better than Rose Hartwick Thorpe's "The White Lady of La Jolla" and has a slight edge over Madge Morris' "At San Diego Bay"; it gives an enthusiastic answer to the question;

> What shall be said of the sun-born Pueblo
> This town sudden born in the path of the sun?
> This town of St. James, of the calm San Diego,
> As suddenly born as if shot from a gun?

But most representative in its sentiments is the poem Joaquin Miller wrote for the dedication of the San Diego College of Letters, an ambitious and short-lived venture started by Harr Wagner and his friends at Pacific Beach. "The Larger College" expressed the rationale of culture seekers in the West, particularly in the stanza which read:

> Behold this sea, that sapphire sky!
> Where Nature does so much for man,
> Shall man not set his standard high,
> And hold some higher, holier plan?
> Some loftier plan than ever planned
> By outworn book of outworn land?

~~~~~

Southern California writers of the era of booms can be classified as visitors, promoters, adventurers, and health seekers, the last category extending to some degree into the other three and certainly proving in the long run to be most productive. The country was still sufficiently out-of-the-way to attract travelers looking for material for books. It naturally had its share of promoters—professional newspapermen and hack writers. It had long been a focus for adventurers, par-

ticularly among the English. But it drew most constantly
from those who looked to the climate to make it possible for
them to live and use their talents. Thus, to a marked degree
it had—and even now has—more than its share of writers
who left their normal economic market in order to build up
health.

Among the books written by visitors to the region, certainly the most influential was Charles Nordhoff's *California:
For Health, Pleasure, and Residence* (1872). Several elements,
in addition to its sound worth, increased the significance of
this book. Nordhoff was known throughout the country as
a competent, reliable, social-minded writer and journalist,
the managing editor, under William Cullen Bryant, of the
New York *Evening Post* during the difficult Civil War years
when the journal stood staunchly behind Lincoln and the
Union cause. A German-born immigrant, Nordhoff had
dedicated his life and writings to fostering an understanding of the democratic way of life in America and to furthering
the national prosperity. He was particularly interested in the
working man, in agriculture, and in coöperative societies and
had published an important study of these groups, titled
Communistic Societies of the United States, in addition to
writing several other books dealing with social and economic
issues. His purpose in visiting the Pacific Coast soon after the
completion of the transcontinental railroad was to get information about the resources of the western slope for travel and
for immigration. Although he dealt with California as a
whole, he paid particular attention to the southern part of
the state, where, he felt, the agricultural possibilities had
hardly been tapped and the climate was especially healthful
for patients with rheumatic and pulmonary diseases. Further,
he was interested in such community ventures as Anaheim
and Riverside, believing that with proper planning the man
with small means could in such places earn an adequate living, gain in health, and create a stimulating cultural environment. Carefully collecting his data and weighing his general-
izations, he produced a book which held out economic and

spiritual hope to thousands caught in the nation-wide depression of the early 'seventies.

Nordhoff's account of California was a practical one. He told about the poor farmers as well as the rich ranch owners, and he stressed the problems which would face the traveler or settler—the price of food, the size of crops, the cost of land and houses, the prevailing temperatures, the number and quality of schools, and the kind of clothing to be worn. His effective use of detail made the comfort he held out to the newcomer very reassuring:

> You can sit out-of-doors almost every day, either to read or write, or in any other occupation; for there are but a few rainy days, and it no sooner stops raining than the sun shines out most brilliantly and kindly. I do not think there were five days, either in Santa Barbara or San Diego, in December, January, and February of this year, in which the tenderest invalid could not pass the greater part of the day out-of-doors with pleasure and benefit . . . but in the evening you will sit by a wood-fire—mostly with the doors and windows open—and at night you sleep under blankets very comfortably.

This statement was typical of the quiet gospel according to Nordhoff; it is not surprising to find that the book went through many editions, that it was the vade mecum of travelers to the West Coast for the next generation, and that a town near Santa Barbara was named after its author. After many years of activity in the East, Nordhoff eventually retired to Coronado, there to complete a life which has been aptly described as "brave, clean, competent, unspoiled, and serene."

The writers of early travel books on Southern California were inclined to follow the pattern set by Nordhoff, concerning themselves primarily with facts, figures, and homely advice and noticeably avoiding the panegyrics which came to be so fashionable during the later boom days. Following in the Nordhoff tradition was *Eine Blume aus dem goldenen Lande oder Los Angeles*, published in Prague in 1878 and written by the young Ludwig Salvator, Archduke of Austria, who had spent the winter of 'seventy-six in Los Angeles as a natural step in his visits to curious places. Earnest, observant, and methodical, the Archduke gave an account to his European friends of the value of Southern California to the foreign settler. The second chapter, for instance, was made up of twenty-five pages of temperature tables and meteorological observations and included the remark: "Earthquakes occur fairly frequently, usually in August." This book, later translated under the title, *Los Angeles in the Sunny Seventies,* told much about the condition of the Indians, the Spanish Californians, and the Anglo-Saxons, prophesied a rich future for the agriculturists, and commented on the cultural institutions which were developing in the land. It was illustrated with sketches conscientiously executed by the nobleman who took his science and his debt to society so seriously.

The perennial promoters of the first era are perhaps best represented by Major Ben Truman and Colonel Tom Fitch. Hack writers and jacks-of-all-trades, they performed with a frontier flourish and boisterous humor quite absent in the men who succeeded them. The step from them to Charles Fletcher Lummis and George Wharton James was a step from the world of the hard-drinking typesetter turned editor and the spread-eagle oratin' lawyer to the world of the professional entertainer of tourists—a world of beards, long hair, eccentric dress, and the flavor of the poseur. Truman and Fitch were survivors of the cow-county days; Lummis and James fitted well into the tourist renaissance.

Benjamin C. Truman, Yankee born and bred, had taught school, set type, and written leaders before the Civil War; during the war he was a brilliant correspondent, served on the staffs of four Union generals, and executed a secret mission for President Andrew Johnson at the end of hostilities, after which he made reports to Congress on Reconstruction measures. Then, in 1866, he came to the Pacific Coast as special agent for the Post Office. In Southern California, far from being enervated by the "sub-tropical climate," he helped to reëstablish the old Butterfield stage line, married a Los Angeles girl, edited newspapers and magazines in San Diego and Los Angeles, acted as chief of the library bureau of the Southern Pacific Railroad, represented Southern California at a dozen world's fairs and exhibitions, and wrote books on the side. These included an account in 1874 of the capture of Tiburcio Vásquez; a huge treatise on duels, *The Field of Honor* (which contained chapters on duels by moonlight, by candlelight, and in the dark); short stories and essays, published collectively as *Occidental Sketches* (1881); and booster books, among which were *Semi-Tropical California* and *Home and Happiness in the Golden State of California*. Genial, energetic, expansive, Truman was a great favorite, whether he was organizing a volunteer fire company or telling of the time he nearly lost his watch in a stage holdup near the edge of Los Angeles—the robber said it wasn't worth stealing. Even his booster rhetoric is made palatable by his mustang humor: "Look this way, ye seekers after homes and happiness, ye honest sons of toil, and ye *pauvres miserables* who are dragging out a horrible life in the purlieus of large eastern cities, Semi-Tropical California welcomes you all."

Thomas Fitch, known as "the Silver-Tongued Orator of the West," was a New Yorker who had reached the Pacific Coast somewhat earlier than Truman, arriving just before the Civil War broke out. During his long and very active career in the West as a lawyer, journalist, and promoter, he lived in various parts of the Coast as well as in Nevada, Utah, Arizona, and even Hawaii. He was a member of the California assembly, of the Arizona assembly, and, as a Representative from Nevada, of the United States Congress. He was one of the group of editors who made Virginia City famous in the early days of the Comstock Lode; he figures as a character in Mark Twain's *Roughing It,* and he fought a famous duel with Joe Goodman and, as a result of Joe's aim, limped for the rest of his life. He was known in Southern California for the magnificent, not to say grandiloquent, technique he displayed both in his auctioneering oratory and his special advertisements. Boosting Santa Monica in 1875, he coined the slogan "The Zenith City of the Sunset Sea"; and operating in the big boom in San Diego, he delighted with such phrases as "Point Loma, with brow of purple and feet of foam."

A few years later, he and his wife, Anna M. Fitch, published a novel, *Better Days; or, A Millionaire of Tomorrow* (1891), which displayed both social purpose and vivid imagination but not much narrative ability. At the climax of the book, the millionaire hero, in an effort to persuade the representatives of the world powers, assembled at Hotel Coronado, to abandon war, staged an early Bikini by blowing up the Coronado Islands with a terrific explosive called "potentite," dropped from an airplane, and by sinking an ironclad with the same destructive agent released from a submarine. Convinced of the immediate necessity of forming an effective world government to maintain peace, the representatives signed a pact and in accord celebrated the event in the Coronado Hotel ballroom, decorated in an appropriate manner: "Suspended from the great dome by ropes of smilax was a gigantic figure of Peace, wrought in white calla lilies, bearing in her right hand a branch from an olive tree, while her left held to her lips a trumpet of yellow jasmine."

Among the adventurers, there was Henryk Sienkiewicz, later to become world-famous as the author of *Quo Vadis* and a host of other novels. The thirty-year-old Sienkiewicz was one of a group of eleven emigré Poles who fled from Russian tyranny in their native land to seek a haven in America in 1876. The group was headed by Helena Modjeska, Poland's leading actress, her second husband, Count Charles Bozenta Chlapowski, and her son, Ralph Modjeska. After having spent many evenings in Poland planning to find happiness "in the far away wilds of America where freedom reigned supreme," they had chosen the little German community of Anaheim as their goal, having heard that it was something of a Utopia in a sun-kissed land, and anticipating less language difficulty there than in an English-speaking community. At Anaheim they tried to work out another Brook Farm experiment in plain living and high thinking, but lack of agricultural experience, personality difficulties, and the postboom depression of the late 'seventies caused them to abandon the farm which one of their members referred to as "a poorly kept graveyard." Madame Modjeska returned to the stage but called Southern California her home for the rest of her illustrious career—a canyon, an island, and a mountain peak are named for her in that region. But Sienkiewicz, after living for a while in a shack at Anaheim Landing and working as a ribbon clerk in Los Angeles, returned to Europe, having spent something more than a year in Southern California.

In time, the Polish novelist drew upon his Southern California experiences for a number of short stories, including "Orso" and "A Comedy of Errors." "Orso" is a circus story, laid in Anaheim, which rings a change on the return of the natural man to the jungle by having the strong man, half Indian, half frontiersman, run away with the lovely girl acrobat to live the simple life in the Santa Ana hills, where cactus fruit served as manna. "A Comedy of Errors," laid in an unnamed boom town where the characters all speak German, is a delightful tale about rival grocers—one a man, the other a woman—who fight so bitterly that they finally get married to end the feud. Perhaps the most amusing episode in their warfare occurs when *he* spreads a rumor that *she* wears padding, and she dispells it by appearing in a low-cut blouse which proves it a base calumny. Sienkiewicz's stories show that he remained a romanticist about Southern California even though it failed to be the Arcadia he had looked for.

Another European novelist who looked for adventure in California in his youth was Horace Annesley Vachell. Vachell was from a good English family, had been trained at Harrow and Sandhurst, and had dabbled in painting at Barbizon. Gifted with a fine body and a brilliant mind, a lover of sports

as well as of the arts, Vachell looked for a spot where he might
have experiences out of the ordinary. His admiration for Bret
Harte's stories led him to California. He arrived in 1881, however, with a copy of Nordhoff rather than Harte under his
arm, for on his way he had been informed that California
wealth was now to be found under the soil, not on top of it.
A display of Brobdingnagian cabbages and onions attracting
his attention to the fruitfulness of the Arroyo Grande settlement, not far from San Luis Obispo, he bought a ranch there.
Not long afterward he married the daughter of C. H. Phillips, an enthusiastic businessman and promoter, who was the
leader in the development of the boom towns called Templeton and Paso Robles.

In the eighteen years that Vachell spent in Southern California, he made and lost a small fortune, learned a great deal
about real-estate speculation and farming, introduced polo to
the West, tried his hand at sport fishing for tuna, and started
his career as a novelist. Before he returned to England, saddened at the death of his wife and the loss of his property in
the depression of the 'nineties, he wrote and published several
novels, using California as the milieu and his experiences
there as a basis for his fiction. In his *Fellow Travellers,* he
paid tribute to his formative period in the West:

Today, looking back, my glance lingers upon the camp-fires in
the foot-hills, upon the beach at Avalon, upon the Pizmo marshes
where canvas-back and mallard flew fast and high over our heads,
upon those Homeric feasts, the barbecues which crowned the
rodeos, the rounding up of the cattle. It was life at first hand. And
it was my capital as a writer, a vivid experience whose variety Time
cannot stale.

In his autobiographical and descriptive books, *Life and
Sport on the Pacific Slope* (1901), *Fellow Travellers* (1923),
and *Distant Fields* (1937), Vachell left a vivid picture of
California society of the 'eighties and 'nineties. It is not entirely a pleasant one, although the genial Vachell was hardly

one to emphasize the seamy side. Life in the San Luis Obispo region moved along with a champagne sparkle in spite of its various pariahs, fools, poverty-stricken wretches, and drunkards. Something of Vachell's concept of that society is symbolized in a scene from his early novel, *The Model of Christian Gay* (1895), in which the hero painted a lovely California girl

. . . standing bareheaded in tall grasses; . . . behind her, the beautiful coast range, stretching far away into a hazy distance of nebulous greys and pinks. Above, a narrow strip of opalescent sky, against which the exquisite shape of her head was superbly outlined. At her feet, a man asleep, his face hidden by some weeds, an empty whisky-flask in his nerveless hand, his whole pose indicative of heavy, drunken stupor.

The two works of fiction in which Vachell best portrayed the life he saw in Southern California are *Bunch Grass* (1912) and *The Procession of Life* (1899), both written after he returned to England. *Bunch Grass* is a collection of short stories in which Vachell sought to portray the changing social attitudes in the period when the San Luis Obispo country passed from pastoral uses such as cattle and sheep raising and was subdivided into innumerable small holdings. He felt justified in following Bret Harte in his character portrayals, for he found the people of the region to be "men and women who were outwardly crude and illiterate but at core kind and chivalrous, and nearly always humorously unconventional." A schoolteacher conquers her fear and wins the admiration of her obstreperous students by bringing a rattlesnake into the classroom. When an old-timer discovers his son to be a horse-thief, his friends connive to give the boy a chance to reform. An old skinflint, known as the hardest man in town, reveals his softer side when he exposes himself to the dreaded diphtheria in order to solace a dying child. *The Procession of Life* is a novel dealing with the boom days in Santa Barbara. Its many themes include the shifting economic position of the old Spanish families, the artificialities of hotel life in a growing community, and the effects of hard work under primitive conditions. Vachell concludes that work is essential to the maturing of his men but nearly disastrous to his women, who find that frontier hardships age them before their time. Vachell's fiction is a fair, painstakingly honest picture of California life of the period.

The health seekers who came to Southern California in the boom days, when so many of the immigrants were "run down," "consumptive," or "ailing," included no Robert Louis Stevenson. It is, indeed, surprising that Stevenson, who was in San Francisco in 1888, resisted the rush to Southern California and sailed to the mid-Pacific in search of a climate which might prove healthful for a tubercular. However, ill-health brought other writers, less talented than Stevenson, who, like their brother ministers, doctors, and businessmen who suffered from rheumatic and pulmonary disorders, added to the growing civilization of the area. Among them were James M. Guinn, from Ohio, who was to write one of the best of the local histories; Charles Dwight Willard, from Michigan, another historian, who also wrote short stories and founded *The Land of Sunshine;* and Charles Frederick Holder, from Massachusetts, who produced a number of excellent books about Southern California outdoor life as well as biographies of Agassiz and Darwin.

Perhaps the ablest of the early writers to come because of ill-health was Theodore Strong Van Dyke, son of Judge John Van Dyke of the Supreme Court of New Jersey, a grandson and namesake of Theodore Strong, the noted Hamilton College mathematician, and brother of John C. Van Dyke, famous professor of art at Rutgers and Princeton, who was later to play so prominent a part in publicizing the beauties of the western deserts. Theodore Strong Van Dyke was born in New Jersey, received his Master of Arts degree from Princeton, and then went into law. He later moved with the Van Dyke family to Minnesota, where he was an assemblyman in 1872 and soon afterward suffered a physical collapse. Coming to Southern

California in 1875, he lived outdoors as much as he could in order to regain his strength, spending much of his time hunting and fishing in the country back of San Diego. Presently, the tall, handsome, blue-eyed Princetonian gained a reputation for his learning and modesty and won the trust and respect of the San Diegans. Becoming an active member of the community, which he came to like in spite of the rawness of the social environment, he informed himself on the possibilities of irrigation, pioneered the building of the first big water project in San Diego County, the Cuyamaca flume, and wrote many articles for local newspapers and journals, such as *The Golden Era* and *The Land of Sunshine*, on the proper use of the land and the wise development of the southern communities. His books about the southland dealt with farming and with hunting. *Southern California* presented facts quietly at the very threshold of the boom, and *Flirtation Camp; or, The Rifle, Rod and Gun in California* offered a very thin coating of fiction to a pleasant account of hunting and outdoor living in the rolling hills near the Mexican border. Most important of his half-dozen volumes, however, is his *Millionaires of a Day* (1890), the best book that has been written about the great boom of the 'eighties.

To Van Dyke, who felt personally responsible for counteracting the influences of the brass bands and the land sharpers, the boom was "the greatest piece of folly that any country has ever seen." He had been in Southern California long enough to see parts of the landscape change from dry, neglected sand hills, pocked with squatters, to orderly ranches, rich from irrigation and scientific farming. This was to be the "promised land" for "farmers by the hundred, tired of vibrating for seven months in the year between the fireplace and the woodpile, dodging cyclones and taking quinine." Here was to come a new kind of migration, one such as the frontier had not seen before: "Emigrants coming in palace-cars instead of 'prairie schooners,' and building fine houses instead of log shanties, and planting flowers and lawn-grass before they planted potatoes or corn." Then people lost their heads. Good farming land (cut into subdivisions to suit the fever of speculation) was allowed to go fallow. Permanent features of great importance to agriculture, such as irrigation projects, were neglected. Men speculated in land in order to pay for their vacations or buy gowns for their wives; they converted a breadbasket into a roulette wheel. "Little it mattered where the land lay. North, south, east, or west, in a hole or on a hill, it was all the same to a man who never saw it, never wanted to see it, and never expected to go near it, but did expect to sell it to some other ass in thirty days for twice what he had paid for it."

Van Dyke's account is presented without rancor; as a matter of fact it is filled with genial satire. Ex-Granger Squizzle, General Tiddlebug, General Milkins, Captain Popsure, Judge Dumpling, Reverend Solomon Sunrise, and Major Bluebottle are all in it together, millionaires of a day. General Milkins expresses the text of the book: " 'But what a piece of stupidity! For a country that can raise what Southern California can and in the quantities that it can, and get the prices for its products that it can, to be making itself dependent for its happiness on selling dry land and town-lots to a lot of crazy greenhorns is positively disgraceful.' " Instead of attempting to develop the country in a reasonable fashion, everyone tried to make a fortune. The letdown was terrible. "I had a half a million dollars wiped out in the crash, and what's worse, $500 of it was cash," moaned one of Van Dyke's characters. "We were a lot of very ordinary toads whirled up by a cyclone until we thought we were eagles sailing with our own wings in the topmost dome of heaven," ruefully admitted another. Van Dyke's *Millionaires of a Day*, which Stewart Edward White was to use as the basis for *The Rose Dawn,* that told the story of the boom for a later generation, had justly come to be accepted as the classic description of one of the most bizarre events in Southern California history.

V

Cultural Hydroponics

In 1882, Oscar Wilde, then making his famous lecture tour through America, wrote from San Francisco to Norman Forbes Robertson: "The railway has offered me a special train and private car to go down the coast to Los Angeles, a sort of Naples here." Whether Wilde's trip below the Tehachapis would have paid returns comparable to the railroad investment must remain a matter of conjecture; the reference indicates, however, that the Southern Pacific was aware of the value of importing culture in the person of one of its most famous examples and exponents. Moreover, the reference to Los Angeles as "a sort of Naples" was strictly in the tradition. Since the stirrings of the early boom of the 'sixties, Southern Californians had been constantly assuring themselves that their "sub-tropical" environment was of a special sort, and, conscious of the former flowering of classical civilizations in similar climate and terrain, had begun to call Southern California the Mediterranean of America and to hope that an appropriate culture would develop there.

The enthusiasm among the newcomers from the Middle West for creating a new Mediterranean culture displayed itself in the choice of names for boom towns: Arcadia, Hesperia, and Morocco; Rialto, Tarragona, and Alhambra; Verona, Venice, and Naples, among others. Of the Mediterranean lands, Italy, with its background of Roman culture, was a favorite, and it became a commonplace to refer to Southern California as "the American Italy." A typical example of this love of association with Italy occurred in the publication of an illustration in *The Golden Era* in May, 1888. It was titled "San Diego—Naples of America," and it consisted of a drawing which represented neither San Diego nor Naples but a good deal of both. The Southern California bay was pictured from a position in which the arc resembled that made by the Bay of Naples; San Miguel was enlarged a little and made to look like an inactive Vesuvius; and the buildings in the foreground were clearly Italian villas rather than Mexican adobes or squatters' shacks. The whole composition reflected an aspiration which was made vocal in articles such as "What We Can Learn from Rome," by Grace Ellery Channing, which appeared in *Out West,* or such books as the Italian-born Peter C. Remondino's *The Mediterranean Shores of America* and Charles Dudley Warner's *Our Italy,* in which Warner compared the approach to Southern California to the approach to Italy over the snowy Alps and adopted the theme: "Here is our Mediterranean! Here is our Italy!"

Grace Ellery Channing, writing from Rome after living in Pasadena, carried the physical comparison even further:

When Charles Dudley Warner christened California "Our Italy," he was not inventing a resemblance. Between the storied Peninsula and our long, narrow State there exists a real analogy. San Francisco, Sacramento, the entire mountainous North with the Santa Clara Valley and Fresno may serve for our wide-awake, commercial Piedmont and our rich and fertile Lombardy; while the temperate counties of the middle South stand for the garden of our Italy—our Tuscany. We should have to concede to San Diego the honor of being our Naples (and who dare affirm we shall always lack a Vesuvius?) while we may perhaps elect Santa Catalina into a Capri, a trifle out of plumb geographically though it be. Beyond

San Diego lie our little-known Calabria and Sicily. All this the
most inapprehensive eye may grasp; if none has yet discovered
those subtler potentialities which may make a City of Rome of our
City of Angels, it is perhaps because few have yet lived intimately
in these removed twin cities.

Having established a physical relationship between Rome
and Los Angeles, Miss Channing went on to predict a cultural
similarity which she felt might develop:

Here we touch the core of the matter. Can all this alikeness be
for nothing? Is it possible for two cities to be born so much alike by
nature, and the destiny of the one bear no natural proportion or
relation to the other?—its geography, climate, scenery, vegetation,
to go for naught, exercise no similar influence upon the race in
constant contact with them? . . . . Caesars and Colosseums and
an Hierarchical Church we do not look to produce on our free
Western shores; but a civilization which shall be to the world in its
day what the Roman civilization at its purest was to its—a city
which shall be to that new civilization what Rome was to the old
—is that unreasonable?

It was but a step from such an expressed hope to a pseudo-
scientific rationalization assuring the growing communities
that the environment would inevitably produce a notable
cultural flowering. Thus, the perennially enthusiastic Dr. J. P.
Widney, in his *California of the South,* written with Walter
Lindley, M.D., in 1888, asserted that the combination of
favorable climate and terrain with the selective factors which
were operating to provide Southern California with an especially fine strain of immigrants would create an exceptional
society. He concluded:

If there is any truth in the law of improvement of race by selection and elimination, and in that other law of the power of climatic
surroundings to influence race development, history shows what
the fruitage may be. It was in the analogue of this climate, as found
about the east shores of the Mediterranean, that, two thousand
years ago, grew up the Graeco-Latin civilization which for cen-

turies swayed the destinies of the world, and to-day, after all the ages, still stamps itself upon the mental life of the races.

One is not surprised at Widney's reasoning when one notes that even as eminent a scientist as David Starr Jordan maintained that because California demanded a more varied ingenuity of her pioneers than did the rest of the country, "the processes of natural selection have favored the survival of the ingenious, and the quality of adequacy has become hereditary."

What with heredity and environment thus provided, there remained only the problem of getting the cultural development started, a problem well recognized by the hordes of settlers from beyond the Rockies as they came to feel at home in the new land. Having no traditions of their own in this region, they resorted to a process comparable to the agricultural device of hydroponics, the science whereby the farmer grows his vegetables rapidly without the benefit of soil. All that is needed is water and a certain number of valuable salts.

The enthusiastic embracing of all things Spanish that overtook the Southern California population in the last quarter of the nineteenth century was a result, to a very large degree, of this strong desire to establish cultural traditions in as short a time as possible. Although an Italo-Roman or even a neo-Greek civilization had at first greater appeal for the hundred thousand Anglo-Saxon settlers who came by emigrant excursion coach and Pullman parlor car in the boom days, the Spanish tradition—stemming, as it did, from the Mediterranean—had many advantages, even though acceptance of it by the preponderately Protestant society involved tribute to an alien Catholicism. It also involved a painful association with the humble Mexican laborer who, by 1890, was already consigned to his Sonoratown on the other side of the railroad track. Moreover, those among the newcomers who knew their history were aware of the fact that California had been but a thinly held outpost of the Spanish empire even in its most prosperous period, and that its missions and garrisons had been peopled mainly by mixed-blooded Mexicans rather than by Spaniards. All these problems could be met, however, by people eager to create a romantic past. The Franciscans could be accepted as pious and picturesque, even while Catholics as a whole remained without the pale. The contemporary Mexican peon could be ignored by assuming that the leading figures of Spanish California had been of the best Castilian blood. And the drama of the history could be made more intense by dressing up the more spectacular elements in the story and by refusing to see California as but a comparatively unimportant sector of the much richer Spanish empire to the south.

In addition to its history and its place names—sonorous, romantic names like Santa Barbara, Santa Monica, San Juan Capistrano, San Buenaventura, Redondo, Escondido—there were actually tangible evidences of its earlier civilization. There were, for instance, the old missions, most of them now in ruins but clearly suitable for easy reconstruction. There were a good many of the old Mexican ranch houses, with their crumbling adobe walls, dirt floors, and tiled roofs. In addition, there were a few local families, such as the De la Guerras and the Coronels, who retained something of the courtesy, if not the affluence, of the old days.

The traditions and legends that were created came in time to be accepted without question. The kindhearted, industrious Franciscans, led by the saintly Serra, had brought civilization and temporary affluence to the docile and grateful California Indians. The great ranchos had soon covered the land; they were lavish in their hospitality and were peopled with brightly dressed *caballeros* and beautiful, fine-tempered *señoritas*. Everyone took it easy in that Arcadia, and there was nothing of the push and shove of modern commercial life. The adobe houses were cool and comfortable; the tinkling guitars and the lovely mission bells brought music to a quiet land; and everywhere courtesy, generosity, and lightheartedness reigned supreme. It all fitted in with the synthetic Spanish place names that were being coined by the avid culture seekers: La Serena ("serene"), Chula Vista ("pretty view"), Encanto ("enchantment"), Descanso ("place of rest"), and Linda Rosa ("pretty rose"). (Only a later generation would coin so flippant a name as El Rancho Mortgage Grande.)

It is easy to ridicule the inhabitants of Southern California who thus turned to Spanish tradition and Spanish folkways—and to poke fun at their descendants, the Kansas Spaniards and Iowa rancheros, the dudes performing with riata or guitar, the broad-bottomed Santa Barbara merchants riding into town in the revived Rancheros Visitadores. But to do so is hardly just. They were merely following a tendency, common throughout the United States, to emphasize the romantic elements in their historical past, even though the material they had to work with was fairly thin and sometimes had to be much altered to meet their needs. The construction of a synthetic Spanish California past was neither more reprehensible nor unnatural than the manufacturing of legends about the Pilgrim Fathers or the building of a tradition of an ideal Southern chivalry. In Southern California, however, the process of creating a past was perhaps more rapidly achieved and can be more clearly traced than elsewhere.

◇◇◇◇

The literary document most important in its influence on the growth of the Spanish tradition in Southern California was the immensely popular *Ramona,* by Helen Hunt Jackson. Appearing in 1884, just before the spectacular boom, it created a nation-wide interest in Southern California, and it served as a sort of romantic guidebook during the tourist rush. There was a good deal of the ironic in the influence of *Ramona:* written as a fictionalized sermon to elicit help for the American Indians, it was accepted as an idealization of all things Spanish; presented as an attack on contemporary conditions in the Ramona country, it was accepted as an idealization of the past. Only in the light of this strange fate of the book can one explain the wholehearted condemnation of Mrs. Jackson by a later reformer, Carey McWilliams, in his *Southern California Country:* "And of course it would be a tourist, a goggle-eyed umbrella-packing tourist, who first discovered the past of Southern California and peopled it with curious creatures of her own invention." Actually, Mrs. Jackson was a practiced reporter of considerable skill who had made three trips to California, in the course of which she spent eleven months in the state. In writing *Ramona* she was motivated not by a desire to create a romantic past or to make money but to point out what she considered to be a disgraceful injustice.

When Helen Fiske Hunt first visited California in 1872 she had but a limited reputation, for, although she had supported herself by her writing for the nine years since the death of her first husband, the naval inventor Edward Bissell Hunt, she had been almost as shy as her neighbor and friend, Emily Dickinson, about public recognition for her work, and had printed her poetry and travel sketches under the initials "H.H.," and her fiction, under a well-guarded nom de plume. Also, like Emily Dickinson, she had successfully dodged the three great causes embraced by her literary sisters—abolitionism, temperance, and female suffrage—in spite of her background as the daughter of a professor at Amherst and protegée of Colonel Thomas Wentworth Higginson, a great moral crusader.

On this first short trip to California, which provided the materials for the western sketches published in *Bits of Travel at Home* (1878), this plump little, fair-skinned, blue-eyed "literary explorer," ebullient and restless, showed her customary independence of taste and importunity of manner by disliking San Francisco but falling in love with Yosemite, where she called everything by its Indian name and insisted that her guide give his horses an extra meal before she would ride on them. On this trip she did not visit Southern California, and she paid no attention to the Spanish Californian past, apparently even failing to go see Mission Dolores in San Francisco. But she left the West with the intention of returning a year later to study the old California missions, which doubtless had been described to her as worthy of attention.

She did not return, however, for nine years. In the meantime she had married William Sharpless Jackson, a Colorado financier and railroad manager, had established her headquarters at Colorado Springs, had traveled a good deal at home and abroad, had written more verse, sketches, and fiction, and, after hearing some Ponca Indians lecture in Boston, had been seized with a desire to do something for the American Indian. Thus, at the age of fifty, for the first time she embraced a cause. In 1880 she collected material for a book at the Astor Library in New York and took part in a spirited controversy with Secretary of the Interior Carl Schurz over the treatment of the reservation Indians in Nebraska. In 1881 she published *A Century of Dishonor,* bound in blood-red covers and stamped with a quotation from Benjamin Franklin: "Look upon your hands! They are stained with the blood of your relations," and sent a copy to each of the members of Congress. This book, a spirited but hardly objective arraignment of federal Indian policy, illustrated injustices that had been done to many tribes of American Indians but did not include any discussion of California tribes.

In December, 1881, soon after *A Century of Dishonor* was published, Mrs. Jackson came to Southern California to obtain material for a series of articles, for the *Century Magazine,* on the California missions and the mission Indians. She arrived at Los Angeles with a letter to the local Catholic bishop, the Right Reverend Francis Mora, who introduced her to Don Antonio Coronel and his young wife, and doubtless to other persons willing to help a writer looking for local-color material dealing with Spanish days. Coronel, whose father had been prominent as a teacher in Los Angeles under the Mexican regime, had served the Mexican government as state treasurer before the invasion by the Americans, had fought well against the invaders, and had held various offices, including that of mayor of Los Angeles, after the conquest. In his old age he had collected many relics of the old times, and, although unable to speak much English, he was quite willing to praise the old regime through the medium of his wife as interpreter, and to encourage Mrs. Jackson in her belief that Spanish Californian life "was a picturesque life, with more of sentiment and gayety in it, more also that was truly dramatic, than will ever be seen again on these sunny shores."

It is unnecessary to review all the contacts Mrs. Jackson made in the winter and spring of 1881–1882 as she traveled about in California in her search for material. Although the evidence indicates that her plans for writing a novel about California Indians did not develop until nearly two years after this trip, and that she wrote every word of *Ramona* thousands of miles away from California, the extraordinarily persistent, tendentious, and to a certain degree nauseating activities of the *Ramona* antiquarians have documented almost every stop which she made, recorded every conversation, and created in addition volumes of apocrypha. Suffice it to say that in addition to Don Antonio Coronel she interviewed many local citizens, perhaps the most helpful of whom were Father A. D. Ubach, for sixteen years the priest in charge of the San Diego area; Mrs. Ezra S. Carr of Pasadena, an ardent student of the Indians and a friend of local and visiting writers, who was herself planning a book about Southern California and at the same time helping to support a sick husband and an extensive botanical collection; and Abbot Kinney, a wealthy resident of Sierra Madre, who had long taken an interest in local subjects and knew something of the legal entanglements in which the Indians were caught. She also visited the places one would expect her to visit: the missions themselves, a few of the extant Spanish ranch houses, such as Camu-

los and Guajome, as many of the remaining Southern California Indian villages as she could reach, and such libraries as
she thought would be of assistance to her. The most important of these were the Franciscan library of the Santa Barbara
Mission and the extremely valuable collection, in San Francisco, of western books, newspapers, and documents which
had been made by Hubert Howe Bancroft, who, with his
corps of specially trained assistants, was in the midst of the
process of writing his thirty-nine-volume history of the Pacific
Coast.

The half-dozen resulting *Century* articles, which reached a
fairly large audience of magazine readers and were later included in her *Glimpses of Three Coasts* (1886), are important
because they gave a more detailed picture of the Spanish
period in California history and the conditions of the Spanish
and Indians in California of the postconquest period than had
yet appeared in English. In fact, Mrs. Jackson's account of
Father Junípero Serra's career, published as "Father Junípero
and his Work," apparently was the first historical survey of the
development of California to draw extensively on the diaries
of Fathers Crespi and Palou and on Palou's life of Serra. At
any rate, her competent use of the materials antedated the
standard historial treatments of Bancroft, Hittell, Engelhardt,
Eldredge, and Chapman. It was not until 1913 that Palou's
life of Serra was translated and published by George Wharton
James and C. Scott Williams, and not until 1926 that Palou's
Noticias and Crespi's diaries were made available by Herbert
E. Bolton in his definitive translations. It is probable, therefore, that Mrs. Jackson found English translations in manuscript in the library of H. H. Bancroft. A curious fact which
points to her use of a manuscript source in her consultation
of Palou is the uniform appearance of the Mallorcan padre's
name, in both magazine and book versions of her article, as
Palon.

Mrs. Jackson expressed great admiration for Serra, although she nowhere showed the extreme symptoms of idolatry

implied in Señora Coronel's statement that she "well remembered Mrs. Jackson sitting in this room, with her hands
folded, looking up with intense earnestness to the picture of
Father Junípero, and saying: 'Ah, faithful, noble, dear old
face; what an unselfish, devoted life you led! All I ask, is to be
permitted to meet you in the other world.' " Her attitude toward Serra was compounded partly of awe for his piety but
more especially of admiration for his enterprise. Like the
countless later adherents to the Serra cult in California,
where there has been for some time a move under way to
canonize the Franciscan padre, she was inclined to value his
good works above his religious zeal. She went at least part of
the way on the road which led to Elbert Hubbard's exaltation
of Serra as a worker and *industrial leader*. "The personality of
a man who could not only convert to Christianity three thousand Indians, but who could set them to work, must surely be
sublimely great . . . These missions which lined the coast from
San Francisco to San Diego, every forty miles, were manual-
training schools, founded on a religious concept." In her
account of the missions, Mrs. Jackson gave some credence to
the reports of unwilling conversions and forced labor among
Mission Indians, but as a whole she thoroughly endorsed the
system.

According to the artist who was sent out by *Century* to
illustrate Mrs. Jackson's series, the understanding was that
her subject was to be "enveloped in the mystery and poetry of
romance." Whether Mrs. Jackson achieved that end is open to
question, but certainly she herself felt the "poetry of romance,"
even to the extent of forgetting much of her anti-Catholic
prejudice, which had been evident during an early trip to
Rome. She generally classified the customs of the Spanish
Californians under the head of picturesque rather than super-
stitious. And, although all the missions were in ruins except
Santa Barbara, the adobe mounds and broken arches, softened by ivy and geraniums, inspired her to declare enthusiastically that their architecture, even in ruins, was "the grandest

in the America of her day." In Los Angeles, where she sought diligently for echoes of the past (with the aid of the Coronels) she detected "a certain indefinable, delicious aroma from the old ignorant, picturesque days"; and she felt that the climate was responsible for the "character, or, to speak more accurately, the lack of character, of the old Mexican and Spanish Californians."

Mrs. Jackson's interest in the California Mission Indians was so stimulated by this trip that she arranged to have Abbot Kinney and herself appointed by the United States government to inquire into the condition of these people. Thus, in 1883 she returned to Los Angeles on her third trip to the West Coast, and in the spring of that year she and Mr. Kinney made a five-week tour of the Southern California Indian villages, after which they filed an important and discerning report with the federal Commissioner of Indian Affairs. Having submitted her report and completed her articles on the missions, Mrs. Jackson then drew upon all the materials she had collected on her several trips, to write *Ramona,* a novel which she hoped would do for the Indians what *Uncle Tom's Cabin* had done for the Negroes. Written shortly before her untimely death from cancer, it contained a fervent plea for help for a people she had found to be much abused. She lived long enough to see the novel become a best seller, as well as to realize that its immediate influence was not what she had hoped. After reading a review in the *Atlantic Monthly* she wrote to a friend: "Not one word for my Indians! I put my heart and soul in the book *for them*. It is a dead failure. The dry-rot is in this nation." In her more sanguine moments, she trusted that in time her purpose would be effected. In such a mood, she wrote words of encouragement to a Saboba Indian who lived in the hills where the prototype of Alessandro had been murdered: "Tell him, if you *can*—about *Ramona:*—tell him that over a hundred thousand people have read that story, and are sorry for the Indians—and that many good people are working to get justice done them by the government." And to

President Cleveland she wrote, four days before her death: "I am dying happier for the belief I have that it is your hand that is destined to strike the first steady blow toward lifting this burden of infamy from our country, and righting the wrongs of the Indian race."

Although *Ramona* undoubtedly played a significant part in bringing to the attention of the Americans the plight of the Indian, this effect was produced as much through the emotional impact of the story as through any graphic portrayal of Indian life contained in the novel. In the novel the purely Indian material is overshadowed by the romance between Ramona and Alessandro; and neither one is very convincingly an Indian. Ramona, we are told, is the daughter of an Indian squaw and a Scotsman named Angus McPhail—a character based, at least in part, on Hugo Reid, whose letters Mrs. Jackson had read. But Ramona, so far as she is human rather than a chromo, is thoroughly a part of her Spanish Mexican background; even under the force of the disasters that come upon her toward the end of the book she remains a *señorita* in trouble, a saintly Castilian at heart. Alessandro, a pure-blooded Indian who is supposed to be the son of a famous San Luis Rey neophyte, in the early part of the book when the narrative still hovers about the Moreno ranch, is as much a pre-Raphaelite figure as Ramona. He is handsome, polite, and well-educated; he reads, writes, and plays the violin. He talks like a drawing-room favorite, and his soul is as pure as the driven snow. In comparing him with the Spanish Felipe (whom Ramona marries after Alessandro's death) Mrs. Jackson further emphasizes the Indian's virtue:

There were many things that Felipe knew, of which Alessandro was profoundly ignorant; but there were others in which Alessandro could have taught Felipe; and when it came to the things of the soul, and of honor, Alessandro's plane was the higher of the two . . . Alessandro was by nature full of veneration and the religious instinct; Felipe had been trained into being a good Catholic.

Under the circumstances, it is deplorable that Alessandro does not, when he is put to the test, better display other traits of the natural man, such as resourcefulness and savage bravery; for, moving as are the descriptions of the dispossessing of the Indians at Temecula and San Pascual, the total effect is sentimental rather than tragic. Any virile Indian traits Alessandro may have had are sacrificed to the formula for producing tears. It is a weak man who is destroyed, merely a type martyr, not a true representative of the mission Indian. His mind is too easily lost, therefore his insanity is not convincing. Dying, he is a completely helpless victim; his death therefore comes as an anticlimax.

In the light of the intent to make the novel a plea for better treatment of the Indians by contemporary Americans, it is ironical that the effect was to a large extent to romanticize the Spanish Californians of preconquest days. Thus, the Ramona Pageant, created years later by the Hemet Chamber of Commerce to bring to the San Jacinto Valley some of the tourists enthralled by the story, ends with a speech by Juan Canito which includes the line, "The story of the Spanish dons is told." Yet *Ramona* clearly is not a story of the Spanish dons. It is laid in Southern California in the 1870's, long after the golden days of the "don" culture, and its two principal characters are a Luiseño Indian with an Italian name and a half-breed girl who had been brought up by the descendants of a Spanish Californian family. Moreover, although the action in the first half of the novel takes place on what had once been an old Spanish (or Mexican) rancho, the owner, Señora Moreno, the widow of a former friend of the notorious Pío Pico, is a selfish harridan whose role is hardly an admirable one. The other main "Spanish" character, Felipe, a weakling whose regeneration toward the end of the novel is as unconvincing as the happy ending which takes him and Ramona to Mexico, adds little to one's respect for the romanticized Spanish Californians.

The acceptance of *Ramona* by Mrs. Jackson's generation as

a picture of an idyllic Spanish California can be attributed partly to the idealization of characters like Father Salvierderra, a personification of pure goodness, who strays in and out of the story to remind one of the holiness and zeal of the Franciscans. Contributing to it also was Alessandro's romanticizing of the past in the face of a miserable present; for he, like many of the real mission Indians with whom Mrs. Jackson talked, looked back upon the mission days as the good time when Indians were fed and clothed and were taught many of the crafts of Western civilization. The readers were, it is feared, much more interested in building up a glorious tradition than in doing anything to protect the helpless Indians from the importunate and ruthless squatters. Thus, as time passed and *Ramona* took its prominent place in the folklore of the region—which named a town after each of the lovers—it came to be looked upon as a eulogy of the old Spanish days; whereas, actually, its plot concerned the persecution of two Indians whose troubles developed because of the stubbornness and cruelty of an old Spanish family.

∽∽∽∽

It remained for Charles Fletcher Lummis to make a real selling point of the Spanish past. It was Lummis who wrote for the Santa Barbara *Morning Press* in a moment of self-revelatory enthusiasm: "We realize today that the old missions are worth more money, are a greater asset, to Southern California, than our oil, our oranges, or even our climate . . . a man is a poor fool who thinks he can do business without sentiment." And yet neither the business nor the sentiment explained all of Lummis; nor for that matter did the not unsubstantiated charges that he was a poseur, a lecher, and a drunkard. He was also a man of extraordinary energy and great bravery, whose neuroses and enthusiasms, like those of many men who move mountains, were mutually stimulating. But especially he was a man with a strong flair for the theatrical.

GEORGE HORATIO
DERBY

HORACE BELL

INA   DONNA   COOLBRITH

MARGARET
COLLIER
GRAHAM

FATHER SALVIERDERRA BLESSING ALESSANDRO

Ramona: California's Greatest Outdoor Play

HELEN HUNT JACKSON

ABBOT KINNEY

CHARLES FLETCHER LUMMIS

GEORGE WHARTON
JAMES

*Photos courtesy
Huntington Library*

MARY AUSTIN

PACIFIC ELECTRIC RAILWAY PAMPHLETS, 1895–1915

CALIFORNIA STATE BUILDING

Panama-California Exposition, San Diego, 1915

With such a flair, Lummis naturally played many parts in his time—that of a Navajo or Zuñi, of a western Thoreau, of a teeth-baring Teddy Roosevelt, but most continuously and consistently that of a Spaniard. In this role he looked, according to Farnsworth Crowder, like a character from San Gabriel Mission. Whether he was dressed in his suit of corduroy—rumor had it that the King of Spain provided a fund each year for a new suit—or in his peon whites, he lived the part, even to the extent of limiting his diet to meat, chili, and olives, maintaining that such food was best suited to the Southwestern climate. When he built his home by the Arroyo Seco with his own hands (plus some help from his Indian friends), he called it "El Alisal," and he dubbed the big sycamore in the patio, where he held his parties and mock trials, "El Alcalde Mayor." His love of singing, particularly to a guitar accompaniment, and the ability of his Mexican cook to double as a Spanish troubadour contributed to his enthusiasm for Spanish Californian and Indian songs, which he diligently collected by means of manuscript transcriptions and phonograph recordings. Of great pride to him was this collection, much of which he transcribed and eventually published in his *Spanish Songs of Old California.* And when freethinking Charles Fletcher Lummis, the son of a Methodist minister, was buried without benefit of clergy, the liturgy of his service was made up of Spanish songs which he had collected.

Lummis had many other projects which reflected his interest in Spanish subjects, among them a Spanish-English encyclopedia which was to cover all topics of importance in Spanish America. He also led a campaign to prevent the alteration of Southern California place names at the time of the Spanish-American War. He wrote *The Awakening of a Nation,* praising the Mexico of his day. And in *The Spanish Pioneers,* addressing the boys of America in an attempt to combat prejudice against the Latin Americans, he declared emphatically, "the Spanish pioneering of the Americas was the largest and longest and most marvellous feat of manhood in all history." He published the first English translations of basic historical documents by Benavides and Escalante in *The Land of Sunshine,* and he helped to inaugurate an interest in adobe architecture. It was a matter of great pride to him that his efforts to popularize the Spanish tradition did not go unrecognized by the Spanish government. As early as 1895, Lummis was able to boast that he had been thanked by the Royal Academy of Spain for his work in clearing up the Spanish reputation in America. And as his crusade continued, he received greetings from the King of Spain, was made a Knight of the Order of Isabel the Catholic, and was the recipient of a special visit from the Duke of Alba (escorted by Douglas Fairbanks) as further indication of the gratitude of the Spanish government.

As one reviews Lummis' career, one is struck with the symbolic nature of his reception on the Southern Californian scene after his adventurous walk from Cincinnati, which he was to describe in *A Tramp Across the Continent.* With his broken arm in a sling, tanned and hardened, after crossing the desert this energetic young man was met, even before he entered Los Angeles, by his new job in the form of Harrison Gray Otis, editor of the Los Angeles *Times.* Otis, who had been publishing Lummis' weekly letters describing the hike and was planning to hire him as soon as he arrived, had walked out from Los Angeles just far enough to reach the appropriate spot to meet the enthusiastic newcomer, "under the shade of the old Franciscan mission" at San Gabriel. That was on the evening of February 1, 1885. "When I pulled off my shoes from tired feet that night," wrote Lummis, "I had walked since leaving Cincinnati in my roundabout course a fraction over 3507 miles. I had been out one hundred and forty-three days, and had crossed eight States and Territories, nearly all of them along their greatest length . . . The longest and happiest 'tramp' ever made for pure pleasure was over; and at nine o'clock next morning I was in harness, as city editor of the Los Angeles *Daily Times.*"

Lummis arrived in Los Angeles just before the big boom and at a time when the Los Angeles *Times,* a Republican daily founded in 1881, was rapidly becoming a power in the community. The doughty Harrison Gray Otis, who had taken over the *Times* six months after it was founded, had been active in Ohio in the newly formed Republican party and had been a Kentucky delegate to the national convention of 1860 which had nominated Lincoln. After service in the Union army and a few years of newspaper editing and "politicking" in Ohio, he had come to California in 1876, eager to ride the crest of Republican favor in Western journalism and politics.

No doubt Otis felt that the twenty-five-year-old "Lum," who had had three years of newspaper experience in Ohio editing the Republican Scioto *Gazette,* who had written vividly of his experiences in crossing the country, and who seemed to exude energy and purpose without stopping to catch his breath, was just the man he needed as an assistant on the growing *Times.* That he was right is evinced by the comment that, at the height of the boom when everything and everybody moved fast, Lummis "passed ordinary people in the street as if they had been hitched." Lummis' references to the three years he worked on the journal, into which he bought as a member of the firm, indicate that he considered his task to be that of a reformer, and Otis' that of an indomitable fighter—the curmudgeon chief himself—although his most pleasurable memory, in later years, of his *Times* career was the part he played as special correspondent to General Crook in the campaign in the deserts of Arizona to capture the elusive Geronimo, an Indian leader whom Lummis was to eulogize in his poem, "The Man Who Yawns." But whether helping to ferment the boom, struggling for the reform of the municipal government, or covering the Indian campaign, Lummis fitted in well and gave his all to the cause. In January, 1888, however, he was stricken with paralysis and realized that, if he were to live, he would have to alter his pace. He departed for New Mexico, where he passed the next six years, spending, according to his statement, much of his time out in the wilds and among the Indians. This was the period of his trial in the desert.

In examining the biographical data bearing on Lummis' career one is impressed by the probable correlation between his physical setbacks and his emotional problems. We are told that an attack of brain fever prevented the Massachussetts boy from graduating with his class at Harvard. On the other side of the record there is the story, roughly covering the same period, of his fathering an illegitimate child in New Hampshire as the result of a vacation romance with a fellow worker in a resort hotel, and of a secret marriage to another young lady and his subsequent removal to his father-in-law's farm in Ohio. Although Lummis at various times atttributed his decision to go West to love of adventure, distaste for Ohio fevers, and a breakdown from tuberculosis, his hike across the continent may have been prompted by marital unrest. It has been suggested that his first wife was "far ahead of her generation" and did not raise objection to his wandering. Later, in the period in which he was working on the *Times*, she joined him in Los Angeles, but soon after, Lummis, ill with paralysis, left for New Mexico, where he fell in love with a blue-eyed Connecticut girl who was teaching at Isleta. A divorce and second marriage for him followed. The former wife and the new bride apparently became good friends. Lummis, never daunted by convention, dedicated his current book, *The Land of Poco Tiempo*, to them both: "To Eva and Dorothea." The parallelism between physical breakdown and marital difficulties was to appear once again, when Lummis suffered an attack of "blindness" coincident with his second divorce. Another period of wandering was followed by another marriage.

Whether his difficulties were physical or psychological, Lummis apparently suffered intensely. His record of his struggles in New Mexico, found in "My Friend Will," the last chapter of *The King of the Broncos*, is a vivid story of his defeat of paralysis by trusting to life in the out-of-doors and to will power. Whatever the circumstances, in the six years he spent in New Mexico Lummis reached the threshold of death and recovered with spirit so renewed that he turned out many magazine contributions, including numerous humorous sketches for *Puck* and *Life;* published six books, dealing principally with Spanish and Indian activities and legends in the Southwest; established a fruitful friendship with the pioneer ethnologist, Adolph F. A. Bandelier, with whom he visited Peru in the Villard expedition of 1892; and returned to Los Angeles in 1894 filled with plans for the future.

The next fifteen years proved to be the most active and important of his frenetic career. Taking over the editorship of *The Land of Sunshine* (later called *Out West),* he made it into a genuinely significant regional journal which bore the stamp of his energy and purpose on almost every page. Through his influence as editor and through his numerous personal contacts he took a leading part in helping the local Indians and restoring the missions. He publicized the climatic attractions of the region and furthered all projects which he thought might enhance the reputation or fortune of Southern California. He entertained visiting celebrities at El Alisal and even dashed off to Washington to tell his friend President Theodore Roosevelt about the attractions of Los Angeles. He continued to pour forth poems, articles, and books which hymned the Lummis faith in the vigorous life and in the glories of the past and hopes for the future of Southern California and the Pacific Southwest. Relinquishing the routine editing of *Out West* to his assistant editor, Charles A. Moody, he served from 1905 to 1910 as librarian of the Los Angeles Public Library, eagerly grasping the opportunity to brand the city's books as if they were cattle, to stamp warning notices on such reference works as he considered untrustworthy, and to write bombastic annual reports in which he told how he planned to make the local library the center of Southwestern scholarship.

With his flamboyant temperament and personal excesses,

Lummis, however, was hardly the person to remain in one position indefinitely. After he left *Out West* and the Los Angeles Public Library, he threw himself into making plans for the Southwest Museum, which was opened in 1914, not without friction and some kindly misrepresentation of the exact part played by Lummis in its development. His was the spirit which started it but not the brains which gave body to the idea nor the pocketbook which made it pass from blueprint to castle with caracole tower. As Lummis grew older, he became more cantankerous toward all who crossed him, more eagerly appreciative of those who saw beyond his excesses to the courage which was always there. When he died in 1928, his body, after being duly displayed in a chief's blanket, was cremated, and the ashes were laid in a niche in the wall at El Alisal. Above them is the inscription:

> He founded the Southwest Museum
> He built this house
> He saved four old missions
> He studied and recorded Spanish America
> He tried to do his share

In composing his inscription, Lummis, who was at heart an honest man in spite of his histrionics, made an accurate estimate of his accomplishments. He was more of a promoter than a man of letters. As a writer with more than a score of books to his credit he was never more than a journalist and publicist. His descriptive books, such as *Some Strange Corners of Our Country* and *The Land of Poco Tiempo,* were essentially pedestrian although they accomplished their purpose of drawing the attention of their readers to the attractions of Southwestern scenery and customs. Curiously, his only extensive work about Southern California, "The Right Hand of the Continent," published serially in *Out West,* never achieved book form. He had no skill at fiction, and his treatment of folk tales in such books as *The Man Who Married the Moon* was uninspired. Although he loved to write poetry, his verses were essentially journalistic, as a perusal of *A Bronco Pegasus* will show. Thus, although he wrote a great deal, his importance lay not in the intrinsic merit of his writing but rather in his influence on others. He was a man who initiated action, an enthusiast with many visions, a spur to those more indolent than he. He was the impresario of the Southern California tourist renaissance.

∽∽∽∽

Because of its importance to Southern California writers, *The Land of Sunshine* was the most noteworthy medium by which Lummis exercised his influence. Back in 1889, Charles Dwight Willard, who had been writing short stories for *The Argonaut* and working on the Los Angeles *Herald,* when he was not convalescing from hemorrhages, had been approached by a wealthy citizen who proposed to publish a regional journal and wanted someone to write short stories for it. "It appears that I am about the only Simon-pure literary character to be found in these parts," Willard confided to his family back in Chicago. The journal, titled *The Pacific Monthly,* had struggled on for a few issues and then had died, but Charles Willard had continued to write short stories and in addition had become secretary of the new Los Angeles Chamber of Commerce and one of the most energetic and talented boosters in a land which was to produce many boosters.

Eventually, Willard decided to start his own journal. According to his letters, he scraped together all of his savings and financed the new venture practically by himself. He chose, however, to remain in the background, and *The Land of Sunshine* appeared in June, 1894, as the work of F. A. Pattee, who was, in fact, but a business manager paid at half-time rates. Willard and his wife wrote much of the new monthly magazine during the first six months of its life, relying principally on descriptive articles about the region. By October he was sufficiently enheartened over its reception to note: "It is always to be a Southern California magazine but it will gradually become less material in its tone." When Willard persuaded Lummis to take over the editorship early in 1895, he was very hopeful. Lummis, Yankee born and Harvard trained, struck him as having a severe conscience and a strict sense of duty: "He is a tireless worker and is throwing his whole soul into the undertaking." As the result of Willard's faith and financing and Lummis' energy and resourcefulness, *The Land of Sunshine* soon had a genuinely significant list of contributors and rallied the first cultural group which Southern California was to know. By the time Lummis changed its name to *Out West* in 1902, insisting that the old title smacked too much of the chamber of commerce and the Sunday school, it was easily the leading literary journal of the Pacific Coast and remained the leader until its demise in 1910.

Although *The Land of Sunshine* never came to be the remunerative investment that Willard had hoped it would be —six months after it started, he wrote: "All the weekly and monthly magazines and papers of San Francisco and Los Angeles combined do not sell as many copies as the *Land of Sunshine* in Los Angeles"—it soon outgrew the painful stage during which Lummis and Willard wrote most of the contents, and their wives contributed articles on Mexican cooking and translations from Spanish documents (Mrs. Eva Frances Lummis was an expert Spanish translator). Short stories began coming in, and, although at first few showed promise, the journal published the best, gradually building up a school of local-color fiction. Charles Willard himself, Yda Addis, Margaret Collier Graham, Lanier Bartlett, Gwendolen Overton, and Mary Austin were representative figures from the local area. And from beyond the mountains and the deserts came work from craftsmen like Eugene Manlove Rhodes, Mary Hallock Foote, and Stewart Edward White. The local poets were as ready as ever with ambitious and uneven verse; Nora May French, Julia Boynton Green, and

Jeanne C. Carr tried their wings alongside better-known poets such as John Vance Cheney, Edwin Markham, and Joaquin Miller. The articles in the magazine dealt with many subjects besides the attractions of the growing Southern California communities, which, however, were accorded considerable space. There were discussions of local and national political issues, essays on science and travel, and art analyses, such as the comments on the paintings of western artists like William Keith, Maynard Dixon, and Gutzon Borglum, who also occasionally provided illustrations. In addition, the journal was profusely and intelligently illustrated with photographs, for Lummis was a good photographer and very much interested in photographic work done by others. There were a number of regular monthly departments: Margaret Collier Graham discussed manners, morals, and the woman's point of view, in "The Angle of Reflection"; William E. Smythe propagandized for more irrigation, better farming methods, and sweeping social reform; and Lummis wrote trenchant and often discerning editorials, in his "The Lion's Den." Lummis also apparently contributed the greater part of the book reviews and saw to it that the magazine rose above the usual flattery of local authors to something resembling an objective critical attitude.

The magazine carried also a large number of somewhat specialized articles which sprang directly from Lummis' keen and sincere interest in the Southwestern Indians. On his trips to Arizona and New Mexico, Lummis had been deeply impressed by the nomadic and pueblo tribes, like the Navajo and Zuñi, who continued their folk arts, danced their tribal dances, and maintained a culture as yet little altered by white influences. He had also become much interested in the relics of earlier civilizations which abound on the mesas and cliffs of the areas near the Colorado River and the Rio Grande. Moreover, his attitude in this field was genuinely enlightened, probably as the result of his association in New Mexico and South America with Adolph F. A. Bandelier, an emigrant from Switzerland who had helped to establish the ethnological approach to the study of the Southwest Indian. Accordingly, no man in Southern California did more to publicize the early findings of the scientists studying the natives, past and present, of these regions than Lummis, although he himself was not a scientist by training nor a detached observer by temperament. In *The Land of Sunshine* he made a special point of describing archaeological and ethnological activity. There were feature articles on pioneers such as Bandelier, Powell, and Cushing; there were also contributions by such men as Washington Matthews, an Irish ethnologist who was studying the Navajos, John C. Fillmore, a Pomona College professor who made promising progress in the examination of aboriginal folk music before his early death in 1898, and David P. Barrows, then writing papers on the Coahuila Indians. Prominent scientists like Frederick W. Hodge and E. L. Hewitt figured in the pages of *The Land of Sunshine,* either as contributing editors or the subjects of articles. In addition, Lummis used the journal to publicize the activities of the Southwest Society of the Archaeological Institute of America, a local group of laymen interested in the scientific study of the Indian, which eventually founded the Southwest Museum, one of the most important centers for the study of aboriginal cultures in America.

Two of the special projects of *The Land of Sunshine* which were to have considerable influence were the Sequoya League and the Landmarks Club, both represented by monthly departments in the journal. The Sequoya League had as its slogan: "To make better Indians by treating them better." By means of this organization Lummis and his companions were able to come to the rescue of the dispossessed Warner's Ranch Indians by raising so large a rumpus that the United States Congress appropriated $100,000 to buy for the Indians land which would support them. They then found the land near Pala and supervised the transfer of the natives to the new site. The organization continued its interest in the unfortunate brothers of Ramona and Alessandro, helping again when a group living at Campo were in distress.

The purpose of the Landmarks Club was to preserve remnants of the Spanish past, particularly the missions. Those of San Gabriel and Santa Barbara, it is true, had never been entirely abandoned; and after the reassignment of the mission chapels to the Catholic Church by the courts and presidential order in 1865, they had been rededicated to church purposes and therefore were fairly well maintained. And with the establishment of a Franciscan novitiate in connection with San Luis Rey in the early 'nineties, that mission was in part restored. But most of the rest, in the half century that they had been neglected, had fallen into ruins; their walls had melted in the rains and turned into mere mounds of earth, and they had been stripped of their wood, tile, and ornaments. It was to these, and especially to San Juan Capistrano, San Fernando, and San Diego, that the Landmarks Club, made up for the most part of Protestants, gave its principal attention. It also did much to rehabilitate the attractive Pala *asistencia* and gave considerable aid to Father J. J. O'Keefe in further restoration of San Luis Rey. By 1902 the movement had become state-wide, and the California Historical Landmarks League was promoted, in San Francisco, with the backing of the Native Sons of the Golden West and William Randolph Hearst. Thus, the movement, which had started with volunteer labor and dollar subscriptions, became a big business venture. Supplementing it was the campaign to turn the old trail connecting the missions into a highway called El Camino Real. The promoters speculated: "What could not the drive from San Diego to Sonoma be made if the State once roused herself to it? Planted and watered and owned as an illustration of forestry, why should it not also as a route of pilgrimage rank with that to Canterbury . . . ?"

Lummis and his friends also supported the annual Los Angeles fiestas, which had swung into action with music, color, and *cascarones* in 1894, just in time to be the subject of the feature article in the brand-new *Land of Sunshine*. As a matter of fact, the journal that year told of three grand fiestas —at Los Angeles, Santa Barbara, and San Diego—all of which were improvements on the winter fiesta which had so pleased novelist E. P. Roe in Santa Barbara eight years earlier. Soon every sizable community in Southern California was putting on its annual show, in which all the pretty girls became *señoritas,* and nearly everyone in town had a chance to ride a horse or appear on a float. The traditions of Spanish California, the Riviera, and old England of morris-dance days were all filtered through a Middle Western imagination to create an institution not quite like anything that had been seen in the world before. As George Wharton James put it:

Does environment affect the spirits of people? Taine, and a score of authorities, literary and scientific, affirm that it does. I do not propose any attempt to answer the question, but merely to state the fact that *something* in California has produced a Festival Spirit not observable to like extent elsewhere on the American Continent . . . Furthermore, the outcome of this spirit is such that I venture the affirmation that California has more varied, distinctive and peculiarly appropriate festivals than any country in the world.

〜〜〜〜〜

Charles Fletcher Lummis' principal rival in the race to provide the new Southwest with a past and a tradition was George Wharton James, the author of the purple passage on the fiestas. In his zeal for unearthing the history of the Spanish Californian days, in his enthusiasm for the preservation of the missions, in his insistence on recognition of the merits of the Mexicans and Indians of the region, and in his whole-hearted devotion to the climate and scenery of the West, James held his own with Lummis in almost every department and even excelled him in the unlimited ceiling of his panegyrics. Although there was a constant feud between the two men, openly acknowledged by Lummis, who was the aggressor, and tacitly accepted by James, who used the coals-of-fire method as his principal weapon, there was a good deal in common between them. Both outlanders, Lummis, a Yankee born in 1859, and James, an Englishman born in 1858, they came to the West about the same time, James in 1881 and Lummis three years later. Both were brought up in fundamentalist households. Lummis' father was a Methodist minister, and James's father was a Methodist choir leader, who helped the boy learn to sing, to lead a choir, to teach Sunday school, and to preach to a congregation in Lincolnshire by the time he was sixteen. Both had plenty of marital difficulties, although Lummis never went through the torture of public castigation as James did when he was "degraded from the pulpit" in Long Beach in 1889 as a result of sensational charges of sex irregularities brought against him by his wife. Both found they could retain their sanity and rebuild their personalities by going to the desert and observing the Indians. Both made a cult of desert living, with emphasis on seminudity, exercise, and bizarre diets, Lummis going in for chili and olives, and James favoring dates and a vegetarian pabulum. Although they resembled each other very little in appearance, for Lummis was little more than five and a half feet tall, thick-lipped, and homely, whereas James was a full six feet in height, pale, and handsome, with "dark hair and liquid eye," they both had more than a touch of the poseur in their professional getups. Lummis went in for corduroy suits, Navajo belts, and cowboy hats; whereas James relied upon the magnetic attraction of his magnificent black beard.

Although Lummis was much the more virile of the two—it is impossible to imagine him writing tracts on "Social Purity" and "Singing through Life with God"—and was certainly the more educated, having had four years at Harvard in contrast to James's lack of schooling, the two were not far apart in much of their thinking. Lummis became a pagan, a sort of freethinker with due respect for the desert gods of the Indians; James followed an equally popular Southern California trail of spiritual philandering. He once wrote: "In religion I'm a Methodist, with leanings towards Roman Catholicism, Presbyterianism, Congregationalism, Christian Science, Theosophy, Buddhism, Confucianism, Universalism, Free-Thought, Seventh-Day Adventism, Frank Wakeley Gunsaulus, Jenkin Lloyd Jones, and Benjamin Fay Mills." Lummis' "My Friend Will" and James's *Quit Your Worrying* both revealed fights against neurotic temperaments. Lummis was an ardent follower of Teddy Roosevelt, whereas James found his salvation in Robert Browning. Lummis liked to think of himself as a historian and archaeologist, whereas James called himself, in *Who's Who in America,* an "explorer and ethnologist." Of course, neither one was trained to be the specialists the terms implied; they were, in fact, energetic exploiters of the new cultural hydroponics, amateur gardeners on a grand scale but unqualified for high positions in the world of art and science.

George Wharton James, born in 1858 and brought up in Gainsborough, Lincolnshire, suffered the fate of a nervous, maladjusted boy, underprivileged, often ill, and always highly imaginative. His father apparently gave him some musical education and encouraged him to master enunciation for public lectures. By the time he came of age, he had adopted history and astronomy as hobbies and had become interested in the Stokes mnemonic system, which was, in later days, to be the basis for lectures in which he recited Southey's "Cataract of Lodore" forward, backward, and at random to illustrate the excellencies of his method.

James left England and came to Nevada in 1881, determined to exploit his talents. A fictional account of his experiences in that state as a lecturer and minister, as well as of his personality and appearance, was given by "A. B. Ward" (Alice Ward Bailey) in *The Sage Brush Parson,* which she wrote in 1906 principally from details which James had given her. In this novel he appears to be something of a blundering fool, kindhearted and unsophisticated, who highly treasured his fine voice, tender ways, and love of flowers and children. A reviewer referred to the fictional character as a St. Anthony in the desert, "tempted by drink, by the unlawful love of a woman, and by the desire to kill." With the real James, it is hard to take the drink seriously, but the woman trouble and the desire to kill appear to be genuine enough. His wife, whom he had left in England after less than a year of married life, turned up in Nevada in 1882, and, after confessing various adulteries of her own, plagued James with accusations of lust for almost every female in town between the ages of ten and sixty. This sort of thing went on for seven years; the harassed James took to the desert at one time, fled to England at another, and, according to contemporary accounts, threatened to beat up his wife with a chair at still a third time. Devoted as he was to editing the *Social Purity Pioneer*—in which, as in *The Guiding Light,* he mixed elementary sex physiology and pleas for premarital continence and the single standard—and to preaching for the Methodist Church, he was still unable to avoid catastrophe. It came in the form of a very unsavory divorce suit in Long Beach in the summer of 1889, with the Methodist Conference first suspending him as a minister and then expelling him from the church.

Not all of James's methods of meeting this major crisis of his life are known, but one remedy seems to have been a period of wandering in the Middle West and in Europe, in the course of which he discovered Robert Browning's poetry:

Browning opened up a new world of life, hope and joy to me . . . When I began to read him, the dark cloud of Pauline theology began to dissipate . . . In "Abt Vogler" I had learned that when God expanded my heart in a desire for good I could absolutely rest assured that sometime, somewhere, somehow, that desire would be fulfilled.

After four years of travel—and much Browning—James reappeared on the Southern California scene. There, as editor of the *Mt. Lowe Echo,* a little journal created to publicize the

funicular railroad and hotel which the visionary Thaddeus
Sobreski Coulincourt Lowe had just established on the mountain named for him, James (now Professor G. Wharton James
rather than the Reverend George W. James) wrote paeans to
nature and praise of its conquerors. "Some years ago I used to
preach sermons regularly, taking my text from the Bible,—
now I only ask to preach irregularly, taking my text from
God's other book, His world—Nature." Thus enheartened
and reborn, James settled down in Pasadena, founded a local
Browning club, made a second and presumably happy marriage, and set about working up a trade as lecturer and publicist of the Southwest, par excellence.

In examining the output of George Wharton James's activity mill from 1895 to his death in 1923 one is impressed with
the amount of energy the man must have had. In addition to
his "exploration" trips into the Colorado Desert and through
the Indian and desert countries of Arizona, Utah, and
Nevada, and in addition to his almost constant lecturing, he
managed to write more than forty books and an uncounted
number of articles—publications which he advertised as dealing with "romance, history, botany, birds, science, and scenic
wonders of California and the Southwest." He also had time
to found and edit *The Basket,* a journal dealing with Indian
basketry; to help with *The Craftsman,* another Indian journal; to edit the revived *Out West* for two years; to run his own
publishing house (which he called both the Arroyo Guild
Press and the Radiant Life Press); to hold Thursday evening
soirées for the culturally thirsty, in his home in Pasadena; to
organize California literary seminars at the San Francisco and
San Diego world fairs of 1915; to raise dates in the Coachella
Valley; and to act as secretary of the Chuckawalla and Palo
Verde Irrigation Association. In addition, he campaigned for
the introduction of Luther Burbank's spineless cactus as a
major farming crop—it was to serve as fodder, food, and
medicinal cure-all for the region—and marketed the George
Wharton James antirattlesnake kit.

In all of this there is the sure mark of the literary racketeer. In fact, Lummis openly accused George of being not only an opportunist but also a liar. In an article titled "Untruthful James" he said: "It is rather well understood by Indians and whites, along some five hundred miles of the Southwest, that Mr. James may tell the truth when he cannot well help it." In fact, Lummis privately referred to James as a "hotel tout," meaning that he was constantly on the lookout for free hotel accommodations and free railroad passes in return for services rendered in exaggerated advertising in his writings and lectures. No doubt there was some truth in Lummis' accusation. Like many other Southern California publicists, James probably sometimes accepted such "courtesies" for his services. Nor was he, when selling his books in advance on a subscription basis, above appealing to a locality in Arizona or Utah in terms which would indicate that his enthusiasm for the region would correlate to some degree with the number of prospective readers. From his earliest appearance in the West, he was given to using the title "Professor" loosely, as if he were a patent-medicine man; and in Nevada and elsewhere he was often derided for placing F.R.A.S., F.R.H.S., and so forth, after his name. His frequent references to his contacts with great men, such as Carlyle and Ruskin, doubtless stemmed from his well-developed sense of salesmanship. He unquestionably borrowed heavily from other writers in making his books, which were frequently merely expansions of his lectures. Many a volume owes as much to scissors and paste as it does to thought and research, but he usually acknowledged his borrowings.

His method was always that of the enthusiast; and his taste, even in sentence structure, was catholic, his fire dispersed. He could announce a lecture on "With God in His Great Out-of-Doors, with Birds, Beasts, Buds, Butterflies, and Blossoms" or could easily write sentences such as this comment on Ina Coolbrith: "Here she first heard the mocking-bird and the meadow-larks, the latter of whose songs she has vivified in human words, so that when William Keith, our greatest and no less literary critic than painter, read them, he wept aloud for very ecstasy of joy." His enthusiasm for all his fellow literary journeymen in California was tremendous and quite uncritical; time after time he came back to one of his favorite subjects for lectures and books, "The Influence of California on Literature." He anticipated all possible approaches for future Taines of the Pacific Coast by boldly announcing four influences which made California literature unique: continent's edge, climate and topography, marvelous history, frontier spirit.

Yet there is something about James that makes one like him even though much of his work is shoddy and his manner is constantly that of the salesman. It is not necessary to agree with the critic who called him a Tolstoy of the West, or to follow along with Fra Elbert Hubbard who made the comment, "When Napoleon met Wolfgang Goethe he said: 'At last I have seen a man.' When George Wharton James made a little journey to Sun-up and spoke one Sunday afternoon in Roycroft Chapel, I mopped for joy, and said the same." The fact remains that in his enthusiasm he collected a great deal of information, much of which is valuable. In his best books, such as *Through Ramona's Country* (1908), *In and Around the Grand Canyon* (1900), *In and Out of the Old Missions* (1905), *The Wonders of the Colorado Desert* (1906), and *Arizona the Wonderland* (1917), he worked carefully and exhaustively (for his period) and weighed his evidence with considerable care. His interests lay in the scenery of the West, the remnants of Spanish California, the character and fate of the Southwest Indians, and the epic of the reclamation of the desert. In stressing these themes he stressed the major factors in Southern California folkways; his writings therefore reflect, albeit crudely, the interests of the country.

VI

The Middle Nordic Period

IN HIS *Libros Californianos* Phil Townsend Hanna has listed six periods in the development of California culture: Barbaric, Spanish-Mexican, Mexican, Early Nordic, Middle Nordic, and Late Nordic. Mr. Hanna has gone further and suggested the musical development which accompanied these periods: "Weirdly barbaric melodies gave way to plain chant; plain chant succumbed before the *alabado;* the *alabado* passed into 'Oh, Susanna'; 'Oh, Susanna' vanished before 'Old Black Joe'; and 'Old Black Joe' has been displaced by 'I Can't Give You Anything but Love, Baby.' " During the decades immediately preceding and following the turn of the century, Southern California was in the Middle Nordic period, and its essentially unpretentious middle-class soul was well attuned to such national folk melodies as "Old Black Joe." For in spite of the eagerness to capitalize on a Spanish past, and in spite of the ballyhoo of the booms, the people were essentially homely in their tastes; the life was pleasantly suburban and rural; and the domestic interests were basically the same as those of the East and the Middle West, the regions which had supplied the bulk of the new settlers. No one felt really at home with the fiestas and the Indian pageants. Good old-fashioned Christmas and the Fourth of July remained the favorite celebrations of the year. No textbooks featuring the activities of Spanish explorers and mission padres were able to compete seriously with McGuffey's readers and Harper's geography, and the excitement of rodeos and fandangos was superficial compared with the emotions aroused by a torchlight political procession or a good old circus parade.

The daily life of the people was not as spectacular as the flamboyantly publicized attempts of men like Lummis and James to graft a Spanish past on an Anglo-Saxon stock, and no novels describing the loves and fears and pleasures of domestic life reached any such public as that which avidly read Helen Hunt Jackson's *Ramona*. But it is possible to catch more than a glimpse of ordinary life by sampling some of the less pretentious books dealing with the region. Two eminently fitted for the purpose are Sarah Bixby Smith's delightful book of reminiscences, *Adobe Days*, and Hiram A. Reid's *History of Pasadena*, perhaps the most detailed and certainly the most lively of the early town chronicles. Mrs. Smith's book gives a remarkably full picture of the activities of a girl in Los Angeles and on a ranch near Long Beach in the 'eighties and 'nineties, and later at a local college founded during the boom. Dr. Reid's history tells of the development of one of the most progressive "home" communities in the area.

Although Mrs. Sarah Bixby Smith, wife of the well-known Los Angeles critic and novelist, Paul Jordan Smith, did not publish *Adobe Days* until 1925, when she was in her mid-fifties, her memories of the years of her childhood and youth, the period covered in her book, were as fresh as if the events had taken place the day before she wrote. A member of the large Bixby-Hathaway-Flint family, which had migrated en masse soon after the gold rush (she could count more than 125 first cousins, most of them in California), Sarah Bixby was born in San Juan Bautista in 1871 and seven years later moved with her family to Los Angeles. After that she spent her winters in the Bixby house in Temple Street near Charity, just below Bunker Hill, and her summers and holidays at one or the other of the two big sheep ranches, Los Cerritos and Los Alamitos, which her uncles, Jotham and John Bixby, had purchased in the late 'sixties. These ranches with their old adobe houses had once been famous Spanish land grants and they covered most of what is now Long Beach.

The Los Angeles that Mrs. Smith remembered was a town of some ten thousand inhabitants who always thought and spoke of San Francisco as the one and only metropolis of the West but were proud that their own town had three daily newspapers and a public library. It was a time when pepper trees still outnumbered the eucalyptus trees, and when the adobe mud of the Los Angeles streets became almost impassible after a rain. "With its first wetting it became very slippery on top of a hard base, but as more water fell and it was kneaded by feet and wheels, it became first like well-chewed gum and then a black porridge." It was a day of bays and sorrels, of phaetons and surries and buckboards, a day when Sarah's aunt delighted in riding to town behind a fine span of Shetland ponies. It was also a time when Sarah and her fellow Angeleños were proud to see "H.M.S. Pinafore" performed in the barnlike Hazard's Pavilion within a year of its first production in London (she did not then know it was being pirated). Other important civic moments for her were the occasions when, as a child of nine, she saw President Rutherford B. Hayes at the time of his visit to Los Angeles in 1880, and when, a year later, she watched the somber catafalque symbolizing the town's mourning for the assassinated Garfield roll through the streets.

But before Sarah was to thrill to the opening of a *real* bookstore in the city—one which no longer carried literature as a side line to drugs and stationery—and before she was to lie awake nights watching the black silhouettes of the eucalyptus trees cast by that "strange and beautiful blue light" which radiated from street lamps in America's first electrically lighted city, she had passed many years filled with childhood games and festivities at home, at the ranches, and at the beach near Los Cerritos. First memories associated themselves with hopscotch and prisoner's base and the "Intry mintry cutry corn" that determined who was "it" for the twilight game of hide-and-seek; later, good times concerned themselves with cribbage and croquet and swinging in a knotted-twine hammock on the porch, or eating sandy, broiled mutton chops at picnics on a beach which was all theirs. For family celebrations all the Bixbys gathered at Los Cerritos or Los Alamitos; Christmas with tree and presents; the Fourth of July with its firecrackers, torpedoes, pinwheels, and rockets; Hallowe'en with its apple-bobbing and its child-carved jack-o'-lanterns. The large family had no difficulty having a good time. More self-sufficient than the present-day family, it even provided its own music: "I recall Sunday evenings at the Alamitos when Uncle John got out his fiddle, and men who had other instruments came into the parlor and we had a concert which included *Arkansas Traveler, Money Musk,* and *Turkey in the Straw."* But all was not fun, even for a child in such a family, for there were mustard plasters for coughs and the hot mustard foot bath which invariably followed the first signs of a runny nose. (The medicine closet contained a bottle of whisky for the male adults to use for bad colds and snake bite, although the Bixbys were strictly a temperance family.) And for parents who knew more about the possibilities of serious illness in a day of high infant mortality, there was always the dread of diphtheria, which carried away more than one of the Bixby youngsters and brought death to hundreds of Southern California children.

Because many of the Bixby tribe had been trained at New England colleges, Sarah was brought up in an atmosphere that was a far cry from the crude environment supposedly an adjunct of the raw West. Unadorned by such characteristics of the period as the "throw," the gilded milking stool with a ribbon bow on its leg, the landscape painted on a palm leaf, and the portiere made of eucalyptus seeds, the pleasant parlor was the center of family life during the evenings. The whole family clustered around the reading lamp or played instructive games: "dominoes, authors, crambo, or logomachy— sugar-coated ways of getting training respectively in addition, names of books and writers, verse-making and spelling." Before she was old enough to do much reading, little Sarah had modeled miniature lead books out of bits of pipe in the blacksmith shop at Los Cerritos. Then came the period when *Sanford and Merton* and *Helen's Babies* were read to her. Still later there was the period when the children sat out under the big eucalyptus tree in the backyard of a Sunday afternoon, assured that Grimm's *Fairy Tales* was a fit subject for Sunday reading because "a book fit to read any day is a book fit to read on Sunday."

Still later, Sarah discovered that the family had a very good library:

In the house were many books . . . The rigid Maine rule of semi-annual housecleaning held sway, and it was often my task to take out, beat, dust and replace all the volumes in the capacious bookcases. There were essays, histories, biographies: sets of Dickens, Thackeray, George Eliot, Hawthorne, Scott, besides scattered novels; Shakespeare was there and a few other dramatists, all the standard poets, Cervantes and Plutarch. These were not only dusted, but read to a great extent. *Harper's Magazine,* with its buff cover adorned with cupids, cornucopias, fruits and flowers, was a regular visitor, as was the *Century* later . . . Several missionary magazines gave knowledge of life in far parts of the world. *Littell's Living Age* came for several years, and, being bound, was at least handled semi-annually. The tri-weekly *New York Tribune* and *Harper's Weekly* (until it turned mug wump) brought news out of the east to supplement what two daily papers afforded. I think father knew where every raw material in the world was produced and where it was manufactured. He used to "poke fun" at me as an educated woman, after I returned from college, because I could not name, characterize and assign to his state every United States Senator.

If Sarah's family had not been able to send her to college, she could at least have taken advantage of the Chautauqua home-study course, as had her Aunt Adelaide, who, like many Southern California women of her time, was very proud of the diploma which showed that she had completed the course. But Sarah did go to college—to Wellesley. Before going East, however, she concluded the Western part of her education in an exciting manner. She was a member of the first senior preparatory class in the pioneer college of Pomona, housed in a former boom hotel at Claremont. Even though there was not a tree on the campus and the college resorted to burning real-estate stakes for fuel, and Professor Brackett had to dispense mathematics and physics over what had been the hotel bar, Sarah Bixby enjoyed every moment and always looked back on her Pomona experience as one of the pleasantest of her life.

Similar in many ways to the environment pictured in Sarah Bixby Smith's memoirs is that described by the historian of Pasadena, the industrious and loquacious Hiram A. Reid, A.M., M.D., sexagenarian prohibitionist and erstwhile Iowa poet who researched as vigorously as he cycled. It was his boast that "The first colony settlers of Pasadena were very largely of the class who keep schoolhouses and churches in the foreground wherever they go." His remark might properly be applied to most of the settlers who chose Southern California for their homes in the Middle Nordic period. The stress was on the humanities, and the Pasadenans concentrated on making their community as refined as the best of towns in the East.

Pasadena resulted from the enthusiasm of a group of Indiana residents to start life anew in California "where life is easy." To this end they organized the Indiana Colony. In the panic of 1873, however, soon after its formation, the Colony ran into difficulties and lost most of its original adherents even before they left home. But those who did come West were augmented, when they arrived, by other newcomers to

California who were willing to join with them in the purchase of Rancho San Pascual on which to start a settlement. In attempting to ascertain the source of these settlers, Dr. Reid consulted the first directory issued in Pasadena, which gave the names and former homes of all permanent residents of the place. Of about two hundred families (Dr. Reid did not bother to count Chinamen and bachelors) more than sixty were from Iowa. Other states followed in this order: From Illinois there were twenty-nine; Massachusetts, twenty-six; Indiana, eighteen; New York, seventeen; and Missouri, eleven. The rest had come from some twenty other states (including eight from California). Canada had furnished eleven of the families; England was represented by nine; and Germany, Scotland, and Sweden had contributed in a minor way.

Under the leadership of Dr. T. B. Elliott and D. M. Berry, both of Indiana, the town was formally established in 1875 and named Pasadena—an abbreviation of a combination of Chippewa words meaning "Crown of the Valley." The town grew very slowly in the 'seventies, having only 391 citizens in the census of 1880, but with the arrival of the Santa Fe Railway and the boom it gained momentum. Incorporated in 1886, it had reached nearly 5,000 population by 1890 (even with the postboom recession), 10,000 after the difficult 'nineties were over, and 30,000 by 1910. Today its population is estimated at more than 100,000.

The first prayer meeting was held in a private home in August, 1874, before anyone was sure that the Indiana Colony had become a reality. A month later the first Sunday-school class met, and early in the next year Presbyterian and Methodist church services were held. It was not long before most of the major Protestant churches, with the Presbyterians and Methodists in the lead, had organized congregations and were building churches.

The first newspaper did not appear until 1883, when the weekly *Chronicle* started. An ephemeral daily sputtered along for a while three years later, and in 1887, in the midst of the boom, the Pasadena *Star* began a noteworthy career. In the following year, the Pasadena *Standard*, dedicated to prohibition and edited by Dr. Reid himself, made its appearance; it carried his famous poem titled "No Saloon in the Valley," one stanza of which read:

> Rise, Pasadena! march and drill
>   To this your bugle's rally—
> A church or school on every hill,
>   and NO SALOON IN THE VALLEY.

The schools, both public and private, developed rapidly, and leading citizens early founded the short-lived Sierra Madre College. Later, they gave their support to the pioneering Throop University, which was one of the most progressive educational experiments in the country. This novel institution was founded by "Father" Amos G. Throop, a beloved philanthropist who had had few educational advantages for himself; it was dedicated to "a higher appreciation of the value and dignity of intelligent labor." Famous tourist hotels, such as the Sierra Madre Villa, the Raymond, and the Green, became little cultural centers in themselves, catering to tourists of discriminating tastes. As if to emphasize its temperance stand, surrounded as it was by vineyard country, the town made Orange Grove Avenue its principal residental street.

Occasionally, to be sure, one catches a glimpse of the influence of the seekers after a Spanish background or notes a bit of pretentiousness in the activities of the community. Berkshire Street was renamed "Elevado" because the Iowans did not want the newcomers to "think hog" the moment they saw the street name. A daily "Spanish conversazione upon subjects of interest to strangers," conducted by Señor Arturo Bandini, was announced as a feature of the Art Loan Exhibition of 1889, a commendable display assembled by Miss Anna Picher. And the sophisticated Valley Hunt Club, devoted to riding to the hounds (and later to the flowers after sponsoring the first Tournament of Roses in 1890), was organized by Charles Frederick Holder. But more fundamental than these activities, more truly representative of their real interests, were the burlesque literary society which met in the shanty schoolhouse in the winter of 1875–76, the Pasadena Library and Village Improvement Society founded by Abbot Kinney in 1882, a half-dozen Chautauqua literary and scientific circles, the Pasadena Academy of Science, the Shakespeare Club, and the Dickens Club. The last had regular clubrooms in the Green Hotel and was pleased to entertain Charles Dickens' son when he came to America. And in his history published in 1895, Dr. Reid lists forty-five local authors in a community of some seventy-five hundred people. Although he used the term "author" with great latitude, the emphasis he placed on literary activity spelled promise for the community.

∽∽∽∽

The pictures drawn by Sarah Bixby Smith and Dr. H. A. Reid were not unique to a particular family or a given area but were truly representative of all the people and all the region. The cultural aspirations of Southern Californians found expression not only in the reconstruction of the missions and the building of an El Camino Real but in the establishing of colleges, Chautauqua centers, libraries, discussion clubs, and many other institutions designed to make life more pleasant and significant for them. In higher education, for example, the local citizens—as elsewhere in America—set about implementing that aspect of the American dream expressed by Timothy Dwight when the nation was young:

> Where slept perennial night shall science rise
> And new-born Oxfords cheer the evening skies.

The colleges that they established had several traits in common: they emulated Eastern, usually New England, institutions like Amherst and Dartmouth, with one modification

—they were all coeducational; they were for the most part founded and supported by Protestant churches; and they came into existence through the peculiar nature of boom economics in the area.

Almost all the major Protestant denominations were represented by colleges started in Southern California within the last three decades of the century: the Southern Methodists, by Wilson College (1874) near Wilmington; the Presbyterians, first by Sierra Madre College (1874) in Pasadena and later by Occidental College (1887) just north of Los Angeles; the Christians by Southern Pacific College (1877) in Downey; the Methodists, by the University of Southern California (1879) in Los Angeles; the Congregationalists, by Pomona College (1877) in Claremont; the German Baptists, or Dunkers, by La Verne College (1891) in Lordsburg; the Quakers, by Whittier College (1891) in Whittier; and the Baptists, belatedly, by Redlands University (1907) in Redlands. Among the nonsectarian institutions there were Santa Barbara College, established in 1869 as the first coeducational college in Southern California, San Diego College of Letters (1887), and Throop University (1891), which later became the California Institute of Technology. Meanwhile, state-supported collegiate institutions began to appear, although they developed at a much slower pace than the private ones. Normal schools were founded—at Los Angeles in 1881 (this later became the University of California at Los Angeles), at San Diego in 1897, and at Santa Barbara in 1909. The California Polytechnic Institution at San Luis Obispo opened in 1901.

The rapid growth of private colleges in what was still a sparsely settled region cannot be attributed entirely to the quality of the settlers or to the high cultural ideals of the area; it came partly because of the economics of the land boom. As *The Golden Era* pointed out, colleges were "great immigration bureaus," and the newly platted community which could boast of a projected college had a distinct advantage over its neighbor. The usual procedure was for a group of citizens planning to subdivide a tract to offer a number of lots to persons interested in forming a college. The plans for the college would improve the value of the remaining lots in the subdivision, and the college would sell some of its lots to pay for its buildings and improvements. The Los Angeles *Times* described the process, in connection with the Occidental University, as follows:

About $50,000 worth of land was donated by different persons for the benefit of the school. From this an abundant reservation was made for the college campus, and the remaining lots were put upon the market for the benefit of the institution. By this means, it will be able to commence operations not only free from debt, but also well endowed . . .

Thus, O. W. Childs, J. G. Downey, and I. W. Hellman—a Protestant, a Catholic, and a Jew—interested in developing the area at the Agricultural Park (now Exposition Park) gave 308 lots to a group of Methodists, headed by Judge Robert M. Widney and Dr. Joseph P. Widney, to develop the University of Southern California. The presence of the college increased land values in the area so much that the new institution prospered mightily, especially during the height of the boom some years after it was founded. In fact, its financial condition at that time became such that it aspired to expand into a great "university system," with the cultural center in Los Angeles and component parts from the middle of the San Joaquin Valley to the Mexican border. These included the Chaffey College of Agriculture at Ontario, the Maclay College of Theology at San Fernando, the San Diego College of Fine Arts, the Freeman College of Applied Sciences at Inglewood, the Monrovia Young Ladies College, the seminaries at Tulare and Escondido, and the observatory planned for Mount Wilson. Only the first two of these materialized, for the collapse of the boom put a check on collegiate expansion in this area. Five years after these ambitious plans were made, President Bovard of the University of Southern California was dead of worry and overwork, the enrollment had dropped to twenty-five, and the resourceful Dr. Joseph P. Widney had taken over, with a policy of retrenchment which was to keep the institution alive, but only barely alive, during the lean years.

Similar difficulties gripped the other hopeful colleges. Occidental was down to six students, and Occidental and Throop lowered their sights by changing their designations from "university" to "college" and "institute." Pomona and La Verne (Lordsburg) managed to survive by moving into abandoned boom hotels; and the process was reversed when the San Diego College of Letters became Hotel Balboa. Wilson, Sierra Madre, Southern Pacific, and Santa Barbara were unable to weather the storm and passed out of existence. If "the college fever" had made these institutions possible, its breaking left them prostrate. Those that did survive, because of the support of their founding denominations and the hardihood of faculty and students, discovered as the century neared its end that Southern California could and would provide plenty of students to assure them fruitful lives.

For those of an older generation denied the advantages of secondary and collegiate training, the contagious spread of the Chautauqua movement was of great benefit. Together with other social and educational movements like the growing adult Sunday school, the cultural lecture series, and the correspondence course, this novel institution gave countless middle-class folk a chance to make up for the deficiencies of their youthful education.

The spread of Chautauqua assemblies after the success of the meetings started in the summer of 1874 by the parent body on the shores of Lake Chautauqua in New York state eventually reached California in the founding of local summer assemblies at Monterey (Pacific Grove) in 1879 and Long Beach in 1884. Long Beach was the logical spot in Southern California for such a development. In 1880, four thousand acres of Rancho Los Cerritos had been optioned to an Englishman named W. E. Willmore, who planned to establish a temperance colony, to be called the American Colony, which he thought would attract retired teachers to the area. Willmore City failed, however, to attract teachers or very many other settlers, and after some four years a group of promoters called the Long Beach Land and Water Company took over Willmore's option, renamed the settlement Long Beach, and established a horsecar connection with the Wilmington–Los Angeles railroad. Their plan to make the small community a center of church and Chautauqua camp meetings blossomed when the Methodist Church promptly arranged to hold its annual summer assemblies there and built the Methodist Tabernacle for that purpose. This was the building in which the Southern California Chautauqua assembly met for ten days each summer.

With its many classes in everything from entomology to music "sight reading," its organized choruses and recreation, and its elaborate series of lectures and musical events, the Chautauqua drew families from all over the region. They came by droves to combine a vacation with worship and education, to spend their time in "profitable leisure." And as they played on the beach and listened to music and lectures, their enthusiasm was unbounded. "The Acropolis crowning that famous height of ancient Athens, overlooking the waters of the Aegean Sea, was not regarded with greater pride by the native Athenian than is our pavilion or amphitheatre by our native Chautauquans, crowning as it does the bluffs of the mighty Pacific, overlooking the ruins and the dreamland of the Montezumas," wrote their historian. Here, during the day, youngsters took part in supervised games while parents discussed Shakespeare's *As You Like It,* the kindergarten movement, and recent archaeological discoveries in the Southwest. Here at eventide the devout Chautauquans chanted the hymn of their Alma Mater:

God bless the hearts that beat as one
Though continents apart;
We greet you, brothers, face to face,
We meet you heart to heart.

The Chautauqua influence was not confined to the annual assembly, however, for many a Southern California resident, like Sarah Bixby's Aunt Adelaide, earned his Chautauqua diploma by joining one of the Chautauqua literary and scientific circles which sprang up in the principal towns. The regular meetings of these groups were given over to discussion and study under the direction of the parent body at Lake Chautauqua, where lessons were planned, books were written, and diplomas were issued to indicate satisfactory completion of the four years of study.

Meanwhile the public library system expanded rapidly, with particularly good collections at Santa Barbara, San Diego, Pasadena, and Los Angeles. That the libraries of Southern California were being used extensively was indicated by figures released in 1893 which showed that the average number of library books annually circulated per citizen was 0.90 in Chicago, 1.61 in Boston, and 5.30 in Los Angeles. Doubtless the Los Angeles record was partly the result of borrowings by tourists, but the figure was nevertheless one to be proud of.

Probably the most notable cultural ferment in the area in the Middle Nordic period was provided, however, by the many phases of what is known by that seriously broad term, the feminist movement. This movement flourished in Southern California, for many of the women, particularly those who came with moneyed families from back East, enjoyed a good deal of leisure. Moreover, the comparative fluidity of social patterns in the new West frequently made it easier for reform movements sponsored by women of this period to germinate and develop. As Arthur M. Schlesinger pointed out in *The Rise of the City,* woman suffrage before the turn of the century was looked upon as "an aberration of the wild

and woolly West." Similarly, the Froebel kindergarten movement was pioneered on the Pacific Coast, under the leadership of Caroline S. Severance and Emma J. C. Marwedel;
equality of opportunity for women in the newly established
colleges was recognized from the first as an axiom; and the
temperance movement, predominantly a feminine social phenomenon, soon found Southern California a worthy stronghold. Accordingly, although there was an early growth of male
fraternal, benevolent, and scientific clubs and societies in the
area, with the establishing of such organizations as the Sunset Club, an excellent male discussion group founded by C.
D. Willard in Los Angeles, the majority of cultural and social
clubs formed in Southern California were created by women.
One of their enthusiastic members wrote: "We have art clubs,
book clubs, dramatic clubs, pottery clubs. We have sewing
circles, philanthropic associations, scientific, literary, religious, athletic, musical, and decorative art societies."

The earliest of these organizations was the Woman's Club
of Los Angeles, founded by Caroline Seymour Severance,
"the mother of clubs," in 1878, just ten years after she had
helped found the first woman's club in America, the New
England Woman's Club of Boston. The time was not yet
ripe, however, for the flourishing of such societies in Southern California, and the venture did not survive. Boom days
brought new life, however; women in Pasadena formed the
Shakespeare Club, and women in Los Angeles started the
Ruskin Club with a very good collection of engravings and
etchings as a nucleus. In 1891, Mrs. Severance, who was once
called "the ethical magnet of Southern California," tried
again and helped found the Friday Morning Club of Los
Angeles. A year later, seven hundred women of the southern
counties banded together to create the Woman's Parliament
of Southern California, a "loose federation of church, club,
fraternal and temperance societies" which met quarterly at
different communities in the area, to get acquainted, promote
worthy projects, and listen to papers on such subjects as

"Plato's Republic" and "The Scarlet Letter for Both." Before long the Women's Congress of the Pacific Coast was meeting in Southern California to consider "the Home from every angle, educationally, aesthetically, economically, politically, sociologically, ethically and from the sanitary point of view." The 'nineties saw the organization of a number of additional clubs in Los Angeles, Pasadena, Redlands, Riverside, San Diego, Santa Barbara, and elsewhere. One of the most successful of these was the Ebell Society of Los Angeles, prompted by the enthusiasm of a young German idealist, Dr. Adrian Ebell, for aiding women to educate themselves.

The California woman-suffrage campaign of 1896, which brought national leaders such as Susan B. Anthony and Carrie Chapman Catt to the Coast, failed in its primary objective of gaining the suffrage for the women of the state; but undoubtedly by eliciting a great deal of coöperative effort it furthered the cause of feminism in the area. In 1900 a California Federation of Women's Clubs was formed; its charter meeting was held in Los Angeles and its first president was Mrs. Robert J. Burdette of that city. And two years later the national General Federation of Women's Clubs chose Los Angeles as the meeting place for its sixth biennial convention, the first to be held in the Far West. By that time Southern California had its full share of flourishing women's organizations, which numbered, among others, the Contemporary Club of Redlands, the Wednesday Morning Club and the Shakespeare Club of San Diego, the Santa Monica Literary Club, the Shakespeare Club of Hueneme, and the Silk Culture Club of Los Angeles.

Although much of the activity in these clubs was doubtless of little importance, there is no question that they helped to foster intellectual interests and especially to encourage creative effort among the more able women. The hearty local support of the Pacific Coast Women's Press Association, one of the most active of the clubs, was but one sign of the literary ferment stirring among the Southern California women. In fact, literary activity during the Middle Nordic period was preponderantly a feminine occupation.

∽∽∽∽

When, under the auspices of the World's Fair Commission of California, the indefatigable Ella Sterling Cummins prepared her *Story of the Files* so that the visitors to the Columbian Exposition at Chicago in 1893 would have an idea of what literature had been written in California, she included a short section on women writers of Southern California, pointing out that the southern part of the state was now producing its own "feminine plants of literature" and implying that the crop would increase as time went on. The region that had a woman, Helen Hunt Jackson, as its principal publicist was indeed to prove a fairly fertile ground for such plants, which were numerous even if not always of the highest quality.

As might be expected, many of the women writers of the area were amateurish versifiers, clubwomen, journalists, and housewives who, in a day when Lummis on *The Land of Sunshine* was ridiculing the innovations of poets like Stephen Crane and William Butler Yeats, were quite naturally wedded to the tried and true poetic techniques. Representative of the heavy rhetoric which often resulted were the poems of Eliza A. Otis, who was described by Mrs. Cummins as "one of the most prolific writers of the age." The wife of the editor of the Los Angeles *Times,* she was as reactionary in her ideas and meters as her husband was in his labor policies; she belonged to the "O crags, O hoary old mounts" school of poetry, described Spanish Californian architecture in stilted diction:

> What though the homes of sun-dried bricks were all
> Their hands did raise to dot th' emerald sward?

and ended her poem on the martyred Garfield with the line: "Friend! Soldier! Statesman! Chief! Hail—and farewell!"

Fortunately, not all of the versifiers of the region were so

ponderous. In addition to writers earlier mentioned, such as
Rose H. Thorpe, Madge Morris, and Dorothea Lummis, there
were the Santa Barbara poets, Rebecca Josephine Walcott
("Cordelia Havens"), who published her *World of Song* in
1878, when the village had but a handful of inhabitants, and
Mrs. Mary Camilla Hall-Wood ("Camilla K. von K."), editor
of the Santa Barbara *Independent,* who broke the rules by
being restless, cynical, and thoroughly pessimistic about
Southern California and life in general in her *Sea-Leaves.*
Another Southern California poet who showed individuality
of thought and delicacy of expression was Olive Percival,
whose *Leaf-Shadows and Rose-Drift* reflects the Oriental influence on American poetry when it was still a novelty; her
little book of poems opens with a quatrain from T'ao Ch'ien
and closes with lines from Chen Hao-tzu. Miss Percival also
left a diary (unpublished) which gives a vivid picture of a
young girl's struggles to make a living and at the same time
find artistic expression in Los Angeles at the turn of the century.

Further spirit of the artist in touch with some of the real-
ities of the modern world can be found in the early verse of
Julia Boynton Green, a Wellesley graduate living in Redlands, who was one of the mainstays of *The Land of Sunshine.* An even more prolific contributor, however, was Nora
May French, who had moved from Aurora, New York, to Los
Angeles when she was six and had grown up in Southern
California, had attended the Normal School and Occidental
College, and had determined that a writing career was what
she wanted most in the world. Search for congenial writing
companions eventually took her to Carmel, where she became one of that little group of writers—George Sterling,
Jack London, Jimmy Hopper, and their satellites—who were
living a Bohemian life by the sandy beach. But there, in
George Sterling's cabin, the twenty-six-year-old idealist com-
mitted suicide on November 14, 1907. Illness, poverty, and
disappointment in love were given as reasons for her death,

the first of a series of suicides which were to play havoc with the writing colony. The qualities of fragility and simplicity and the somewhat mournful mood of Nora May French's poems are glimpsed in a stanza from her "Rain":

> The rain was grey before it fell,
>   And through a world where light had died
> There ran a mournful little wind
>   That shook the trees and cried.

There were also, in Southern California, a good many women writing fiction dealing with the local scene, short stories for *The Land of Sunshine,* the San Francisco *Argonaut,* and other journals, and occasionally a novel. Of considerable reputation in her day but long since forgotten are the stories of Mexican life written by Yda Addis, a Kansas girl who had been brought to Los Angeles as a child and had become an accomplished linguist. Because her realistic sketches were never collected into book form she is remembered principally for her history of Santa Barbara County, published in 1891, the year after she married C. A. Storke, a prominent college teacher, editor, and rancher of Santa Barbara. Similarly evanescent were the tales about Los Angeles Orientals written for *The Land of Sunshine* by Sui Sin Far, a half-breed Chinese girl. Born in England of an English father and a Chinese mother, a "lady of rank and beauty," Sui Sin Far, or Edith Eaton (her Occidental name), worked as a sort of peripatetic stenographer in many of the Coast cities. Another picture of the Orientals in Southern California is found in Mary Stewart Daggett's *The Yellow Angel,* written in the hope of combating the prejudice against the Chinese through the loving characterization of a servant named Sue Chang. Mrs. Daggett, who came to Pasadena in 1888, wrote two other novels dealing with the region: *Mariposilla* told of a family of tourists who repaid the kindness of some Spanish Californians by mistreating them and ended with the suicide of a Mexican girl after she was abandoned by a wealthy young American; and *The Higher Court* portrayed the life of a Catholic priest in Protestant Pasadena.

The principal successors to Helen Hunt Jackson in the treatment of Indian and Spanish Californian themes were Constance Goddard Du Bois and Marah Ellis Ryan. Miss Du Bois, who had become an active member of the Woman's National Indian Association in Waterbury, Connecticut, came to California determined to carry on the crusade started by *Ramona*. In turn she joined the contributing staff of *The Land of Sunshine;* published serially in that journal the novels, "A Soul in Bronze" and "The Raven of Capistrano," the latter never issued in book form; familiarized herself with the religion and mythology of the Potrero and La Jolla Indians; and came to be a competent amateur anthropologist, working under the sponsorship of the American Museum of Natural History and the University of California, where A. L. Kroeber directed her work. Unfortunately, Miss Du Bois * paid little attention to the racial history and cultural traits of the Indians she portrayed in *A Soul in Bronze* (1898). Instead, she told the incredible story of Antonio Lachusa, a mission Indian who had been adopted by a wealthy, sentimental woman and given a fine education in Europe and the Orient. When he returned to his native village, filled with a knowledge of astronomy, higher mathematics, and the poetry of Keats, he dedicated his efforts not to the improvement of the state of his fellow Indians but to wooing a foolish white girl who was "not prepared for the startling adventures of Western life." Eventually, Lachusa was sent to San Quentin for a murder he did not commit and spent the rest of his life as a model prisoner, translating the Septuagint from Greek into English as his contribution to culture.

Mrs. Marah Ellis Ryan's *For the Soul of Rafael* (1906) capitalized more on the Spanish Californian tradition than on the hard fate of the Indians. The book was handsomely

---

* Constance Du Bois should not be confused with Cora Du Bois, another University of California anthropologist.

printed, with fancy borders, photographs of the characters in *rebozo* or *sarape* posing before mission walls, and inserts of the words and music of a number of the Spanish and Mexican folk songs which Charles Lummis had collected. Mrs. Ryan, a Pennsylvania romancer who had been an actress for a while, when she came out to Southern California prepared herself for her task in a truly wholehearted manner by renting a room in Mission San Juan Capistrano and saturating herself in the atmosphere. The resulting novel, dealing with melodramatic intrigue among the dispossessed Californians in the period between the conquest and the Civil War, has as its principal characters a proud Castilian matriarch who acts as arbitrarily as Señora Moreno of *Ramona,* her weak son who indulges in clandestine affairs described with mildly titillating eroticism by the author, and a heroine who has in her veins Aztec blood that leads her to murder and frequent rides beneath the stars. The novel shows how far out of hand the Spanish Californian theme had got by the turn of the century.

After exposure to Mrs. Ryan's hothouse Spaniards it is a pleasure to feel the fresh out-of-doors in Kate Douglas Wiggin's charming little novel about youthful hikes and camping trips in the California hills, *A Summer in a Cañon* (1889). In this juvenile and in her memoirs, *My Garden of Memory,* the author of *Rebecca of Sunnybrook Farm* told about the good times she had while growing up at Santa Barbara, where not even the illness and death of her stepfather and the consequent family poverty that sent her into kindergarten teaching took all the joy out of life. "How intense everything is in Southern California!" she wrote. "The fruit so immense, the cañons so deep, the trees so big, the hills so high, the rain so wet, and the drought so dry."

The feeling of the land is present also in *Hilda Strafford* (1897), an interesting novel by an English writer and feminist, Beatrice Harraden, who spent some time in the country back of San Diego attempting to recover her health. (She was the coauthor, with Dr. William A. Edwards, of a down-to-earth book titled *Two Health Seekers in Southern California*.) Her novel dealt with the failure of a homesick English bride to master the "drudgery and desolation" of life on an isolated Southern California lemon ranch. Whereas the heroine fails to adjust herself to the unfamiliar country, her friend—whom she hopes in vain will become her lover—learns by hard experience to love the region.

In addition to the poets and novelists there was of course no dearth of women writers willing and frequently able to write articles and books on everything from the missions to the rising oil and aviation businesses. For instance, Mrs. A. S. C. Forbes (Harrie Rebecca Piper Forbes), a California immigrant from Pennsylvania by way of Kansas, wrote articles and books on the mission and rancho past, erected plaques, raised flags, and variously decorated historic spots. It was she who evolved the ubiquitous mission bells, used to mark the horse-and-buggy El Camino Real.

In the meantime, local residents interested in Indian baskets turned to the articles by Jeanne C. Carr (Mrs. Ezra Carr) of Pasadena or went to buy the baskets from Eve Lummis at El Alisal. Bird enthusiasts read the charming *A-Birding on a Bronco* (1896) written, after two summers near San Diego, by an Eastern ornithologist named Florence A. Merriam, or followed the articles and books of Mrs. Elizabeth Grinnell, who had spent ten years with her physician husband among the Plains Indians before she brought her son, Joseph Grinnell, to Pasadena to be educated at Throop Institute. They both served on the board of contributors of *The Land of Sunshine* and became well-known authorities on western bird and animal life.

And there was the dean of local writers, Jessie Benton Frémont, who spent the last fifteen years of her very active life in Los Angeles, where she wrote her *Far West Sketches* (1890), contributed occasionally to *The Land of Sunshine*, and encouraged the younger writers who flocked to her. The women of that city paid fitting tribute to this remarkable woman when they presented to her a home, called "The Retreat." As the coauthor of Frémont's reports and as an idol of the nation, this daughter of Senator Thomas Hart Benton had exerted as much influence on expanding America as any woman of her day.

~~~~

With the exception of Mary Austin, the three most talented feminine contributors to *The Land of Sunshine* were Charlotte Perkins, Grace Ellery Channing, and Margaret Collier Graham. Charlotte Perkins was the most radical of the three, gaining in time a nation-wide reputation as an ardent feminist and reformer. A great-granddaughter of Lyman Beecher, and a grandniece of Henry Ward Beecher and Harriet Beecher Stowe, with the energy of the Beecher blood she approached the many issues which she embraced. As she put it when she began her long and notable lecture career, "I had plenty to say and the Beecher faculty for saying it." In her childhood, in Connecticut, this ancestry had been an important element, when her restless, brilliant father, Frederick Beecher Perkins, had deserted his family and thus brought poverty and debt as environmental factors to influence a sensitive child. It came to haunt her again after her marriage in 1884, in Rhode Island, to a young painter, Charles Walter Stetson. The marriage at first appeared to be very happy, but soon Charlotte began to suffer almost unbearable depression, and the birth a year later of a child, whom she dearly loved, merely intensified it. The best nerve specialist in the country, Dr. S. Weir Mitchell, promptly diagnosed her as a Beecher and had little patience for her troubles: "He had a prejudice against the Beechers. 'I've had two women of your blood here already,' he told me scornfully." Charlotte tried her best to follow his advice and save her marriage by devoting herself to her husband and child and avoiding books and ideas, but her mad desire to crawl away and die simply grew worse.

Thus caught in a morass of emotions which she could not at all understand, she decided that the best thing to do was to make a trip to Pasadena to see her closest Providence friends, the Channings. Dr. William F. Channing, the son of the eminent Unitarian leader, William Ellery Channing, had taken his daughter west in 1885 for her health and had found Southern California an attractive place to settle. There Grace Ellery Channing enthusiastically greeted her sick friend. Life in Pasadena restored Charlotte Perkins' health, and in time, confident that she could now make a success of her marriage, she returned to her anxious husband and child. But she very soon found that she was still unable to be a satisfactory wife and mother and came so near to collapse that she and Stetson agreed that an amicable separation was the only solution. Accordingly, Charlotte returned to Pasadena, took a little cottage near the Channings, and threw herself into feverish activity. She gave art lessons and designed gift cards. She and Grace spent night after night collaborating on plays, which were never produced. She accepted the editorship of a literary magazine, which Charles Frederick Holder was promoting, and, before the venture collapsed, read a number of manuscripts submitted for publication. She acted humorous parts in local amateur dramatic productions, and she decorated the auditorium of the new Pasadena opera house. And above all, she wrote—poems, articles, sketches.

In time much of her writing was accepted, and not infrequently a small check came with the acceptance. Then a genuine thrill came when, after the publication of her satirical poem "Similar Cases" in the *Nationalist* of April, 1890, she received a letter from William Dean Howells stating "We have had nothing since the Biglow Papers half so good for a good cause." He had liked her trenchant attack on reactionaries who opposed all progress on the grounds that one cannot alter human nature. He had been pleased with the little Eohippus who scandalized his Eocene neighbors with his avowed intention of becoming a horse, and the Anthropoidal Ape who enraged his companions by announcing he was going to become a man. The poem was, in fact, widely read and came to be much quoted. Then she added strength to her growing reputation by writing a magazine sketch which appeared in 1892 under the title, "The Yellow Wallpaper," in which she described very movingly how a woman went mad obeying the kind of advice she had been given by Dr. S. Weir Mitchell. One of the most vivid early examples of psychological portrayal of a mind bordering on the edge of insanity, it left a vivid impression on Charlotte Perkins' contemporaries.

Her growing literary reputation only in part compensated for the emotional turmoil and hostile criticism attendant upon her domestic misfortunes. Finding that genuine incompatibility was not a legal ground for divorce, she suffered the humiliation of obtaining a divorce by subterfuge. Then, when Stetson married Grace Channing with her full approval, she found the public bitterly opposed to her continued friendships with her former husband and girlhood companion. And when she arranged to have her child cared for by its father and stepmother, she was violently labeled "an unnatural mother." The result was that she threw herself with increased vigor into championing a new position for women. Becoming a wanderer, she lectured throughout the country on woman's rights. And she wrote *Women and Economics,* a book which, in clearly stating the case for the psychological and economic independence of women, is a milestone in the progress of feminism comparable to Mary Wollstonecraft's *A Vindication of the Rights of Women.*

Frequently Charlotte returned to Southern California, and for years she was a fairly regular contributor of poems and articles to *The Land of Sunshine,* which carried her name in its masthead as one of its imposing list of stockholders and contributors. Even after leaving the West permanently, on her marriage in Chicago to her cousin, George Houghton Gilman, she continued to contribute to the Western jour-

nal for some time. Many of her Southern California poems
are included in her *In This Our World,* published in 1893.

In contrast to the perfervid prose and the pert, sometimes
biting, poetry of Charlotte Perkins, of the lithe figure, burning black eyes, and blunt language, was the carefully polished
work of the fragile, subdued, conservative Grace Ellery Channing (Stetson). Grace had early attempted a novel about
Southern California, but it had come to nothing. Then, when
The Land of Sunshine was founded she began writing for it
and in so doing found the field of her particular talents: short
stories, poems, and articles. So close became her association
with the young journal that in 1898 her appointment as assistant editor was announced. Soon afterward she settled in Italy
with her painter husband, but she continued sending her writing home—stories and articles on life in Rome as well as
material dealing with California. Her *The Sister of a Saint,
and Other Stories* (1895) is praiseworthy for its careful work-
manship and its vignettes of life in Southern California and
in Italy. Less commendable is her book of poems, *Sea Drift*
(1899), containing the best of her verses, most of which dealt
with the nature she had learned to love in Southern California. Typical is the one titled "California of the South," which
ended with the stanza:

> This is the land of the poet's desire;
> This is the Beautiful's indwelling place;
> Land of the new dawn and late sunset's fire,
> Lo, she laughs like a child in the grim East's face!
> And a thousand years shall be born and expire
> Ere her youth shall have dimmed its immortal grace.

There was nothing particularly spectacular or unusual
about the life of Margaret Collier Graham; in its major features it seems almost a prototype of the lives of many of the
Southern California women of her day. Born in Iowa in 1850,
she was educated in the public schools at Keokuk, and at Mon-
mouth College in Illinois, from which she was graduated in

1869. Four years later she married Donald M. Graham, and in 1876 they came west for his health, settling first in Anaheim and later in Pasadena. In search of an outdoor occupation, her husband grew strawberries and, having the horses and vehicles for the job, took the first contract for carrying the mail from Los Angeles to Pasadena.

In the boom years the Grahams had their experience with real-estate ventures, for they and Mrs. Graham's brother, William Collier, and F. H. Heald bought and subdivided the Laguna Ranch, which included a lake and medicinal hot springs which ran into it. Somehow reminded of Hamlet's remark to Horatio, "But what is your affair in Elsinore? We'll teach you to drink deep ere you depart," Mrs. Graham suggested Elsinore as the name for both the lake and the settlement at the hot springs. (There is no truth in the local legend that the name arose from the answer a Mexican gave when asked how the water tasted: "Like 'ell, señor.") She may also be responsible for naming Wildomar, at the southern end of the lake, by combining the first syllables of the given names of the three family partners: *Wil*liam Collier, *Do*nald Graham, and *Mar*garet Graham.

Probably the family enjoyed at least moderate prosperity during this period, and it may have been of these days that Mrs. Graham wrote, "I haved lived in California since 1876 and have in consequence no desire to go to heaven." But the small good fortune seems to have been shortlived, for Mrs. Graham's championing of the right of women to enter all professions and her insistence that *every* woman should be prepared to support herself in an emergency suggest that she had none too easy a time after the death of her husband in 1893. (Doubtless she would have subscribed to Charlotte Perkins' idea that an agency be established in Southern California to provide work for the widows of tubercular husbands.) It was at this time that she took to the lecture platform, where she boldly and wittily defended her ideas, daring even to ask: "Is it not possible that she [the contemporary woman] would do less harm in the labor market than in domestic life?" And for two years she conducted a department in *The Land of Sunshine* called "The Angle of Reflection," in which she discussed in polished aphorisms such universal topics as the value of will power, the pursuit of happiness, and the necessity of good taste. Here she wrote such sentences as: "The man who is perpetually looking for his rights is very likely to be neglectful of his duties"; "Discontent is the offspring of irresponsibility"; and "Sweetness, serenity, dignity, self-sacrifice—all the qualities that go to the making of the highest motherhood and the noblest fatherhood—are no protection against poverty." Her main interest, however, lay in writing her carefully polished short stories. These appeared in Eastern magazines such as *Harper's* and the *Atlantic Monthly* and were then published in Boston by Houghton Mifflin under the titles, *Stories of the Foot-hills* (1895) and *The Wizard's Daughter, and Other Stories* (1905). She herself was "as interesting as her stories," according to President David Starr Jordan of Stanford. After years of pain from a chronic illness, she died in 1910. Some of her essays and speeches were posthumously issued in a book called *Do They Really Respect Us?* in which she discussed the "universal contempt" held by men for intellectual women.

Clear evidence of her character, taste, and skill are her little handful of stories by which she sought "to reveal the humanity that lies beneath the unpromising exteriors, to open . . . the recesses of human motives, to trace the threads of human influences." In these effective tales, laid for the most part in the rural districts near Anaheim and Elsinore, she conscientiously followed her models, William Dean Howells and Sarah Orne Jewett, in seeking for a quiet realism. Like Sarah Orne Jewett, she chose her characters from the types she felt were most characteristic of the local scene. She portrayed tubercular invalids pathetically eager for a bit of sunshine, ministers whose fundamentalism seemed strangely out of place in the pagan hill country, farmers who tenaciously attempted to gain a livelihood in a land they did not understand. Her drama usually lay in a turn of character. In "Idy" a prohibitionist, a poverty-stricken invalid, roots up his vineyard after discovering that he has been deceived into buying wine grapes for raisin grapes. In "Alex Randall's Conversion" a husband converted to Methodism breaks his wife's heart when his new religious zeal causes him to confess an old scandal. In "Lib" a girl with an illegitimate child proudly refuses to marry the scoundrel who had fathered it. The excellence of these stories is partly the result of Mrs. Graham's carefully worded, aphoristic style. She captures the feeling of the country in such phrases as "tar and honey and spice from the sage and the eucalyptus, with now and then a warmer puff of some new wild fragrance from far up the mountain-side" and "There was a sunshiny dullness about the place, like the smiles of a vapid woman." The reader does not soon forget her description of an improvident homesteader's farm:

The redwood shanty; a dozen orange-trees, rapidly diminishing in size and number by reason of neglect and gophers; a clump of slender, smoky eucalypti; a patch of perennial tomato-vines; and a few acres of what Barney Wilson called "veteran barley"—it had been sown once, and had "volunteered" ever since—constituted these additions to the value of the land, if not to the landscape, upon which Parker based his homestead rights.

Here is the substance of rural Southern California of the 'nineties, done with loving skill. Margaret Collier Graham's fiction deserves a much wider audience than it has received.

VII

The Desert Grows Friendly

UNTIL THE TURN of the century, the desert had been a most formidable barrier for the Southern Californians. It lay on three sides of them: from the dusty reaches of the southern San Joaquin Valley it extended past the desiccating sands of the fearful Mojave and Colorado basins to the barren reaches of Baja California across which Junípero Serra and his companions had struggled 1769. These were the deserts which had been so cruel to Pattie and Frémont and Manly and the Jayhawkers, which had been crossed by the tired men of the Mormon Battalion and Kearny's Army of the West, which in fact had kept California isolated for two centuries of busy colonization in other parts of the Western Hemisphere.

The struggle to cross the deserts, to mine in them, and to irrigate them had been a difficult one, filled with magnificent gestures and powerful dramas. The very place names of the region are a record of it. The heat was remembered in the Spanish Caliente and the Greek Thermal. The aridity was symbolized in the desert-plant names given to communities and railroad sidings: Mesquite, Ocotillo, and Cactus; and in place names emphasizing the salty and bitter: Saline, Salada, Saltus, Salton, Amargosa, and Badwater. Watered spots took natural oases names—Palm Springs, Twenty-nine Palms, and Indian Wells. Ironic wags labeled one-tank railroad stops Siberia and Klondike, and settlers who hoped that there was romance in the desert used the names Arabia, Mecca, and Bagdad. The last was applied to a mining town in San Bernardino County which has been called by climatologists the most arid spot in the United States, having an average annual mean rainfall of 2.3 inches. More appropriate is the name of the place having the highest mean temperature of any recorded spot in the nation—Furnace Creek in Death Valley. Legend has it that the near-by Funeral Mountains were named for four dead Jayhawkers. Perhaps most imaginative of all was the naming of a Mojave volcanic crater Pisgah after the mountain of that name northeast of the Dead Sea from which Moses gained his glimpse of the Promised Land.

To those who succeeded in crossing the Mojave or the Colorado deserts, the "promised land" was the Los Angeles plain below the Sierra Madre or one of the coastal valleys which embouched on the Pacific from Point Conception to the Mexican border. Yet these were not natural paradises. It seems a paradox to use the word "desert" for an area in which today live more than four million people, but by the climatologist and geographer the greater part of even the more favored Southern California terrain is classified as desert, and the rest, except for the high mountain places, is called semiarid. Near the coast, as a traveler moves north he passes through localities where the mean annual rainfall rises above the ten-inch line, below which the term "desert" is correctly used. But he finds only fifteen inches at Los Angeles, eighteen at Santa Barbara, and must go to the higher parts of the mountains near Santa Ana or Sierra Madre before he finds moisture enough to indicate that he no longer is in a semiarid land. Rugged mountains, the concentration of rain in winter, rapid erosion on slopes not adequately protected by vegetation or resistant layers of soil, the absence of alluvial valleys, unstable river courses on the structural plains below, and summer des-

iccation all help to give the area the problems of arid countries. It is a land of the sun and a land of flash floods. It is a
land in which Mark Twain's quip about the California river
—he said that he fell in and "came out all dusty"—is apt for
most of the year. It is a land in which there was no irrigation
before the coming of the white man; and the acorns, which
kept the Indians alive, were of no use to the colonists from
other lands. When the Spanish explored and settled Southern
California, they brought their own food, and, even in so
favored a region as that bordering San Diego Bay, they had
difficulty getting enough wood and drinking water to make
even a small community survive.

Careful use of subsurface waters, maximum utilization of
the winter runoff, and the bringing in of water from spots as
far away as the other side of the Sierra (from Owen's Valley)
and the Colorado River eventually created a garden of much
of the region, for the arid land under irrigation offered many
advantages over normally watered areas. But the early settlers
never forgot that the terrain was naturally a dry one. Their
view has been ably recorded by Mrs. Sarah Bixby Smith who,
in her *Adobe Days,* described the outlook in what is now
Long Beach.

The southern houses were each placed on the brow of a mesa,
with a view across a characteristic California river which might
be a dangerous torrent or a strip of dry sand, according to the
season of the year. The eyes could follow across flat lands, treeless
except for a few low-growing willows, to far blue mysterious
mountains. It was a very empty land, empty of people and towns,
of trees and cultivated fields.

And when she enrolled in the new Pomona College at Claremont, she noticed that the desert seemed impervious to the
hesitant settlement:

Such was Claremont in 1889; no streets, no walks, just a few
spots reclaimed from the desert, connected by trails or sandy roads;
all the rest sage, cactus, stones, an occasional oak or sycamore . . .

Rabbits scuttled between the bushes, lizards and horned toads enjoyed the climate, rattlesnakes found a peaceful home, and at night coyotes ranged and sang.

It is for these reasons, the presence of the surrounding desert and the memories of a dry time in a dry land, that the literature of Southern California has been much concerned with the desert. The early attitude toward the desert, when it lay as a deathtrap for men approaching the inland island of Southern California and, after they arrived, continued like an underlying motif in a symphony of a tenuously held land, was one which emphasized its treachery, its ugliness, and its formidable terrors. The feeling of the settlers about this wasteland was essentially that voiced by Benjamin F. Taylor in his *Between the Gates:*

Here are the cruel, glittering plains, flinty to the feet, fiery to the eye, "and not a drop to drink" in thousands of square miles of desolation. No ruins here but the wrecks and ruins of all the Christian seasons of the year, shut out from the blessed promises of seed-time and harvest, and sending back fierce answer to the noon. It is the crumbling skeleton of Nature, hopeless of burial and bleaching in the sun.

Even after the completion of the railroad, travelers found the desert stark, drab, and painful. The discomforts of travel by crude Pullman and even cruder emigrant car possibly helped to delay the discovery that the desert had its attractions. Thus, Charlotte Perkins, who in her "A Nevada Desert" described the dreary landscape as she saw it from her railroad coach in the early 1890's, wrote of "an aching, blinding, barren, endless plain." It was "corpse-colored with white mounds of alkali,"

> Hairy with sage-brush, slimy after rain,
> Burnt with the sky's hot scorn, and still
>   again
> Sullenly burning back against the sky.

When she submitted the poem to Thomas Bailey Aldrich, editor of the *Atlantic Monthly,* he rejected it because it did not contain a spot of color.

The lack of color and the horror were expressed by many another local poet. This, for instance, was the mood of Madge Morris, wife of the editor of *The Golden Era* (in San Diego) when she wrote her "To the Colorado Desert," in which she turgidly, rhetorically, and unequivocally expressed the attitude of the early settler toward the desert at his threshold. This was the treatment of the desert that suited the declamation classes of the local schools.

> Thou brown, bare-breasted, voiceless mystery,
> Hot sphinx of nature, cactus-crowned, what hast thou done?
> Unclothed and mute as when the groans of chaos turned
> Thy naked burning bosom to the sun.
> The mountain silences have speech, the rivers sing,
> Thou answerest never unto anything.
> Pink-throated lizards pant in thy slim shade;
> The horned toad runs rustling in the heat;
> The shadowy gray coyote, born afraid,
> Steals to some brackish spring and laps, and prowls
> Away; and howls, and howls, and howls, and howls,
> Until the solitude is shaken with an added loneliness.
> Thy sharp mescal shoots up a giant stalk,
> Its century of yearning, to the sunburnt skies,
> And drips rare honey from the lips
> Of yellow waxen flowers, and dies.
> Some lengthwise sun-dried shapes with feet and hands
> And thirsty mouths pressed on the sweltering sands,
> Mark here and there a gruesome graveless spot
> Where some one drank thy scorching hotness, and is not.
> God must have made thee in His anger, and forgot.

God was forgiven for making the desert, before another generation had moved across its forbidding surface; in fact, within a few years it was to go through a change in esteem remarkable and bizarre. A day was to come when the very ani-

mals of the desert were to be cherished for their beauty, its
flowers were to attract thousands of eager week-end nature
lovers, and its aridity was to be a source of aesthetic inspiration and moral strengthening.

The first major breach in the traditional attitude toward
the desert was, in fact, made by an art professor in 1901. The
attack of the aesthetician was followed two years later by the
assault by a moralist, who struck with the combined ammuni-
tions of transcendentalism and primitivism. John C. Van Dyke,
in *The Desert,* led the way, and Mary Austin, in *The Land of
Little Rain,* completed the rout. The cleanup and war profit-
eering were left for the many followers who, in the 1900's and
the succeeding decade, continued in the same direction and, in
passing, invented most of the phrases—now clichés—that were
to advertise the desert far and wide. A. J. Burdick's *The Mystic
Mid-Region* (1904), George Wharton James's *The Wonders of
the Colorado Desert* (1906), and J. Smeaton Chase's *California
Desert Trails* (1919) expanded the discursive approach, and
such writers as Gwendolen Overton, Idah Meacham Strobridge, Stewart Edward White, and Zane Grey modified, expanded, or exaggerated the fictional aspects.

◇◇◇◇

"The desert had gone a-begging for a word of praise these
many years," wrote John C. Van Dyke in *The Desert.* "It
never had a sacred poet; it has in me only a lover." And an
ardent and discerning lover he proved to be. Librarian at the
New Brunswick Theological Seminary in New Jersey, popular lecturer on modern art trends at Rutgers College, and, as
critic for the *Century Magazine,* one of the nation's favorite
essayists in the field of art appreciation, he visited the West in
the mood of an explorer expecting to find a new world. With
his extraordinary acuteness of vision, his love of natural
scenery, and his enthusiasm for the experiments in color and
light being made by contemporary artists, he was the logical
man to discover the beauties of the desert.

His older brother, Theodore S. Van Dyke, who had so clearly shown in his books about Southern California that he preferred the brown hills back of San Diego to the tawdry congestion of the boom towns, was a good person to act as a guide for the art enthusiast. The younger man was not looking for new towns, not interested in boom economy. Even the settled sections of Southern California seemed to him but tenuously held anomalies in a desert land:

> The cultivated portion of the land is but a flower-garden beside the unbroken foot-hills and the untenanted valleys. As you look down upon them, the terra-cotta of the granite shows through the chaparral of the hills; and the sands of the valleys have the glitter of the desert. You know intuitively that all this country was planned by Nature to be a desert. Down to the water-edge of the Pacific she once carried the light, air, and life of the Mohave and the Colorado.

Accordingly, John Van Dyke turned his back on the villages of the coastal plain and found his delight in the vast reaches of the Mojave and Colorado deserts, hoping that they might never become settled land. "Some sections must lie fallow that other sections may produce . . . The deserts should never be reclaimed. They are the breathing-spaces of the west and should be preserved forever."

To one who was sympathetic with the efforts of Monet, Cézanne, and others of the plein-air school to capture sunlight on canvas, the desert lands were intoxicants. Light, light, light, was his theme. Here was sunlight such as Cézanne had never seen. "Pure sunlight requires for its existence pure air, and the Old World has little of it left," he wrote. "The chief glory of the desert is its broad blaze of omnipresent light." Here, also, were line and form in proper relationship to light and color. "In sublimity—the superlative degree of beauty—what land can equal the desert with its wide plains, its grim mountains, and its expanding canopy of sky?" Here was mass in simplicity, line handled almost as by an abstractionist.

"There is a simplicity about large masses . . . that is inviting and ennobling. And there is something very restful about the horizontal line."

But best of all to this art enthusiast's eye was the subordination of form to color in the desert. "The landscape that is the simplest in form and the finest in color is by all odds the most beautiful," he proclaimed. "There you have the most decorative landscape in the world, a landscape all color, a dream landscape." It was this color even more than the light that he loved; and he fully realized the paradox that the dust which made the color effects possible cut down on the purity of air which allowed the dazzling light. Since, however, he was in love with the desert, he compromised by embracing dust and scorning humidity; and he clung to the idea that the desert air was purer than other air, even though a sandstorm might hover on the horizon. "Yet despite the fact that desert air is dust-laden and must be thickened somewhat, there is something almost inexplicable about it. It seems so thin, so rarified," he explained. Yes, Van Dyke was thankful for the dust, which slowed down the blue rays in the spectrum and accounted for the glorious reds, yellows, and browns of the desert. "The stronger the wind, and the more of dust and sand, the brighter the coloring," he observed.

Whatever the cause—pure air or dry air or dusty air—the effects were almost infinite in variety, almost violent in intensity. A shaft of sandstone in the desert, perhaps a dull ochre or even gray in neutral light, would change from blue to topaz to glowing red within a half hour. The sunbeams "stain the ledges of copper with turquoise, they burn the buttes to a terra-cotta red, they paint the sands with rose and violet, and they key the air to the hue of the opal." Even desert clouds appeared more brilliant and fiery than elsewhere on the globe, and of an evening a dome of granite shone "amethystine, golden, crimson, or perhaps lively purple."

It was the same gray desert that had disturbed Charlotte Perkins, but it was a desert seen under different conditions and by different eyes. Not only were the conditions under which the traveler saw the desert more pleasant, but the desert was beginning to fit into the contemporary taste in art. As Van Dyke said of the Colorado River, which, although it suggested blood to him, he did not find repugnant: "On the contrary, that deep red contrasted with the green of the banks and the blue of the sky makes a very beautiful color harmony." In fact, Americans were beginning to realize that they had outlived the Hudson River School. Just as dissonant notes in music were beginning to sound pleasant to their ears, discordant shapes introduced occasionally into otherwise regular landscapes began to please their eyes. They began to like the angular lines of the ocotillo and the menacing pattern of the cholla, and to see the beauty in the geometric design of the horned toad and in the orange and black diamonds of the Gila monster. As for colors, the artist went as far as Maxfield Parrish, not dreaming that in time he might catch up with a Georgia O'Keeffe.

Van Dyke was fully cognizant of the trend of American art, although he did not envisage the extent of the revolution. In his introduction to *The Desert* he suggested that much about the desert might be appreciated only through an acquired taste: "One begins by admiring the Hudson-River landscape and ends by loving the desolation of the Sahara." He discussed the ingenuity of the design of desert plants, suggesting that their functional nature might be related to their beauty. And he warned that the desert-lover must broaden his classical taste, suggesting that one test of the beautiful object might be whether it was "appropriate to its setting." Thus, the interest that led one to admire the peasants of Millet or the burghers of Rodin might cause one to appreciate greasewood and cactus. It would not be long before the inhabitants of Southern California would welcome the making of a national monument of an area which abounded in Manly's "cabbage tree," the Joshua tree, and Arizona would pass stringent laws to prevent tourists from removing cholla from the desert sands beside the transcontinental highways.

It was inevitable that Van Dyke, as an American naturist as well as an art critic, should see in the desert more than its beauty. Like most of the writers of his generation who were to discover the desert, he found God at home there and man hardly welcome. Man was an enemy of nature, disturbing her balance and marring her landscape; even the Indian, according to Van Dyke, failed to see the beauty of the silvery sheen in the mesquite. The law of nature was a law from which there was no appeal, and the desert was a part of nature. It offered a place of worship, an escape from a harried civilization, a sublimity and a mystery. Sleeping under the stars in the desert was a cathartic experience. "Around us stretches the great sand-wrapped desert whose mystery no man knows, and not even the Sphinx could reveal." "Is it not true that bulk and breadth are primary and essential qualities of the sublime in landscape? And is it not the sublime that we feel in immensity and mystery? . . . And quite as impressive as the mysteries are the silences." One suspects that, after nearly a century, Natty Bumppo had reached the desert. One is certain of it when he comes to the writings of Mary Austin, who brought transcendentalism to Southern California, carrying all of Deerslayer's instincts and Rousseau's principles in her bag.

$\infty\infty\infty$

The wedding of temperament and tradition in Mary Austin is well indicated in her remark explaining why she wrote *The Land of Little Rain* (she often spoke of herself in the third person): "She was bound to have written something of the kind no matter about what country, for to Mary all places were beautiful and interesting so long as they were outdoors." She not infrequently asserted that her course in writing was charted by forces beyond her, as in her famous remark—in the preface to her autobiography, *Earth Horizon*—that long before she had lived the first third of her life, it was clear "that I would write imaginatively, not only of people, but of the scene, the totality which is called Nature, and that I would give myself intransigently to the quality of experience called Folk, and to the frame of behavior known as Mystical." As she came to be more imbued with mysticism, fitting her own particular brand into one of her most effective concepts, that under the right spiritual circumstances man automatically adjusted himself perfectly to his environment, she asserted frequently that forces operated through her—forces such as she felt expressed in the primitivism of the Indian, the voice of the desert, or even God in a walnut tree. Somewhat skeptical, one suggests that it is perhaps more plausible to explain Mary Austin on the basis of a lonely childhood, an uncomfortable later life in which she found nature more friendly than man, a keen ability at perception and recording of impressions, and an appreciation of transcendental thought as expressed by Emerson, Thoreau, and John Muir. Like dozens of writers before her who had been products of the romantic revolt, she accepted certain tenets common to American transcendentalists: that nature heals, has a wisdom of her own, is permeated with the spirit of God, and offers a convenient environment in which to indulge in transcendental rapture. Her significance as a writer resulted in part from the fact that she arrived at the desert at the right time, and in part from her very great ability at expressing herself.

That desert she saw first in 1888, when as twenty-year-old Mary Hunter she crossed the alkali flats and purple-sage country of Utah in a tourist coach on the Union Pacific Railroad. As she gazed on the sands glistening beneath a summer sun, "the sight-seer's interest relaxed and allowed Mary to be happily absorbed into its vast space and silence, faintly stirred by the sense of something expected, familiar yet remote in the marching landscape line." There was little in her past that would account for this feeling of familiarity with the desert.

The daughter of a Yorkshire emigrant father and a pioneer mother, she had grown up in the midwestern town of Carlinville, Illinois. Her youthful environment, described most competently in *Earth Horizon,* centered around the home, the church, and the farm; its legends clustered around the Mississippi River and the Civil War. It was a quiet family life in which the crusades of a Frances Willard or the disturbing challenges of a Henry George or a "bobingersoll" seemed more vital than the pursuit of gold or homestead land into the Great American Desert.

Such an environment offered comparatively meager opportunities for the intellectual development of the eager, precocious, homely, adolescent girl who cherished a love for a liberal father who died when she was very young, who never seemed quite to "belong" as far as the rest of the family was concerned (although she yearned for a better understanding with her plucky, church-active mother), and who hoped that some day she might justify her existence by writing books "of all kinds." Her world of art centered around Ruskin's *Seven Lamps of Architecture* and Emerson's *Essays,* and her world of adventure around Beadle's Dime Novels, read surreptitiously, supplemented by trips into the countryside. Her world of revolt seemed to be associated principally with the reading of books like Hugh Miller's *Old Red Sandstone* and Thoreau's *Walden.* But that the grain of rebellion was vital is indicated by the fact that the woman who emerged was to be banned from the Methodist Church for teaching "the Higher Criticism." The banishment might have come even if she had never listened to Paiute medicine men in campodies on Western deserts.

The Hunters came west as one family among thousands attracted by the Southern California boom of the 'eighties. By the time they arrived, however, the postboom reaction was fully established, and Mary first saw the new land as a lovely and challenging landscape already marred by commercialism. It had started on the path which resulted, in "all the uses of natural beauty slavered over with the impudicity of a purely material culture." She was pleased when the family decided to leave the boom town of Monrovia, near Los Angeles, where her brother had been working in a drugstore, and go north to homestead in the hill country which lay between Los Angeles and the San Joaquin Valley. There followed four years of struggle—high in the Tejon Pass, down by the Grapevine and Rose Station, and in the sand hills near Bakersfield—four years that convinced Mary Hunter that the inexperienced homesteader was but a poor match for drought, loneliness, and the men who controlled the water in the Sierra streams. But, though the Hunter family did little more than keep up the struggle, Mary learned to love the desert, to watch the flocks, to listen to folklore from the sheepherders and Mexicans, to garner history and tales about the Indians from the lips of Edward Fitzgerald Beale, and to discover that she could find friends among the outcasts and fringe-livers even though her own social group ostracized her for her friendship with them.

By 1892 she had married Stafford Wallace Austin and was reasonably sure that life would be good in the new home to which he took her, in Lone Pine, a little town at the southern end of Owens Valley. The story of the next fifteen years was, however, one of considerable personal tragedy. The destruction of the hopes of the settlers of Owens Valley, which had begun to develop into a fruitful agricultural area but was forced to revert to desert so that San Fernando Valley and Los Angeles might have more water, seemed an appropriate accompaniment to an unhappy marriage, the pain of bearing and rearing a subnormal child, the antagonism of communities which even today will not tolerate Mary Austin's writings, and the conflicts within her which took so long to be resolved. There were compensations, however; in this period Mary Austin proved herself as a writer. The essays, short stories, and novels which make up the eight books which she wrote about California owe most of their virtues to this period when

Mary Austin, at odds with society, was learning to know the desert and the Indian.

Thus, Mary Austin found comfort when a Paiute *mahala* nursed her baby and brought dried meadow-lark's tongues to make it talk more readily. She was so unhappy in her family life, so at odds with the community, and so eager to learn to write that she came to spend much time at the Paiute campodies, among the "brown wickiups in the chaparral like wasp's nests." There she joined the *mahalas,* the Indian women, in gathering roots and seeds, she marveled at the lack of reticence in the tribal meetings, she listened in awe to the tales of Shoshone land told by members of a wandering people. She even became convinced of the existence of some Indian in her own blood—"a single isolated gene of that far-off and slightly mythical Indian ancestor"—which made her understand the Indian way of doing things. Her sympathy with the economic distress of the Indian, her violent dislike of *mahala*-chasing by the town toughs, and her admiration for Indian fortitude all helped her to come to the defense of the Indians "because they were the most conspicuously defeated and offended against group at hand." She began to study Indian verse, Indian wisdom, Indian art. Her tribute to this experience was effusive: "She entered into their lives, the life of the campody, the strange secret life of the tribe, the struggles of Whiteness with Darkness, the struggle of individual soul with the Friend-of-the-Soul-of-Man. She learned what it meant; how to prevail; how to measure her strength against it. Learning that, she learned to write."

This was her view late in life when she wrote *Earth Horizon* (1932). In the Owens Valley days, however, she was aware that the Indians were not enough, that she needed contact with fellow craftsmen in a congenial atmosphere. This atmosphere she sought by going to San Francisco and to Los Angeles, although in the long run the warming companionship of writers in search of similar goals was fully realized only in Carmel. Although in her autobiography Mary Austin asserts that, at the time she began writing her sketches and tales, "there was nothing of the West but Bret Harte and the interdicted dime novels," she went unerringly to Ina Coolbrith in San Francisco and Charles Lummis in Los Angeles for the congenial atmosphere that she had not been able to find in her own home. In particular, the several months that she spent in 1899 with the "Arroyo Seco" group down below the Sierra Madre apparently fanned into flame the talent which she had for some time nourished in the spark. Friendships with both Dorothea and Eva Lummis, encouragement from Charles Lummis (she wrote to Houghton in 1902 that Lummis was "my first and warmest friend in the West"), and welcome from the *Land of Sunshine* group enheartened her during a time when the bitter ashes of disappointment in marriage and motherhood were still on her lips. Although in time she lost most of her enthusiasm for Lummis ("Mr. Lummis did not take to her, nor she to him. . . . Mary shrank from him a little; thought him romantic; felt that he rested too much on the lesser achievement: on working too many hours a day; on sleeping too little; on drinking too much; on his wife's translation of Spanish documents" she wrote thirty years later), at the moment and for some years to come she benefited from the stimulation she received in "the long, dark, barbaric hall" where Charles Lummis entertained guests with Spanish food and Indian songs. The group shared not only her interest in writing but also her love of the desert and the Indian; and, no doubt, Charlotte Perkins and other members of the group encouraged her militant feminism.

A visitor of the time remembers Mrs. Austin, whom she met at a Lummis soirée, as a person "not very much in love with civilization, preferring the desert with its ever changing beauty, and the grave, thoughtful, brown people who inhabit it." This description accords well with the thumbnail sketch written by Mary herself about the same time: "You are to figure to yourself a small, plain, brown woman, with too much hair, always a little sick, and always busy about the fields and mesas in a manner, so they say in the villages, as if I should like to see anybody stop me." Contact with the Los Angeles writing group was not to last for any length of time, however, for Mrs. Austin felt that her duty lay in returning to her husband, who would not consent to leave the desert for the orange groves. But it brought opportunities to publish in *Out West* a number of sketches and poems, as well as a juvenile serial titled "The Truscott Luck," and through it she received a stimulant which revived a flagging *amour-propre*—an invitation to lecture to students at the normal school (now the University of California at Los Angeles) on desert flora and fauna. Only a few years earlier she had been refused a certificate to teach in a Bakersfield district school, because her mathematics was deplorable and her personality "was anything but appealing."

She went back to Owens Valley, beloved by her for its water trails and Basque herders if not for its narrow-minded settlers, and lived for several years more in the towns that were "strung along the foot of the Sierra Wall"—Big Pine, Bishop, Independence, and most attractive to her of all, the half-Mexican Lone Pine. Before she left for good, and while she still considered Carmel only a congenial place to go in the summer, she wrote *The Land of Little Rain* (1903) and *The Flock* (1906), as well as a number of lesser books. In her work she was not unaided by trail breakers, for she had a John Muir to lend a transcendental glow to the mountains which towered above her, and a John C. Van Dyke to declare the beauties of a desert land, the aesthetic values of which were not least among its attractions for her. But her principal interest lay in combining the appeal of the natural life with the picturesqueness of the folkways, with always a diapason of desert call beneath the melody.

Her approach in her sketches was essentially realistic. Although she sometimes, as in "Jimtown," rang the changes on the Harte formula that eccentricity plus costume produces local color, she exclaimed eagerly: "With all my seeking into desert places there are three things that of my knowledge I have not seen—a man who has rediscovered a lost mine, the heirs of one who died from the bite of a sidewinder, and a shepherd who is insane." Her distrust of the Helen Hunt Jackson formula for sugar candy was clearly stated. She had little sympathy for "the factitious effort of everybody to recreate a sense of the past out of the sentiment for the Old Missions, out of 'Ramona,' a second-rate romance very popular at the time." (In *The Flock* she wrote: "*What* is it in the Castilian strain that makes it possible for a girl to stick a rose behind her ear and cause you to forget the smell of garlic and the reek of unwashed walls?") Her forte was, indeed, the presentation of the totality of Nature within the special phase which she called "the accent of folk experience," and the assertion of mystical values which she claimed as her own and the treatment of which at their best surely earned her the degree of M.A.E. (Master of the American Environment) which Carl Van Doren once facetiously suggested that she be granted.

Most important of Mary Austin's writings about the deserts and sagebrush plateaus were *The Land of Little Rain,* in which she wrote in a moving, sensitive style of the desert, from coyotes and hawks to pocket miners and campodies, and *The Flock,* a minor American classic dealing with the lives of sheep and herders. In writing *The Flock* she rejoiced that "the dust of the shuffling hoofs is in my eyes." So sympathetic is her picture of shepherd life that the reader will not quarrel with her when he reads: "When the fire kindles and savory meat seethes in the pot, when there is a drowsy blether from the flock, and far down the mesa the twilight twinkle of shepherd fires, when there is a hint of blossom underfoot and a heavenly whiteness on the hills, one harks back without effort to Judea and the nativity." And this sympathy is based on full and detailed knowledge of her subject; only Mary Austin could speak with certainty of the young lambs who were principally legs, "the connecting body being merely a contrivance for converting milk into more leg." Again, in her book about California titled *Lands of the Sun* (1927), Mary Austin, as in *The Land of Little Rain,* caught that sense for man upon the land which makes her nature writing so distinguished.

She was not so fortunate in her fiction, however, although she handled the tale better than the novel. The gleanings from quiet talks with Paiute and Shoshone Indians, from gossip in Mrs. Dodge's boardinghouse in Lone Pine, from nightlong rides beside the stagedrivers on the long run down from Bishop to Mojave, resulted in the Indian tales of *The Basket Woman* (1904) and the yarns of desert rats and frustrated women in *Lost Borders* (1909). When she turned to the novel, in *Isidro* (1905) she wrote an improbable and somewhat tedious book in which not even the sensitive nature descriptions make up for the cloak-and-sword fustian of a lost heiress in disguise as a shepherd boy. And in *The Ford* (1917), a somewhat better book, her lack of skill in handling narrative and character is only partly balanced by her concern with the issues of feminism and reclamation. Her third California novel, *Santa Lucia* (1908), lies beyond the reaches of the desert and of Southern California. But in her Indian plays, *The Arrowmaker* and *Fire,* she portrayed with considerable force the tribal emotions of the desert peoples.

In addition to a number of lesser themes in Mary Austin's books—her assertion of the rightness of women's judgment, her love for the peasant life of the Mexican immigrant, her devotion to the wisdom and simplicity of Indian life—there is the constant and dominant theme of the arid lands that reach from the Santa Lucia Range to the Kaibab Plateau and beyond the Colorado into the Navajo country. Although Mrs. Austin consistently links death with beauty and admits that the desert sucks men dry, as a whole her theme illustrates the old Spanish proverb: "The lands of the sun expand the soul." She was glad to affirm that "the secret charm of the desert is the secret of life triumphant," and to rejoice: "For all the toll the desert takes of a man it gives compensations, deep breaths, deep sleep, and the communion of the stars." And she insisted that she drew strength, both physical and spiritual, from the wastelands; the girl who had caused raised eyebrows in Bakersfield by letting down her hair and wandering over the desert in the moonlight was proud at a later date to be known as "a desert woman, competent, rugged, self-reliant, unconventional—a *chisera*." Certainly the name of *chisera*, Indian medicine woman, was more appropriate to her character than the epithet "God's mother-in-law," used at a later day by some of the younger generation, impatient with her claims to mystical powers.

Besides strength, life in the desert brought wisdom. When she wrote in *Lost Borders* that "Out there where the boundary of soul and sense is as faint as a trail in a sand-storm, I have seen things happen that I do not believe myself," Mary Austin was thinking of more than bizarre happenings in a land where convention breaks down. Just as the very names of the desert land—Ubehebe, Pharanagat, Resting Springs, Dead Man's Gulch, Funeral Mountains—meant more than romance to her, she was speaking of something besides the picturesque when she assured her readers that in the desert a great many myths come true. The desert was a land where the herder could speak to his sheep directly, without the aid of language, as if there were a more primitive tongue common to nature and man. It was a land from which emanated a natural rhythm, a rhythm indigenous and atavistic. From this concept was to come Mary Austin's theory of the rightness of Amerindian rhythm in American poetry, which she was to express in her controversial *The American Rhythm* (1923).

Finally, there was virtue in the desert. An ethical determinant of great force, it was interpreted by Mary Austin in terms many an earlier mystic had used. "Great souls that go into the desert come out mystics," she wrote—"saints and prophets—declaring unutterable things: Buddha, Mahomet, and the Galilean, convincing of the casual nature of human relations, because the desert itself has no use for the formal side of man's affairs." And yet, it is not Mary Austin's faith in the desert as a source of strength, wisdom, and virtue which gives truly lasting quality to her work; it is, rather, her skill in picturing the desert in its many moods. If part of this is due to her applying to greasewood and cactus Emerson's dictum that "the occult relation between man and vegetable" is the "greatest delight that the fields and woods can minister," the effect is still very moving, if not always rational. Whether it is her most appropriate tribute to the eucalyptus, with its complete adaptability to the Southern California landscape which it so enhances, or her comment on the founding of the city of Los Angeles, where the spirit of Our Lady the Queen of the Angels hovered "snow-whitened amid tall candles of the stars, while south and west the coyote barked the menace of the unwatered lands," she writes as a poet. So it is with her description of the reach of the land:

The range of which San Bernardino and San Jacinto are outposts carries the artemisia desertward until the shifting, root resisting sand defeats it. South again about the Salton Sea it holds its own with cactus and palo verde. Its eastern border, like that of the wild tribes along the Mohave line, is lost. Over Kaibab it goes and beyond the Colorado to the Painted Desert.

And, when reading Mary Austin, one is almost willing to believe in the heaven of the Shoshone: "It will be tawny gold underfoot, walled up with jacinth and jasper, ribbed with chalcedony, and yet no hymn-book heaven, but the free air and free spaces of Shoshone land."

∾∾∾∾

As the attitude toward the desert shifted, the writers who described it found a new list of adjectives and comparisons. It was no longer fashionable to refer to it as "more desolate and terrible than Dante's wildest dream of the Inferno"; instead, one wrote enthusiastically of Palestine, Araby, and Egypt. The inscrutable smile of the Sphinx rested on the Mojave; and Ishmael, Esau, and even Nimrod were claimed as early and worthy members of the "Most Ancient Order of Lovers of the Desert." One author was reminded of Kinglake's *Eothen,* another was heartened by the thought that the Chaldeans were a desert people, still another named his hero Elijah, and a fourth realized as he gazed on the desert at night just why Abraham became a great Biblical leader.

After John C. Van Dyke's *The Desert,* the writers of books descriptive of the deserts, particularly of the Mojave and Colorado, took it for granted that their readers would recognize their aesthetic appeal. For instance, in 1904, A. J. Burdick issued a down-to-earth book for travelers, *The Mystic Mid-Region,* which contained a good deal of practical information about the desert country in the eastern reaches of Southern California. In it he spoke of the beauty of the landscape and actually praised Death Valley (which had filled men's minds with horror since the days of Manly and his friends). It was "not wanting in beauty," he wrote, and, "Color effects such as artist never dreamed of are here to be seen." The aspects of the "lure of the desert" (already a stock phrase) which Burdick stressed, however, were its mystery and its oddities. "There is a mystery about the desert which is both fascinating and repellant," he wrote. Part of its attraction were the *strange* plants, such as the yucca, greasewood, and soap plant, and its *curious* animals, such as the centipede and the Gila monster. Burdick seemed to experience particular joy in discovering the virtues of land lying below sea level, and he certainly approved of the spirit of the *Submarine,* published at Indio twenty-two feet below sea level, which boasted of being "the most low-down paper on earth."

A much more formidable and detailed tribute to the attractions of the desert was that of George Wharton James in *The Wonders of the Colorado Desert;* in this James drew extensively on his experiences in the desert, his talks with old-timers, and his reading of practically everything that had been written about the region. Although it is marked by James's usual excesses, it is full of information and is very valuable in other ways. James found beauty and mystery in the desert; he also found adventure, wisdom, morality, health, and philosophy. No man to take things by halves, he discarded most of his clothes, used the hot springs as his bathtub, delivered orisons to the sunrise, and went in for a diet of dates and nuts. He was particularly enthusiastic about the health-giving aspects of desert life. "The desert is God's greatest health-giving laboratory. It is the manufactory of health where are to be found purest sunshine, purest air, purest soil. Disease flies away in such presences." He was writing on the threshold of the era when the desert, made habitable by new devices, was to become a boon to the tubercular, the arthritic, and the nervously exhausted. And in his emphasis on health and longevity he was but continuing the tradition of earlier days in Southern California. The long lives of the Indians of the region had been proverbial ever since the day when Vizcaíno had seen at San Diego an Indian woman, believed to be one hundred and fifty years old, who "had wrinkles on her belly which looked like a goldsmith's bellows, and the navel protruded bigger than a gourd."

The theme that the desert improved one's health was one of the ideas taken up by another enthusiast for the Southwest, J. P. Widney, who carried the idea farther and found in the desert the environment which would improve the race through selectivity and the passing on of acquired traits. A charter member of the Los Angeles Medical Society and the president of University of Southern California from 1890 to 1895, Widney, for more than a half century, took a prominent part in the discussion of most issues facing the citizens of the area. In his old age (he lived to be ninety-seven) he assumed something of the manner and prerogatives of Moses, expressing theories very sweeping in their inclusiveness. Such was his plan to bore through the Sierra Madre, extend the city limits of Los Angeles to the Mojave, and erect "a hundred miles of mountain-slope sanitariums, facing upon the broad slope of the desert." He even managed to figure out how the plan could be carried out without costing the city a dollar.

In 1907, Widney published his *Race Life of the Aryan Peoples,* the first of a series of publications in which he put forth the concept that a new racial type with advanced cultural traits was certain in time to emerge from the desert lands of the Southwest. He believed, above everything else, that living on the desert would lead men to worship a universal God, and that in this area would spring up a religion which would appeal to all peoples. In coming to such conclusions he was, of course, in tune with the peculiar brand of nonsectarian religious fervor which has created many new cults in the Southern California region. The church which Widney founded stemmed in part from his natural philanthropy and faith, in part from his concern for the economically unfortunate in Los Angeles, and in part from his enthusiasm for the desert.

A quieter reaction to the arid lands is found in the books written by a pleasant English naturalist-turned-Californian, J. Smeaton Chase. In his *California Trails* he wrote competently of the attractions of the Colorado Desert; he was particularly skillful in describing desert animals and plants. In this book and in the small companion volume, *Our Araby: Palm Springs and the Garden of the Sun,* Chase stressed the last of the elements in the lure of the desert which were to remain permanent parts of the folk concept of the subject. To Chase, the desert was not only beautiful and inspiring; it was a potential playhouse for visitors tired or harassed by the strain of modern living. It is true that his view was cheerful enough, and he was no jaded fugitive from city life; he did not talk in terms of escape from hypertension or boredom but merely chatted of the joys of simple pleasures at a desert oasis. In his invitation to the tired city-dweller to come "in time for a cup of tea and a desert sunset" he was but anticipating the day when the New York financier or the Hollywood movie actor would be invited out to rough it for a while and take a little sun, with a highball in one hand and the racing form in the other.

As time went on, the desert came to serve, often effectively, as a source of beauty, mystery, excitement, health, recreation, escape, and religion. Today one reads in tourist literature the following sort of blurb without remembering that the desert once was a synonym for Hell:

At gay resort oases play all you will, but sometime, for your soul's sake, make good your escape from noisy groups and go questing in the desert. Go not on any practical errand, just walk into it alone, a few rods, a few miles, like some hazy old prospector answering the mystery of its call. Clothe your body and your mind properly, wear stout garments and leave petty thoughts behind. The desert is no place for frills and foibles. It is a wide, honest space under a wide, honest sky; a shrine of long thoughts, a realm of profound intimations.

∞∞∞

Local fiction writers not only took the message of Kipling and the technique of Harte to the desert country, but at the same time reflected the changing attitude toward the arid lands. As the mood changed, their fiction came to reflect a more serious purpose than the stories in Beadle's Dime Novels and the boys' adventures written by Captain Mayne Reid which had used the desert as an environmental influence principally productive of adventure. Like the essayists, they discovered that the desert was a source of strength of arm, keenness of eye, and regeneration of soul—a land where a man could be a man.

When Gwendolen Overton, a twenty-six-year-old Los Angeles resident who had spent most of her youth in army camps in the Apache land of New Mexico and Arizona, published her *The Heritage of Unrest* in 1901, she followed the older pattern, picturing the desert as "a waste of glittering sand and white dust," of air that "waved and quivered with incredible heat," of a land where "at night malaria rose from the ground, the coyote barked and whined at the light of the brilliant stars, and the wildcat prowled deliberately." It was a pre–Van Dyke desert. This harsh land was the birthplace of Miss Overton's half-breed Apache heroine, most of whose troubles resulted from the death of her white father from desert thirst, and from the savage character of the Indian blood, desert blood, inherited from her mother. Because of her desert heritage, which was only thinly covered by an education in the East, she was restless, impassive in the face of suffering, and had a taste for cruelty—any violent action, such as the goring of a man by a bull, was a matter of intense fascination to her and aroused in her very unladylike impulses. To Miss Overton, who knew it well, the desert was a place that tried the souls of the soldiers forced to pass time in the frontier posts. Her mood was similar to that of John Russell McCarthy in his vivid poem on Anza's journey from Sonora to Southern California:

> And under the steel blue frying pan
> Whose fires were lit when time began
>> Men sizzle and stew
>> The glare-time through
> On the road to California.

Mrs. Idah Meacham Strobridge, who like Gwendolen Overton was a contributor to and sponsor of *The Land of Sunshine* and lived not far from Lummis in the artists' colony which had grown up in the Arroyo Seco, took quite a different attitude toward the desert in her collection of short stories and sketches, *In Miner's Mirage Land,* which she issued from her own Artemisia Bindery in 1904. A somewhat older woman than Miss Overton, born in Moraga Valley near Oakland in 1855 and educated at Mills College, she reflected a mature and long-standing love of the desert, particularly that haunting and little-known section of northern Nevada called the Black Rock country. Her vignettes of desert life, which reflect some of the quality of vision that is found in the *Lost Borders* sketches of

Mary Austin, whom she greatly admired, are essentially realistic in tone. In her first volume, as well as in the later *The Loom of the Desert* and *The Land of Purple Shadows*, she pictured desert life as arduous, particularly from the point of view of the woman settler, but she never let her readers forget that she loved the country in spite of its hardships. She was probably the first writer to capitalize "the Desert" when she referred to it; and she spoke of it with awe: "I can only tell you the charm of the Desert, when you, too, have learned to love it." To her, also, "the Desert" was animate: "And once there, unprejudiced, the voice by and by will make itself heard as it whispers in your ear. And when you can lay your head upon its breast, and hear its heart-beats you will know a rest that is absolute and infinite."

Mrs. Strobridge's modest, quiet stories reached only a small public, for they appeared in book form only in the limited editions from her bindery, where she herself assembled the sheets. Quite another public read the Western romances of Stewart Edward White and Zane Grey and their followers, which soon began to roll from the Eastern presses. A taste for the desert and the rugged life had become epidemic in America; the same enthusiasm which gripped Gutzon Borglum as he modeled horses and cowboys in his studio back of Pasadena, that attracted young artists such as Carl Eytel and Maynard Dixon to go to the desert for subjects for their paintings, was stimulating a new school of Western writers.

Stewart Edward White, who had passed much of his boyhood in Southern California, had portrayed the strenuous life as it was lived in the Black Hills of South Dakota and in the lumber camps of his native Michigan before he turned to the Far West for a locale for his fiction. Then he found that the Southwestern desert was an ideal setting for his skillful blending of realism, folklore, and pleas for the outdoor life—a successful formula already established in *The Westerners* and *The Blazed Trail*. His *Arizona Nights*, which appeared in 1907, was a better book than Wister's *The Virginian*, often called the classic of cowboy fiction, and it may in the long run have had a more pervasive influence. (The little-known Eugene Manlove Rhodes was also publishing his first stories of cowboy life in *The Land of Sunshine* while Wister and White were reaching a larger public.) In *Arizona Nights*, a collection of stories told under the stars, White sometimes portrayed the desert as cruel but more often as a stimulant to adventure. And prominent among the stories is "The Remittance Man," which tells about an heir to an English estate who gave up his fortune to return to "the wide places" and renew his life as a cow hand. His explanation for his behavior was accepted with approval by his companions as a proper tribute to the lure of the desert country: " 'I've come back to the Big Country, where the pay is poor and the work is hard and the comfort small, but where a man and his soul meet their Maker face to face.' "

Zane Grey, who, like Mary Austin, insisted that he had some Indian blood in his ancestry, and who prided himself on being a descendant of the pioneer after whom his birthplace, Zanesville, Ohio, was named, did not succumb to the lure of the desert country until he had given up careers of baseball playing and dentistry in Pennsylvania. He had always been determined to write, even while working at these other professions, but no one except his wife had any confidence that he could do so. In 1908, when he was thirty-three years old, he seized the opportunity to go to the Kaibab and Lee's Ferry country of southern Utah and northern Arizona as a ghost writer for Colonel C. J. (Buffalo) Jones, who was looking for someone to persuade the world that he could capture mountain lions with a lariat. Grey failed to place his book about Buffalo Jones with a publisher, but he used some of his material in writing his first romance, *The Heritage of the Desert*. Later trips with John Wetherill into the Navajo country provided him with background and ideas for his immensely popular *Riders of the Purple Sage*, issued in 1912, and *The Rainbow Trail,* which soon followed it. He eventually settled in Southern California, at Altadena, where he continued to exploit the desert, and man upon the desert, for the rest of his prolific writing career. His sixty-odd books are said to have sold more than thirteen million copies.

Zane Grey's success resulted partly from the timeliness of his theme, partly from his skill at picturing remote and spectacular parts of the Southwest, such as the enchanting Navajo Mountain region, and partly from his truly ingenuous enthusiasm for the adventure and morality of the desert. There is no question that he sincerely believed desert life improved a man's character; he often said he wrote to correct the false thesis of the naturalists that wild life brought out the beast beneath the skin. He praised romance and idealism and loathed the stark-naked realists who showed the elemental man retrograding to a brute. "My own investigation, my reading of frontier history, my long strife to explore the lonely and hidden wilderness of the West, have proved to me that hard men of the open also climb to the heights of nobility and sacrifice, to a supreme proof of the evolution of man, to a realization of God," he wrote as his *apologia.*

His romances are but poorly contrived blendings of scenery, adventure, and moralizing. They have, however, something of that impelling narrative tug found in Cooper and Scott. In theme, Zane Grey early adapted the popular interpretation of evolutionary processes to his purpose; desert men grew "lean, keen-eyed and silent," infinitely resourceful, because they were tempered in the flaming furnace of the fiery desert life. Just as only the hardiest plants survived in the desert, only the strongest men had a chance. Here is a sort of wedding of popular Darwin and Frederick Jackson Turner. Grey's heroes are nearly all Easterners who find regeneration in the desert. Wanderers with shady pasts never clearly understood, doubters of Protestant creeds found to be inadequate, they become strong and sometimes ruthless (when necessary to effect a moral end), but above all they develop into stern proponents of spiritual values in their new environment. Shefford, in *The Rainbow Trail,* is typical:

The desert had transformed Shefford. The elements had entered into his muscle and bone, into the very fiber of his heart. Sun, wind, sand, cold, storm, space, stone, the poison cactus, and racking toil, the terrible loneliness—the iron of the desert man, the cruelty of the desert savage, the wildness of the mustang, the ferocity of hawk and wolf, the bitter struggle of every surviving thing—these were as if they had been melted and merged together and now made a dark and passionate stream that was his throbbing blood. He realized what he had become and gloried in it.

With the heroes of Zane Grey, the desert had come into its own.

VIII

The Drama of Reclamation

"THE STRUGGLE of men with men is at best a sick and squalid affair for one of the parties; but men contriving against the gods for possession of the earth is your true epic," wrote Mary Austin in *The Lands of the Sun*. In doing so, she put her finger on the most promising subject for literary treatment in the arid countries of the Pacific Southwest, man's reclamation of the land. The literary output on this subject ranges from Kate Sanborn's aphorism, "irrigate, cultivate, and exaggerate, in her *A Truthful Woman in Southern California,* to William E. Smythe's imaginative and stirring plea for a new social order in *The Conquest of Arid America*. It varies from the bathos of the line in a local poem which reads "He walks with God who walks the flume" to the influential histrionics, meretricious and flamboyant though they be, of Harold Bell Wright's *The Winning of Barbara Worth*. It marches from such inadequate verse as A. J. Burdick's:

> Where now but lurks grim, ghastly, burning death,
> The violet may shed its fragrant breath.

to the vision and descriptive force that Mary Austin achieves in *The Ford*. Unfortunately, however, the subject has not to date produced the epic, either in poetry or prose, which it merits.

Irrigation, of course, had long been used in California; it had been introduced by the Spanish padres, who showed great ingenuity in using the limited and irregular flow of the local streams to water their gardens. But in the disorganized period after secularization of the missions, irrigation nearly disappeared, except for the *zanja* which watered the gardens in Los Angeles; and after the conquest, in the decades, when cattle and wheat ranching flourished, there was no need for systematic water control. By the late 'fifties, however, the German colonists at Anaheim were using the old Spanish irrigation methods to make their communal vineyards successful; and when in the 'seventies and 'eighties the settlers poured in from Indiana and Missouri and other Middle Western states, they quickly showed their ingenuity in obtaining water in a land where rainfall was not enough for their purposes, as it had been in their former homes. This was the era of individual engineering: on his property the farmer built small dams to check the runoff; bored artesian wells to release the liquid gold from a high water table where the pressure was intense; and, when the pressure slackened, installed first windmills and later engines or motors to pump the water. Such purely individual efforts in time gave way to efforts of nonprofit organizations such as the mutual water companies, and eventually whole communities entered the picture. These undertook more extensive projects and built storage dams in the mountains to catch the runoff, dams from which long flumes ran many miles through the hill country. Or they drove tunnels into the hills to tap underground currents and found that the old Spanish adage that "the rivers of California run bottom upward" was true.

Among the successful coöperative ventures of this early period, that of Riverside was the most prominent, earning an almost magic name. Under the leadership of J. W. North, the Riverside Colony turned the old Jurupa rancho into one of the wealthiest properties in the state. True, the introduction of the navel orange from Brazil and the discovery that the hill slopes were less subject to frosts than the bottom lands were both essential in this development, but so also was irrigation. The venture would not have been possible had not North and his companions been able to bring an ample water supply to the orange groves by building a $50,000 distribution canal which tapped the mountains back of the community.

Another such project was the work of George Chaffey, the most farsighted and ingenious of the early irrigators, who led the waters from beneath Mount San Antonio ("Old Baldy") to Etiwanda, to be divided equitably among the settlers whose membership in a mutual water company meant relief from the frustration created by the legal recognition of riparian water rights, a recognition which seemed for a time to doom anything like a democratic development of irrigation sources. George Chaffey carried on to create Ontario, with its utilization of hydroelectric power and its lavish display of gushing water in the fountain in front of the railway station, which for many years stood as a symbol of abundant water in a thirsty land.

George Chaffey played an important early role in the reclamation of the Imperial Valley also, and had all the men later connected with it been as capable and social-minded as he, the valley might never have faced the famous disasters of 1905–1907, when the entire area nearly reverted to the Salton Sea. It was a comparatively simple matter to tap the Colorado River, with its natural high dikes, to obtain water to irrigate the formidable desert in southeastern California, which had once been a neck of the Gulf of California and lay below sea level where the water could reach it by means of gravity. But the California Development Company found it easier to make the cut in the artery than to stem the flow when the need arose for strong controls. Its shabby, ill-considered improvisations of a dry year were washed out in a flood year, and, had not the Southern Pacific Railroad put all its resources into closing the gap, most of Imperial Valley would have been irretrievably ruined. As it was, many a new house and many a green acre had been swallowed up and the New River had cut a trench hundreds of feet wide through the heart of the land before the river was returned to its original course. The nearly disastrous results of the venture showed that the time had certainly come when the state and federal govrnments were better fitted than the individual or company to make the desert bloom.

The drama of man against nature, in which man was inept and shortsighted, was not repeated when Los Angeles made its first long reach for water by building the Owens River aqueduct. Here it was careful and thorough and, many insist, sinister and secret, planning which supplied the drama. When, in 1908, the 250-mile aqueduct which was to bring water from the lower Owens Valley was started, plans had been drawn up and costs had been estimated that proved to be accurate right up to the date in November, 1913, when the water from the highest part of the Sierra began flowing into the San Fernando Valley. The engineering was worked out beautifully, and the achievement was the fit subject for nation-wide praise. The social consequences, resulting in the apparently permanent ruin of the farming lands of Owens Valley, were less fortunate. The results, which reached at times the proportion of a sectional civil war, are felt to this day.

The Owens River aqueduct was but the first of several major ventures to bring water from the outside to feed the thirsty soil south of the Tehachapis. More water brought more settlers and more farms; these in turn demanded more water. And so the problem was created which is still unsolved today, in spite of the building of Hoover Dam and the Colorado River aqueduct. Now the talk is of bringing water from the Columbia River or of distilling it from the ocean by means of huge solar evaporating systems.

The subject of the finding and use of water has been a recurrent theme in fiction dealing with Southern California, although it has by no means received the treatment it deserves. American novelists, long skillful at describing the social situation in America, have not as yet, with a few exceptions like Frank Norris and George R. Stewart, succeeded effectively in utilizing the rich imaginative drama provided by American technological skills. And in the treatment of the reclamation theme in Southern California, the conquest of the desert has usually been subordinated to the portrayal of social or domestic problems. Thus, Beatrice Harraden, in *Hilda Strafford,* treating the period when irrigating was an individual effort, tells of the futile and agonizing efforts of a lemon rancher to build a reservoir to meet the demands of the dry years, only to have it washed out during the floods; but the main interest of the story is the bad effect of farming on the domestic life of Hilda Strafford. The short tales of Margaret Collier Graham are motivated primarily by the moral problems faced by local settlers, although the search for water enters into many of them. For instance, it furnishes a plot for "The Wizard's Daughter," in which a deaf "professor" confounds an engineer by finding water with an electric divining machine; and it provides a theme for "The Withrow Water Right," in which a desperate farmer protects with a gun the headwaters of his irrigation ditch, which is about to be taken over by a development company.

A more ambitious attempt to utilize the reclamation theme in this early era is found in Frank Lewis Nason's *The Vision of Elijah Berl* (1905). This is the story of the moral struggles that come to a New England Calvinist in Southern California in an area in the Redlands region saltily described by one of the characters as follows: " 'Lucky thing the Lord didn't start in makin' man in this section . . . he wouldn't have had water enough to have pasted him together with.' " Elijah Berl, almost singlehanded, tries to set up an entire irrigation system in order to get rich quick on an orange-ranch development scheme. His aim he states magniloquently:

When these great, barren, red hillsides are all covered with orchards; with beautiful houses and thousands of happy, prosperous people; when the snows and rains of the San Bernardinos, instead of running to waste, will flow through tunnels and canals and make the desert bloom as a rose; then they will say that this is the work of one man, of me, Elijah Berl!

The trouble is that he can't go it alone. He has to borrow money, an act that leads him to moral turpitude; and he has to hire a pretty secretary, a circumstance which, of course, arouses erotic complications, hard for a strict Yankee to handle. But he does build his dam and his flume, and he lives almost long enough to see an end to his bit of desert. Thinking he has been mistreated by his creditors and his engineer, however, poor Elijah tries to destroy his own dam; naturally, he learns his mistake at the last moment and sacrifices his life in saving the dam. This noble act makes his widow feel that her marriage was worth while after all. And the scene closes with Uncle Sid trotting the baby and planning for the next generation, which will presumably not have so many moral problems.

Of the novels dealing with reclamation, *The Winning of Barbara Worth* (1911), by Harold Bell Wright, was the most popular, attaining a sale of more than a million and a half copies. As a youth, Wright had determined to be a painter, but later he had turned to the ministry and in time had come to Southern California as pastor of the Redlands Christian Church. His heart was not entirely in the ministry, however, for he had already reached a larger public than his congregation through his two novels, *The Shepherd of the Hills* and *The Calling of Dan Matthews*. Accordingly, he resigned his pulpit and moved to the Imperial Valley, which he had decided to use as the setting for his third sermon in fiction, *The Winning of Barbara Worth*. While working on this novel he lived near the town of Imperial on the Tecolote Ranch, where, while attempting to build up his frail health by outdoor living and the construction of an "arrow-reed house" with his own hands, he acquainted himself with the local scene and the people connected with the irrigation project. In his declaration at the beginning of the book he thanked various well-known engineers for their aid, and he dedicated the book to the promoter, W. F. Holt, the founder of Holtville and presumably the prototype for Jefferson Worth.

The themes which Wright used included some of the most timeworn stereotypes in popular fiction, as well as a few ideas which were just beginning to become a part of American folklore. There was, of course, the rescue of the child from the desert, quite properly a girl child who grew into a woman whose eyes revealed "the wholesome, challenging lure of an unmarred womanhood." * Inevitably the child's presence brought reformation and kindness to the heart of the austere Jefferson Worth, her guardian, who had had hardly a friend before he found her in the desert. She grew up to be a true desert child, never as happy as when she was riding the open country in the sunset, mounted on her faithful horse. All sorts of people fell in love with her, including Abe Lee, himself a foundling of the desert, and Willard Holmes, an engineer of good family from back East. Abe, who is Natty Bumppo in still another disguise, learned that his role was to be the brother rather than the lover. But fortunately he had a desert to turn to; silhouetted against the sky at the end of the novel, he was granted a happiness "greater, it may be, than the joy of possession." Barbara Worth's eventual choice of Willard Holmes to be her mate and the father of her children came as the logical result of Wright's desire to reform the East to meet Western terms. Holmes had the best of blood and education—all he needed to find himself was contact with a truly moral environment. He had considerable difficulty at first adjusting himself to "the mighty expanse of desert that lay as it was fashioned by the creative forces that formed the world." In a moment of crisis, he confessed to

---

* Quotations from Wright's *The Winning of Barbara Worth* used by permission of Appleton-Century-Crofts, Inc.

Barbara Worth: " 'I am out of place in the big desert. I should have stayed at home. I wish—I wish you had never wakened me to the possibilities of life—real life.' " But he came around all right in the end.

This theme of the superiority of the West over the East permeates the novel. The reader is assured that the West was ages old before the East was discovered, and that if Columbus had come first to the western coast New England would still be "an uninhabitable, howling wilderness." Moreover, as one character from the West puts it, "the only difference between the East and the West seems to be that you *have* ancestors and we are *going to be* ancestors."

Somehow mixed up with this juxtaposition of not entirely consistent ideas is the contrast drawn between the evils of absentee capital and the virtues of local investment—or at least local participation in the acts made possible by the investment. Quite ignoring the fact that it was local mismanagement that caused the mess in the Imperial Valley, and eastern capital—eventually paid back by the federal government—that came to the rescue, Wright made the villains of his novel the absentee stockholders in the development company (the time-honored mortgage holders and bankers in a new role), and the heroes the engineers and promoters that were on the spot, ready to do or die. "Face to face with the unconquered forces of nature, nothing remained but the real strength or weakness of the individual himself," he wrote. All is to be won by "the methods of a man laboring with his brother men, sharing their hardships, sharing their returns; a man using money as a workman uses his tools to fashion and build and develop, adding thus to the welfare of human kind." Wright apparently was too close to the scene in both time and space to see that many of his hero promoters of the Imperial Valley had been irresponsible and shortsighted and had, as a consequence, nearly destroyed it. He did not have sufficient perspective to see that the development could have been done safely only by the federal government, which would have secured treaty rights, made surveys covering the entire western watershed, and built a dam upstream to prevent disaster. These conclusions came only later, after shoddy financing and promoting had done much damage.

As for the drama of the book, it concerns the fight of man against nature (and against other men), with the surveyors, engineers, and real-estate promoters as the Christian soldiers of the conflict. Their world-embracing goal is "the progress and the future of the great Reclamation work, of its value not only to our own nation but to the over-crowded nations beyond the seas, and of its place in the great forward march of the race." Unfortunately, however, Wright failed to make the best use of the climax of his novel, the truly remarkable fight the Southern Pacific made to stop the Colorado River in its apparently inexorable flow into the valley. The many attempts to divert the river, the intricate organization necessary to move materials to the site, the alarming collapse of whole farms and even towns, and the eventual victory are treated in rapid summary with little telling dramatic effect. Instead, Wright makes the climax of his book the ridiculous ride of his hero on a buckskin pony from San Diego to Mexicali to bring in much-needed money to pay back wages. That, and the desert were all that he had to offer.

Ednah Aiken in her *The River,* which appeared three years after *The Winning of Barbara Worth,* did a better job in describing the fight to divert the river into its old channel, but did not do as good a job as she should have done, for she allowed her interest in a tedious domestic triangle to dull her novel beyond repair. The humors of engineers and their bitchy wives and understanding sisters, sweating out their emotions in the tents and ramshackle huts of the Imperial Valley construction settlements while the river is undercutting the main street, fail to impress the reader. Not even the assurance that the engineers were the soldiers of the desert is convincing, for the introduction of the camp retainers vitiates the results on the battlefield. The most interesting feature of this novel is the presentation of a minor character named Brandon, a "lunger" turned newspaperman, who expresses many of the more important concepts that have arisen from the reclamation movement.

∽∽∽∽

Whether the benefits obtained by the draining of Owens Valley to obtain water for the Los Angeles area ethically out-balanced the dubious methods utilized in effecting the plan is a matter for the historians to decide. But the fiction based upon the project reflects a philosophy current at the time, which had its seamy side, to say the least. In no place is this better seen than in Peter B. Kyne's *The Long Chance,* which appeared in 1914. Although much of this story deals with the fate of yet another desert orphan—female of course—who lived down in the heart of the Mojave, and with the kindheartedness of a saloonkeeper named Hennage (a reincarnation of Harte's Oakhurst) who treasured a pressed rose petal right up to his sacrificial end, the significant action concerns the efforts of a red-headed wanderer named Bob McGraw to improve nature with the aid of his wits and his six gun. McGraw goes into "the great, hot, panting hungry heart of Inyo," where, by exploring a bit, he discovers and lays claim to hidden sites for dam and reservoir, which, together with the tunnel he plans to build for $50,000, add up to a reclamation project. Without a cent he sets out on his devious way. He obtains capital by blackmailing the villain, a promoter who represents unscrupulous absentee investment, and by tricking the government by filing false claims, the shady legality of which is expounded at length throughout an entire chapter. But McGraw's aims in all this are above reproach. He dreams of creating a model farming land for the poverty-stricken of the eastern slums—a wonderland fully equipped with free electricity, gas, and water. " 'I'm going to convert an Eden out of an abandoned Hell,' " he boasts, adding that he is going to accomplish this reform through the aid of the "God of the Square Deal." He hopes some day to look down from the slope of Kearsage and say: " 'That is mine. I helped to create it, and I did it for love. I finished what the Almighty commenced, and the job was worthwhile.' " Needless to say, he succeeds in bilking the government, unmasking the wicked promoter, and winning the orphan girl. The model community is not in sight at the end of the novel, however. Southern Californians who eventually learned that a former mayor of Los Angeles had posed as the employee of the United States Reclamation Service in order to buy up lands in Owens Valley surreptitiously, that a leading representative of the same service had resigned to work for the Los Angeles Water Board, taking his notes and maps with him, and that the Secretary of the Interior had declared a wilderness of sagebrush and cactus a forest reserve in order to keep it out of the hands of homesteaders, might well ponder upon the ethics of exploitation as exemplified by Kyne's Bob McGraw.

Mary Austin, who suffered through the days when it became clear that Owens Valley was to be sacrificed, also pondered those values. At the time that the first moves in the gambit became apparent, she was living in Independence, where her husband, the register of the Land Office, was protesting to Washington against the machinations of Fred Eaton and J. B. Lippincott. She says, in *Earth Horizon,* that she knew "that the land of Inyo would be desolated, and the cruelty and deception smote her beyond belief. There was nothing more for her in Southern California." Before she left Inyo, she made two prophecies. One, that Los Angeles would some day feel the moral responsibility for its acts, came true, she felt, when dynamiting of the aqueduct led to forced arbitration twenty years later. The other, that the City ("the City" is always Los Angeles to Inyo people) would be destroyed by the land itself, is a prophecy—stated in somewhat cryptic terms—that has not yet come true.

When Mary Austin wrote *The Ford,* published in 1917,

she drew upon her experiences in Owens Valley, merging them with many of the impressions she held of the southern San Joaquin Valley, where she had lived before moving to Inyo. She laid the action of this realistic account of economic inequality and social unrest in "Tierra Longa," a fictitious valley which resembled both Owens Valley and the country around Bakersfield. The novel is a story of reclamation in the broadest sense. Among other things, it tells much about the failure of the people to unite to defend their future, and it paints a shaded rather than a black-and-white picture of the role of the strong man in developing a desert area. More confused in its theme and less forceful in its drama than Frank Norris' *The Octopus,* it nevertheless merits a place beside that novel as an account of man's effort to remake nature.

For the attempt to conquer aridity is indeed the theme of *The Ford.* As an introduction to this theme, Mary Austin describes vividly a Southern California drought. The young folks, helpless in their plight, could do no more than talk despairingly of the thousands of cubic inches of water, of the refreshing streams that would have been available had there been scientific irrigation. The rest of the book deals with attempts to get that irrigation.

The story is frequently interrupted by detailed and important digressions, detrimental to the flow of the narrative but of much interest. There was the oil boom in which everyone thought he was going to get rich, and everyone except T. Rickard went broke. There were the machinations of this same T. Rickard, whose efforts in the long run paid dividends for the entire community, but not without posing a moral problem. "It came over him again that the key to the Old Man's success was, after all, knowledge, knowledge of land and minerals, knowledge of law, and, more than everything else, knowledge of men, knowledge of everything except that strange, ineradicable quality of men called righteousness." There was the failure, time after time, of the farmers to get together for their own interests. The community sense was lacking. And, taken from Mrs. Austin's Owens Valley experiences, there were the devious methods used by Elwood in obtaining options to purchase the land, so that he, or his masters, would control the water supply. The people, assuming that he was working for the United States Reclamation Service since he was provided with official surveys, trusted Elwood and made it possible for him to take up options right and left. Actually, however, the surveys had been given him by a former employee of the Reclamation Service; and Elwood, no government employee, was, in fact, working to take up the land so that the water might be funneled into the city hundreds of miles away. Mary Austin tells us that Elwood had

. . . looted the wilderness; he had led the river captive . . . He had climbed up Indian Gate and from thence he had had a vision; a vision of the river dammed and stored, not to unending fruitfulness, as Steven Brent had seen it, but of an arched, concreted aqueduct leading from the Gate to the city's faucets; a vision worthy of the most exalted cult of Locality.

In the end, however, the city found its water elsewhere, and the valley was saved. Thus, Tierra Longa escaped the fate of Owens Valley.

∽∽∽∽

In some verses titled "The Spirit of the Desert" a budding poet in San Diego expressed an article of faith that appeared often in the reclamation story:

> Then with the petals, and pollen, and sand,
> We built beautiful houses along the shore
> *Just alike for the rich and the poor.*

The assumption that the irrigation age would provide alleviation of economic maladjustment was constantly cropping up in books of the time. Too much of a realist to expect any sweeping social changes, Mary Austin concerned herself, in *The Ford,* with the problems facing the little people in availing themselves of the benefits of irrigation. Without capital and without unity they were fighting an uphill battle for their betterment, but they had a chance. Harold Bell Wright's seer, in *The Winning of Barbara Worth,* saw the Imperial Valley as a home for small farmers, heroes in the drama of man against nature. And Peter B. Kyne's Bob McGraw, in *The Long Chance,* considered himself to be a social benefactor. " 'I'm going to make thirty-two thousand acres of barren waste bloom and furnish clean, unsullied wealth for a few thousand poor, crushed devils that have been slaughtered and maimed under the Juggernaut of our Christian civilization,' " he boasted. In Ednah Aiken's *The River,* the social prophet is Brandon, the newspaperman who had come down the river with John Wesley Powell, that fabulous visionary of the West whose plans for reclamation had been as daring as his explorations. Brandon preached a gospel of a new way of life, a new democratic society of small landholders, self-sufficient and reliant, which would be created by the concentrated and controlled agriculture made possible by irrigation. To him Riverside was "the unreal dream of the socialist come true," and the Imperial Valley was to be the poor man's paradise. Unaware of the time when absentee landlordism and peon labor would be twin curses of the Valley, he asserted with complete confidence that the reclaimed land was to support a bit of Jeffersonian democracy.

Brandon was but echoing the ideas of William Ellsworth Smythe, sometimes called the Peter the Hermit of the irrigation crusade, who expressed more vividly and effectively than anyone else the social hopes that accompanied the reclamation movement. Smythe, a Massachusetts boy, had early absorbed the faith of Horace Greeley in the future of the West and in the virtue of colonies organized along Fourieristic principles. Moving to Nebraska, he found his mission in life when the droughts of the early 'nineties caused widespread distress. Having seen something of irrigation in the course of a trip to New Mexico, Smythe, in his capacity as editor of a local newspaper, led a crusade for irrigation in Nebraska to save the farmlands. The movement spread rapidly and with great success. "To my mind," wrote Smythe, "irrigation seemed the biggest thing in the world. It was not merely a matter of ditches and acres, but a philosophy, a religion and a programme of practical statesmanship rolled into one." A man of great energy, clear mind, and unlimited optimism, he devoted the rest of his life to the cause. In 1891 he founded a periodical called the *Irrigation Age,* the same year he organized the first National Irrigation Congress, and in 1893 he came out to Los Angeles to lead the first International Irrigation Congress. He wrote a number of books on his subject, the most important of which were *The Conquest of Arid America* (1900) and *Constructive Democracy: The Economics of a Square Deal* (1905). After establishing a colony in Idaho on the basis of his ideals, he moved his headquarters to Southern California at the turn of the century, where he founded a number of colonies, edited the *California Farmer,* and contributed to numerous journals. For a considerable period he ran a monthly department in *Out West.* He also took an active part in politics as a progressive, he organized conventions and lectured all over the country, and he helped with a number of government surveys. In San Diego, where he lived for a long while, he was prominent in civic affairs and wrote a most creditable local history.

Smythe's thesis, as expressed in *The Conquest of Arid America* and in numerous other places, was that aridity was a great blessing. It was not an accident, in his opinion, that many of the older civilizations—Egyptian, Palestinian, Persian, Arabian, Aztec, Incan—had developed in lands of low mean rainfalls. And he was convinced that "the better half of the United States" lay west of the forty-ninth parallel, in the regions in which farmers could not depend on seasonal rains for their crops. His reasoning was cogent enough. The West was fortunately arid. The minerals and salts which had been leached out of the ground in rainy zones here lay rich for the farmer's use. "The valuable ingredients of the soil which are soluble have been washed out of the land in humid regions, like our eastern States, by the rains of the centuries. On the other hand, these elements have been accumulating in the arid soil of the West during the same centuries." Smythe believed that irrigation in itself was a fertilizing process, partly because the silt carried by irrigation water increased fertility. Most important of all, the Western farmer was not at the mercy of the weather. "In the whole range of human industry nothing is so crude, uncalculating, and unscientific as the childlike dependence on the mood of the clouds for the moisture essential to the production of the staple necessities of life. . . . Rain is the poor dependence of those who cannot obtain the advantages of irrigation," he asserted. The scientific irrigation farmer was no longer subject to the ravishes of drought and flood; he got his water when he wanted it and in the quantity he desired, and he was able to distribute it according to the varying needs of his crops. To Smythe it was a symbol that Eden was an irrigated land: "A river went out of Eden to water the garden," he quoted. And he reminded his readers of the saying in Proverbs: " 'Make this valley full of ditches, for ye shall not see wind, neither shall ye see rain, yet this valley shall be full of water.' "

Smythe, the disciple of Greeley, was not satisfied with the conviction that irrigation produced more fruitfulness than seasonal rainfall but saw also in the practice a great opportunity for associative enterprise, indeed, a real necessity for coöperative organization. At the same time, he reasoned that irrigation made it possible for a family to be self-sustaining on a small plot without hiring labor; in fact, the large farm was out of the question. "The essence of the industrial life which springs from irrigation is its democracy. The first great law which irrigation lays down is this: There shall be no monopoly of land. This edict it enforces by the remorseless operation of its own economy. . . . A large farm under irrigation is a misfortune; a great farm, a calamity. Only the small farm pays." Moreover, the very smallness of the holdings would make it possible for the landowner to live close to an urban center. Thus the farmer would have the advantages not only of economic security but also of the proximity of cultural offerings.

Smythe's enthusiastic writings in *Out West* on the Owens River project seem somewhat pathetic. On the thousands of acres of San Fernando Valley to be watered with Sierra snows, proud and resourceful democrats were to live on an acre apiece, growing vegetables, small fruit, and poultry. It would be one great garden filled with beautiful homes. Electric cars would take the sturdy farmers in to Los Angeles to the theater or the opera whenever they wished to go. "The neighborhood of Los Angeles will supply the highest refinement which has ever come to the life of the common man." Ironic, indeed, when one learns that almost all of San Fernando Valley was bought up for a song by a few financiers before the Owens Valley aqueduct was put in, and that the promoters of the valley (and the aqueduct) later sold to the common man at a thousandfold the cost.

Smythe never stopped at words; he put his ideas into operation. Down at San Ysidro, near the Mexican border, he started a "Little Landers" community in 1908. The Lower Otay Dam provided controlled irrigation. For an average price of five hundred dollars, well within the limits of the purse of the sturdy democrat, the settlers each bought his acre of farmland and his lot in town and pledged himself to improving them within six months of purchase. The village was built around a park, and life prospered, with "a little land and a living." Then, in 1916, the citizens of San Diego, plagued by years of drought, hired the famous rain maker, Charles M. Hatfield, to bring moisture out of the skies with his extraordinary paraphenalia of open tanks filled with secret mixtures. (It is said that he produced forty inches of rain in three hours on the Mojave Desert near Randsburg.) Hatfield set to work, and the rains poured down. They came so fast that San Diego was isolated from the rest of the world. A second effort followed, in spite of the protests of the city council, and Lower Otay Dam was washed out. With it went the community of Little Landers, victims of the haphazard ways of nature (aided by a magician) in the face of man's best scientific efforts.

And yet Smythe's spirit lives on. There are many in California who live on their small holdings, and many more who insist that the economic welfare of the state agricultural lands —such lands as those developed by the great Central Valley Project—depends upon a displacing of large holdings with small farms, thus encouraging individual initiative. Time will tell.

IX

Pacific Electric

AFTER WEATHERING the dark days that followed the depression of 1893, Southern California was ready for another tremendous spurt, and by 1906 she was in the midst of her third boom, which brought more tourists and settlers, produced more towns, and enlarged further her established cities. But this boom was somewhat different from the earlier ones, for not only was Southern California growing physically but she was also maturing psychologically. As Harry Carr wrote of Los Angeles, "When it [the Spanish-American War] began we were still a hick town. When it ended, we began to grow into a city." The enthusiasm of the expanding, the boisterously expanding, society was comparable to that of the earlier periods of rapid growth, and in 1915 it was climaxed by the twin expositions at San Francisco and San Diego, celebrating the completion of the Panama Canal. Two years later, doughboys were training in California camps to go overseas, the Yanks were coming, and an era had ended.

How rapidly the newcomers arrived during this period can be learned from the figures. The population of the ten southern counties grew from 227,052 in 1890 to 337,328 in 1900, to 808,445 in 1910, and reached 1,423,756 by 1920. The number of Southern California communities having more than 2,500 people increased from ten in 1890, just after the Big Boom, to forty-six in 1920, when the world was returning to peacetime conditions. Los Angeles, spreading out like an organism which grows by cell division, absorbed mile after mile of area as its population increased. That doubled between 1890 and 1900, rising from 50,395 to 102,479; it tripled in the next decade, reaching 319,198 in 1910; and it hit the half-million mark in 1920, when it was 576,673.

With the increase of population came economic development, the result partly of the ingenuity of man, partly of the luck of the region, which had become almost legendary. Even the outside world seemed to be helping. Continued prosperity in the Midwest and East brought tourists, settlers, and buyers for Far Western products. Through the Spanish-American War the United States acquired an active empire in the Pacific, automatically increasing the importance of California ports. In 1905 the Japanese defeated the Russians in the Far East. The effect of their victory was, in America, to stir into action amateur and professional strategists who pushed for the enlarging and strengthening of West Coast fortifications and military installations—and the Pacific fleet began to grow and to become a more and more familiar sight in Southern California waters. The partial destruction of San Francisco by earthquake and fire in 1906 for a time diverted from the north to the south the flow of both settlers and business. The development of a good harbor at Wilmington and the opening of the Panama Canal in 1914 made possible the growth of trade with the East Coast and with the Orient. And World War I brought to Southern California her share of industrial expansion.

The growth of Southern California was manifest in many ways. In the economic field it was symbolized by a series of "firsts": the first trainload shipment of oranges in 1886, the discovery by E. L. Doheny of oil within the city limits of Los Angeles in 1892, the appropriation of money by Congress for a deep-water harbor at Wilmington in 1896, the inauguration of the Imperial Valley reclamation project in 1900, the primitive beginnings of the motion picture industry in 1910, the first Western air meet, in the same year, at Dominguez Field, the completion of the Owens Valley aqueduct in 1913, and the establishing of the Douglas Aircraft factory in Santa Monica in 1920. Political and social currents also indicated a changing society: the local adoption, in the period from 1905 to 1920, of the direct primary, the initiative and referendum, female suffrage, and prohibition; the emergence of Hiram Johnson to break the hold of the Southern Pacific; and the darker events which revealed the rift between labor and capital in a land dedicated on the one hand to the open shop and on the other to political agitation. The dynamiting of the *Times* building in 1910, the parts played by Clarence Darrow and Lincoln Steffens after the confession of the McNamaras, and the mobbing of the I.W.W. speech demonstrators in San Diego the next year were all milestones on a rocky road. Culturally, the change is shown by the birth of many famous institutions of the region. As has been mentioned earlier, the Pasadena Battle of Flowers (later called the Tournament of Roses) was started in 1890, and Los Angeles had its first annual fiesta four years later. The Mission Play was inaugurated at San Gabriel in 1912. Hollywood became Hollywood with the premiere of D. W. Griffith's *The Birth of a Nation* in 1915; and in the following year the amateurs and professionals of Hollywood and Los Angeles combined to give an outdoor performance of *Julius Caesar,* which in turn gave birth to the outdoor performance of Edwin Arnold's *The Light of Asia.* This in its turn gave birth, by miraculous processes, to a local passion play called the Pilgrimage Play and to the Hollywood Bowl. By 1920, Southern California had become her now-familiar self—breezy, brassy, aspiring, a hyperbolic representative of the nation as a whole.

By the time America entered World War I, Southern Cali-

fornia had come to be one of the principal playgrounds of
the nation, unpretentious on the whole, and quite naïve. It
was a sort of middle-class Methodist paradise, with enough
sunshine and oranges to give color, enough innovations in
the way of airplanes and automobiles and cafeterias to lend
excitement, and enough ruggedness—with its jack rabbits and
stingarees and hiking trails and surf bathing—to provide adventure. As good a way to get a glimpse of those days as any
other is to follow the experiences of the comic characters in
the humorous book called *Tourist Tales of California,* by
Sara White Isaman, published in 1907. In a monologue delivered in "hick" dialect (later made "literary" by Will Rogers, mayor of Beverly Hills) Aunt Pheba Harrison tells her
niece about the experiences she and Uncle Hiram had when
they sold the Nebraska farm and went to Southern California to see the sights. After a trip west in a tourist coach, in
which they boiled coffee and baked potatoes on the little stove
at the end of the car, they found California sunshine to replace Nebraska snow, explored the mysteries of an apartment
with a disappearing bed, and visited cafeterias where one
bought twice as much as he could eat. They had their difficulties trying to devour tamales with the shucks on, sampling
olives straight from the tree, and fighting the fleas at the
beach. They made a trip up Mount Lowe on the funicular,
explored Orange Grove Avenue and Busch Gardens in Pasadena, visited the old mission at San Gabriel, walked the pike
and went in swimming at Long Beach, ate at the ship restau-
rant and had their fortunes told at Venice, got seasick going
to Catalina Island, and gawked at the ostrich farm, the alli-
gator farm, and the fiesta of flowers. Finally, they bought a
house out Westlake Park way, picked up an automobile,
which snorted and coughed its way to the Nebraska State
picnic, and made arrangements to rent a cottage at the beach
for the summer. At the end of the book they were polishing
up their language, planning to take in a little culture, and

talking with the enthusiasm of the newly converted Southern California booster.

One of the phenomena that aroused most enthusiasm in Uncle Hiram and Aunt Pheba was the remarkable public transportation system always ready to carry them on the grand tour.

> Then we felt so glad and free,
> We started out to see
>   Los Angeles, the good old tourist town;
> From the ocean to Mt. Lowe
> Sight seein' we did go—
>   Rode them trolley cars for miles and miles around.

For these were the days of the Big Red Cars, when Southern California boasted one of the best electric interurban systems in the nation, or, for that matter, in the world, and the mournful hoot of the red cars was as omnipresent, as insistent, and as exciting a part of the land as the crash of the breakers at Santa Monica. Henry Huntington's interurbans were a great boon and a dominating factor in the Southern California of the early part of the twentieth century. This was the era of the Pacific Electric.

Back in the 'seventies, when Robert Widney introduced the horsecar to Los Angeles, he had been forced to redesign the carriage in order to keep the vehicles on the track when they took the curves. In contrast was the equipment of the Pacific Electric, which, in 1913, inspired a publicity man to write an article for *Sunset Magazine* titled "The Red Car of Empire." In this panegyric he grew lyrical about "the crimson chariot," "the red car with the invisible wings," "the flitting red car" which said to the suburban dweller: " 'I'll just wipe distance off the map, and your life shall be one long cocktail of orange blossoms, ocean beaches, and Spring Street.' " Other statements in his article were perhaps less poetic but somewhat more informative.

Los Angeles is the center and heart of the most highly developed interurban electric system in the world. . . . Within a radius of thirty-five miles of Los Angeles, there are forty-two incorporated cities and towns with countless country homes between. All these are literally of one body, of the healthiest and most rapidly growing body in America. The arterial system that holds them together is the double trackage of the interurban electric road. The red corpuscles that race to the end of every farthest vein to proclaim and carry the abundant life are the flitting crimson cars.

By the time this description was written, the up-to-date system developed by Henry E. Huntington between 1900 and 1910 had been expanded by acquisition of all the interurban lines in the area. It covered more than a thousand miles, with tracks going out from Los Angeles north as far as San Fernando, east as far as Riverside, south as far as Newport Beach, and west to the ocean. (Henry E. Huntington had once had dreams of sending the red cars up to Santa Barbara and down to San Diego, but these never came true.) The hundred million dollar corporation carried 225,000 persons 73,000 miles a day in its 600 cars, at between one-half and three-quarters of a cent a mile. It transported mail, sugar beets, oranges, tourists, and commuters who wanted "to sleep in the woods and have an office in the city." Yet at the same time it kept something of the small town quality and was genuinely proud to boast that it once held up the departure of a car while a widow rustled the dozenth egg in order to earn her mite and support her wee babe. It was unquestionably a first-class transportation system, far superior to anything the Southern Californian grumbles at today. As such it exercised an important influence on the pattern of the developing Los Angeles, which came to have loosely knit residental districts far removed from the business areas, a condition which has been referred to as "six suburbs in search of a city."

Both tourists and residents used the red-car system generously for recreation and education. Groups frequently chartered private cars for Sunday-school picnics, singing trolley parties, and moonlight streetcar excursions. It was great fun to return from a weiner roast at Redondo on the *Mermaid,* poppies barely visible along the tracks in the moonlight, and youngsters out on the wicker seats in the open section in the back of the car, singing "Down Went McGinty" and "After the Ball." One could always make the round trip to any of the beaches for fifty cents, and the famous daylong tours were not expensive. These rivaled the earlier Santa Fe Railway excursion trips on "The Old Kite Route," which went from Los Angeles along the foothills to Redlands and back to Los Angeles via the Santa Ana Canyon and the Fullerton valley —"No scene twice seen on the kite-shaped track." The Pacific Electric daily offered three "specials": the Balloon Trip, a swing down to the beach at Santa Monica, then through the boom towns of Venice, Manhattan Beach, and Hermosa Beach, on to Redondo, and back by way of Culver City; the Old Mission Trip, which mixed orange trees and ostriches with Mission San Gabriel; and the Triangle Trip, down to Long Beach, Balboa, and Santa Ana, with glimpses of forests of oil derricks, fields of sugar beets (the agricultural enthusiasm of the moment), and groves of almonds, lemons, and oranges. Best of all, there was the Orange Empire Excursion, run only twice a week, which took one to San Bernardino, Redlands, and Riverside. The high points of this expedition were the trip by tally-ho up to Smiley Heights near Redlands and the stop for lunch at Riverside Inn.

Henry E. Huntington built up his Pacific Electric empire rapidly and solidly, with the same shrewdness that had been shown by his more famous uncle, Collis P. Huntington, the most ruthless and most efficient of the Big Four, a man known throughout the country as "the Colossus of the Pacific." Born in Oneonta, New York, in 1850, the year his Uncle Collis reached California, the keen, acquisitive nephew hitched his wagon to the family star not long after the first transcontinental railroad was completed, and, after years of able administration in the Eastern branches of the Huntington empire, had come West as Collis' right hand man on the West Coast. He was more than an able lieutenant, for the childless uncle treated him almost as a son. (The family relationship was actually closer than that of nephew-uncle; Henry Huntington's first wife was the sister of Collis' adopted daughter; his second wife was Collis' widow.) One of his early duties in the West, the reorganization of San Francisco's traction system in the 'nineties, was, as it turned out, training for his later career. For after his uncle's death in 1900, Henry Huntington soon became the owner of the Los Angeles street railways, the developer of the Pacific Electric system, and the most extensive landowner in Southern California.

The emphasis in popular anecdotes shifted as the nephew's ability and strength became apparent. Before Collis' death, according to Horace Vachell, the yarn went around that the notoriously stingy C. P. Huntington acidly replied to a Los Angeles cabby when the latter remonstrated that he was not as generous with his tips as his nephew: "After all, I am not so lucky as to have a rich uncle." After the Henry Huntington empire had been established, a classic story, told about many another American financier, was adapted to fit the local hero. A small boy, after stopping at the Huntington Hotel, traveling down Huntington Boulevard on a Huntington electric car, and passing through Huntington Park, finally reached Huntington Beach and asked his mother whether God still owned the ocean or had sold it to Mr. Huntington.

There was a great difference between uncle and nephew, however. The man of iron who had put money-making before everything else and had scoffed at his partner's new Western university as "Stanford's circus" might indeed have been startled if he had known how his nephew was going to dispose of the Huntington fortune. Less than ten years after Collis Huntington's death Henry Huntington retired from active business affairs and started to accumulate the finest private library of his day, which was to become an almost unparalleled storehouse of documents and books dealing with

English and American history and culture, and to build up one of America's best art collections, which would include a peerless group of eighteenth-century English paintings. Such was the man who made the Pacific Electric the symbol of the period.

~~~~~

Two show spots of the Pacific Electric empire which in their aspirations and in their limitations were typical of the spirit of Southern California in the period between the Spanish-American War and World War I were Venice and the Riverside Mission Inn. Both were products of flamboyant imaginations; both attempted to transport parts of the European past to the American present; both were prompted as much by an enthusiasm for culture as by a desire to make money. Their immense popularity showed how fully they appealed to the folk imagination.

Venice was the product of the curious mind of Abbot Kinney, Helen Hunt Jackson's fellow commissioner, who has been described as "a student of law and medicine, commission merchant, botanical expert, cigarette manufacturer, and member of the United States Geological Survey." Ever since Kinney had inherited half of the Sweet Caporal fortune before he was thirty, the blue-eyed, sorrel-thatched adventurer had been looking for interesting things to do. For a while he roamed in Africa and Asia; then, in 1880, he settled near Pasadena, on the ranch which he named Kinneyloa—"Kinney" for himself and "loa" for the Hawaiian word for hill. After touring the Indian country with Mrs. Jackson, he became an enthusiast for marriage, and, finding a mate—whom he called another Helen Hunt Jackson—in the daughter of a San Francisco judge, proceeded to illustrate the theories of "creative reproduction," which he had put forth in his *Tasks by Twilight,* by fathering nine children. In the meantime and in between he helped to develop Yosemite as a national park, aided in securing the local enactment of the Australian ballot law, furthered the establishment of federal forest reserves, pioneered in the use of the eucalyptus tree in California, helped to found public libraries at Pasadena and Venice, and edited and published a local agricultural journal titled *Los Angeles Saturday Post; Fruit, Forest, and Farm* (1900–1906).

When Mrs. Jackson pictured Kinney in her story for children, *The Hunter Cats of Connorloa,* she described him as a wealthy retired man, finding pleasure in writing and science. As he once put it, he believed in culture and familiarity with literature as a means of development of a well-rounded character but not as a sole outlet for one's mental energies. In addition to helping with the report on the California Indians, he wrote books titled *Under the Shadow of the Dragon, Money, Protection vs. Free Trade, The Australian Ballot, The Eucalyptus, Forest and Water, The Conquest of Death,* and *Tasks by Twilight.* The last two are perhaps the most interesting, because they were manuals of social philosophy and sex education for his growing family; he felt that the two most important principles to be followed in improving society were the recognition of the right of the individual to enjoy what he earned and the exercise of creative reproduction. Pledged to a sort of modified Lamarckian evolutionary theory, he believed it possible to improve the race by persuading the best folks to mate with the best folks, to live well in a congenial environment such as Southern California, and to produce many children better than themselves.

In developing his Venice of America, Kinney entertained the optimistic idea that he could create a center of culture overnight by providing the surroundings that would attract settlers of taste and ability. As Newmark put it, "the dreams of his prime became the realities of his more advanced age"; as the doge of a new Venice, he would provide select entertainment for the cultured, good music for the masses, laboratories for the scientist, and a wholesome playground for the children. Characteristically, he threw all his resources into developing Venice once he decided on the venture. Promptly, sixteen miles of canal were dredged, weeping willows and gum trees were planted, and Italian villas were built. Gondolas and singing gondoliers were brought from the old Venice, as were pigeons, whose descendants still beg popcorn near the dismantled pier. The architecture of Windward Avenue, with the second stories of its Italian Renaissance buildings projecting over arcades, was intended to conform with that of the square of St. Mark, and a St. Mark's Hotel further carried out the motif. The art galleries included an Oriental building with a permanent Japanese display sponsored by the local Nisei; the aquarium was designed as a laboratory for studying Pacific marine life; the pier with its ship cafe was one of the best on the Coast, with a concert pavilion at its ocean end where Ellory's Famous Italian Band played and Madame Johnstone Bishop and other fine singers sang to the accompaniment of the great organ. A Chautauqua was inaugurated, bringing men of letters and scientists and musicians. Kinney hoped that there would be created a true folk university. Other plans included a deep-water harbor (Redondo and Santa Monica also talked in such terms) which would accommodate the largest ocean-going vessels.

But Venice was not able to survive on culture alone, much as Kinney had hoped it would. Even such stellar attractions as Benjamin F. Mills, the well-known liberal religious leader and evangelist, and Sarah Bernhardt, whose private train stood for two days in Venice while the actress played "Camille" at the end of the pier, failed to bring all the moneyed settlers he had envisaged. However, if Venice did not entirely meet the desires of the old folk from Iowa, it soon came to be a paradise for the children. Concessions from a Midway Plaisance in Portland, Oregon, and the huge Ferris wheel from the Chicago Fair, a big warm salt-water plunge, a miniature train, and a shoot-the-chutes added to cultured Venice a section which was probably the most pleasurable fun house America was ever to see. It was a Coney Island without a blasé person in sight, a carnival without a hangover. For perhaps ten years it retained its character, but changing tastes, social deterioration, annexation to Los Angeles, and local option gradually brought the serpent into Eden. When the day came that one could get a drink at Venice when he could get it nowhere else, the resort was doomed. Today it is little more than a slum at the edge of the water, although plans have been made to turn it into a municipal recreation center. Most of the canals have been filled in, because of their threats to sanitation; oil derricks have replaced Venetian villas; the miniature train no longer toots its whistle; the pier has been razed; the ship cafe is gone; the Renaissance palaces on Windward Avenue look like the tin shacks they really are; and the gondoliers' sons are no doubt running Bingo games. The old-timers in the local "greasy spoons" maintain that Venice went to pieces because Kinney's sons did not have the vision of their father, that "creative reproduction" failed to produce results. A much sounder explanation, however, lies in a changing world rather than in a eugenic failure.

On the opposite flank of the Pacific Electric empire, nestling in the Santa Ana hills, was Riverside, the home of the navel orange and the site of Southern California's most missionized institution, Frank Miller's Mission Inn. In 1874, soon after the arrival of the two Washington navels which were to become the parents of all Southern California's navel orange trees, Christopher Columbus Miller, a "location engineer" from Wisconsin, arrived with his family, to act as engineer for the colony development company. The big irrigation ditch which he designed proved to be a little slow in paying dividends; the company gave its engineer a block of colony land for back wages; and son Frank helped his father to make the adobe bricks that were used to build the Glenwood Tavern, a modest forerunner of the hostelry that was to be erected around it twenty-five years later. Frank Miller, a sensitive, imaginative boy with much the sort of rural Protestant background which Hamlin Garland had known, dreamed in those days principally about making a modest living and getting married. But as more and more people came to Southern California and a lively interest in the Spanish past began to take its many forms, Miller conceived the idea of expanding the inn into a kind of shrine, not only illustrating the architecture and furnishings of the mission days but incorporating many of the features of Mediterranean civilizations of the Old World. Spurred on by an unquenchable thirst for the romantic, the former farm boy who had seen no galleries and visited no cities set about building "the Alhambra" of the Pacific Coast. He was greatly aided by the financial backing of Henry Huntington and Charles M. Loring; by the architectural abilities of Arthur B. Benton, Myron Hunt, and Stanley Wilson; by the enthusiasm of such passionate pilgrims as David Starr Jordan, Sir Rabindranath Tagore, Jacob Riis, Zona Gale, Edwin Markham, and Carrie Jacobs Bond; and especially by the thirst of the Southern Californians for cultural symbols.

The growth of the Mission Inn as it developed wing by wing—the Mission wings of 1902, the Cloister wing in 1910, the Spanish wings in 1914, and the Rotunda internacional in 1930—reflected the growing sophistication of the region. Starting as a simple adobe structure, the Inn passed through the period in which Alhambra gargoyles were wedded to mission bell towers and eventually reached a time when El Mundo, "the international cocktail lounge," vied in popularity with St. Francis Chapel, the favorite marriage spot for flyers from near-by March Field. From the beginning of its period of expansion, the hotel ("a center of a peculiar kind, technically an Inn, but really a museum, a gallery, a collector's event") developed in a frankly eclectic manner, furnishing its delighted patrons with what was described as "the World Tour through Mission Inn." Typical was the Spanish patio: the west wall had come from Seville, the bell tower from Pala, the misereres from the Alhambra, and the ambulatory "wide enough for a banquet table" from a Spanish cloister; the clock tower was a replica of Anton's clock tower at Nuremberg upon which was inscribed the quotation: "Where there is no vision, the people perish." Eventually, the structure, which included everything from shrines to catacombs, exhibited "an astonishing variety of architectural forms, arcades, buttresses, flying buttresses, balconies, turrets, domes, pinnacles, made of concrete, and glazed and unglazed tile."

From the penthouses for writers, with latches instead of locks, to the Presidential suite, with its particularly ample chair built especially for Mr. Taft, the inn mingled informality with romance; the motto which hung in the Mission lobby told the visitor: "Ye canna expec' to be baith gran an comf'table." Frank Miller, who came to be known as the Master of the Inn, saw to it that his guests felt "like members of a great house party in some way moved back in time and scene to the days of the Mission Fathers." There was always something new to look at, from Ramona's spinning wheel to the great bell collection, which included a Manchurian gong, a Dutch landlord's bell, two church bells from the San Francisco fire, a cowbell inscribed "Paulus III Pontifex Maximus," a facsimile of Big Ben, and hundreds of other bells. "The palm-lined paseo winds round about, and over all rises the square belltower, whence float the chimes of morn and even." As if to give the hospitality of the Inn religious sanction, it was dedicated to the twin spirits of Junípero Serra and St. Francis. The only things lacking were the brown robes, which all Californians persist in thinking Franciscan padres wore in California missions.

Of an evening, particularly on Sunday, guests were invited to gather in the Cloister music room, which had some of the features of the baronial hall of a Spanish castle, and in addition a cathedral organ, wooden beams, and a minstrels' gallery modeled on those at Mission San Miguel, and decorations of swords, banners, and paintings. Most impressive of all were the stained glass windows portraying nuns and monks listening in rapt attention to the first Mrs. Miller, dressed as St. Cecilia, playing the organ, which was her favorite instrument.

A pet macaw, a traditional inhabitant of the central patio, was pictured in the upper corner of the window. In this atmosphere guests sat, expansive in voice and catholic in convictions, and sang while digesting their good dinners. The Mission Inn songbook gave a wide choice of secular and religious music, including a Jewish hymn, several songs by Mary Baker Eddy, a number of Latin church poems of an early period, and many camp-meeting favorites such as "What a Friend We Have in Jesus."

The constant mixture of the religious and secular in the Mission Inn did not seem particularly incongruous to the predominantly Protestant clientele of the institution, which did everything possible to make true Archer Huntington's remark to Frank Miller, "any enterprise which has an historical background and a religious significance has as good a chance of permanent success as anything on this earth." On the contrary, they were quite delighted with church architecture in a secular building, "with statues of saints in the dining room and in close proximity to the ballroom." "On the outside wall," boasted the official handbook,

St. Christopher . . . greets the arriving traveller and wishes him well at leaving, while St. Francis, Patron Saint of the Inn, as a weathervane on the Adobe chimney, blesses all sojourning guests. In the kitchen, various well-known saints look down benignly, inserts of Madonnas are interspersed with coats of arms, and signs 'Smile' and 'Don't Worry' keep the culinary staff in good fettle.

"You are confronted by sentiment, philosophy, consolation and inspiration whichever way you look," commented an enthusiastic visitor.

It is not surprising to find that the sunrise Easter services on near-by Mount Rubidoux, said to be the first of such services in America, were closely associated with the Mission Inn. Frank Miller, aided by Henry E. Huntington, led in the project of making Mount Rubidoux into a park, building a road to its summit, and erecting there a huge cross to commemorate Father Serra (who had probably never come within miles of the place). In 1909, Jacob Riis stood beside Miller in the shadow of that cross and suggested that a sunrise service be held there. For once Miller was a doubter: "No," he said, "you couldn't get them to come here for that. No one but Catholics would go out in the dark to sing and pray." But Riis insisted, and two days later a hundred people climbed the mountain in the dark to participate in a nonsectarian service as the first rays of light colored the horizon.

It was in this same year that Carrie Jacobs Bond was so thrilled by the sunset as seen from Mount Rubidoux that she rushed down to her room at the Mission Inn and dashed off "The End of a Perfect Day." The lyric of the song was soon printed on cards to be distributed as mementos for the dinner guests, and a room was set aside for any future visits to the hotel that Mrs. Bond might wish to make. Soon the song became very popular; it fitted into funeral services, particularly in Southern California, as effectively as its composer's "I Love You Truly" did into wedding ceremonies. Carrie Jacobs Bond, who settled down in Southern California for the rest of her life, was not a composer of sacred music; but in this area her songs seemed to fit into religious ceremonies with as little incongruity as the hotel rooms of the Mission Inn served as chapels.

〰〰〰

Probably the most notable cultural product to emerge from the Mission Inn was the famous Mission Play, which was performed almost daily in San Gabriel for sixteen years and was the high point of many a tourist's visit to Southern California. The idea first occurred to Mr. Miller when he attended the Passion Play in Oberammergau and became convinced that something of the sort should be undertaken in his part of the world. On his way home he discussed it with Dr. Henry Van Dyke, in New York, who referred him to Dr. David Starr Jordan, in Palo Alto. Dr. Jordan declared that the very man to write a great religious pageant for Southern California was John Steven McGroarty, the bard of Verdugo Hills. Upon investigation, Mr. Miller found that McGroarty was indeed the man, and, after persuading General Otis to give his employee a couple of months off from writing editorials for the Los Angeles *Times,* he took McGroarty up to Mount Rubidoux, where, "beneath the shadow of the cross erected to the memory of Father Junípero Serra, the plan was unfolded."

McGroarty was an ardent Irish Catholic from Pennsylvania who, after trying his hand at schoolteaching and practicing law in the East and in Montana, came to Los Angeles in 1901, when he was forty, and went to work for Otis on the *Times.* He had already written some rather pleasant newspaper verses before coming West; and his poems about California, which had appeared in the daily press and in such volumes as *Just California* (1903) and *Wander Songs* (1908), had won him considerable local fame. The best known of these was his poem about El Camino Real titled "The King's Highway," two stanzas of which read as follows:

It's a long road and sunny, and the fairest in the world—
There are peaks that rise above it in their snowy mantles curled,
And it leads from the mountains through a hedge of chaparral,
Down to the waters where the sea gulls call.

It's a long road and sunny, it's a long road and old,
And the brown padres made it for the flocks of the fold;
They made it for the sandals of the sinner-folk that trod
From the fields in the open to the shelter-house of God.

A good fellow who was properly modest about his poetry, McGroarty undoubtedly knew that his talent lay more in promotion than in poetics. He wrote several books about California, thinly disguised as history; he apparently had an interest in the Grafton Publishing Company, which published the *West Coast Magazine* (edited by McGroarty) from 1906 to 1914; and he promoted an ambitious real-estate development in the Verdugo Hills. He went to Congress as a Townsendite in the early 'thirties, was made Poet Laureate of California in 1933, and shared with Charles Lummis the honor of being made a knight of the Order of Isabel the Catholic for making notable contributions to the Spanish tradition in Southern California.

McGroarty's Mission Play, which opened in 1912 in a specially designed theater near Mission San Gabriel under the able direction of Henry Kabierske, was primarily a pageant which effectively utilized all the color available in the rich lode of Spanish Californian materials. The play, strenuously supporting the policies of Serra and his fellow Franciscans at the expense of Portolá and his military companions, opened with a prologue contrasting the Specter of the Faded Military Glory of the Spanish Conquest with the Spirit of the Ever-living Faith of the Cross of Christ; and throughout the performance the knaves, clowns, and villains were Spanish soldiers. The Indians, presented first as brutish, became lovable and competent under the mission system, brokenhearted and dissolute after its decline. The first act was concerned with the establishing at San Diego of the first of the missions and used as a climax the answer to Serra's prayers, the timely arrival of a supply ship after everyone else in the party had given up and was in favor of returning to Mexico. Typical of the "poetry" of the play is the speech by Serra in this act:

"How beautiful is this land of California; How bright are the waters of yonder bay—that noble and lovely Harbor of the Sun: The wild grape grows in the valleys and the roses are like the roses of Castile. How my soul longs to bring this land under the banner of our Lord and Saviour."

The second act portrayed the missions at their height fifteen years later. The scene was Carmel Mission, the occasion was a gathering of priests to report to Serra on their progress, the drama lay in the continuing conflict between Serra and the military, and the color was concentrated in an elaborate festival in which the Indians displayed the products they had made under mission supervision.

The last act, which was laid at Mission San Juan Capistrano in the 1840's after secularization had brought disaster, was of necessity an anticlimax and rested for its appeal on sentiment rather than drama. In addition to presenting a rather awkward lament for the departure of the glory of the mission, it suffered from being constructed around the improbable character of a fictional benefactress of Spanish lineage, Señora Doña Josefa de la Cortina de Argüello, who expired from an Indian's bullet just as the play came to an end. There was no particular reason for her to die, unless perhaps the actress who played the part was proud of her skill in portraying death scenes. She was Princess Lazarovich-Hrebelianovich, formerly Eleanor Calhoun, the daughter of Judge E. E. Calhoun, who was rounding off a dramatic career by lending her ability, money, and title (she had married a Serbian prince) to the cause of rebuilding mission romance. After she left the company, the part was revised and the bullet omitted.

Clearly, the attraction of the Mission Play was not primarily its history, its poetry, or its drama, but rather its unquestionably excellent values as pageantry. There was appeal in the richness of the costumes, with muleteers in rough boleros and slashed breeches, Catalonian soldiers as black-bearded as pirates, sandaled padres in their brown robes, and bespangled Spanish dancing girls; in the exciting movement of Indian war dances and Spanish fandangos; and in the lilting melodies of songs like "La Golondrina" heard for the first time by California audiences. Here was truly a brightly colored tapestry for a once-barren land.

∽∽∽∽

Not all the writings of the period seem today to be as forced and artificial as McGroarty's Mission Play, William H. Holcomb's *Old Mission Rhymes,* or Irish-born, Wisconsin-bred George Ward Burton's versified effusions for the Los Angeles *Times,* republished in *Burton's Book* (1909), which can be quickly characterized by quoting a single typical line: "Glory over me! I have seen Yosemite!" In contrast was the quiet, restrained verse of John Vance Cheney, for example, who, by the time he settled near San Diego soon after the turn of the century, was already an old man with an established reputation as a minor but competent poet. While writing his eleven volumes of poetry Cheney had supported himself by serving as librarian at Sacramento, San Francisco, and Chicago. It was when he was at the Newberry Library in Chicago that he had paid tribute to John Phoenix' exploits in San Diego by editing the Caxton Club edition of *Phoenixiana*. The son of a musician and himself a lover of music, he had tried, like Sidney Lanier, to capture something of the spirit of the kindred art in his verse. In spite of this somewhat experimental attempt he was, however, essentially a conservative in literature—and also in politics. He distrusted Whitman and abhorred free verse; and he won the $750 offered by C. P. Huntington for the most successful answer to Edwin Markham's "The Man with the Hoe," thus helping to rout radicalism.

Cheney's principal literary output during his days in San Diego (from 1903 to his death in 1921) was his book of poems titled *At the Silver Gate* (1911). Here he wrote sensitively of his hopes and fears, of natural objects such as the desert ("A great bare brain, a disillusioned mind") and the coyote ("In the sage-brush is whelped a fuzzy thing"), and of the brave acts of Serra and his followers. Among the best of his poems is his tribute to Padre Jaime, who was the first Franciscan to be martyred in California. In this poem, titled "The Wooden Cross in the Weeds," Cheney pictured the horror of the murderous attack on San Diego Mission:

> The savage, with his ax and brand,
> Could not Heaven's warrior understand.
>   "Seek Him, love Him, my children!" so he cried
> On the raw ranks of native men,
> Who only struck, and struck again,
>   And left him with the arrows in his side.

· A factual prose approach to this subject of the missions is found in the sober and reliable history written by the Reverend Zephyrin Engelhardt, O.F.M. Engelhardt, a German-born Franciscan, who had learned to know Indians when he was a missionary in Michigan, took up his residence in 1900 in the Franciscan Seminary connected with Mission Santa Barbara. Having earlier given evidence of his ability as a scholar and writer, he was appointed official historian of the order in California and spent his full time for the remaining thirty-four years of his life piecing together the records of the Franciscan venture in the area. The result, his *The Missions and Missionaries of California* (1908–1916), remains a basic and important historical document.

But in spite of the value to the scholar of Engelhardt's work, the best book to tell the traveler to California about the missions is probably *The California Padres and Their Missions* (1915) by J. Smeaton Chase and Charles Francis Saunders. By dividing their book between straightforward accounts of the missions, past and present, and legends and short stories connected with them, the authors turned out an attractive and helpful volume, marked by a simple, unaffected style that reveals the personalities of the two pleasant writers. The Englishman, J. Smeaton Chase, was a professional social worker (a settlement resident) and an amateur botanist. It was in the latter capacity that he wrote, in addition to his volume on Palm Springs, where he spent the latter part of his life, a handful of chatty books which include *California Coast Trails, California Desert Trails,* and *Cone-bearing Trees of the California Mountains.*

Much more prolific was Charles Francis Saunders, a Pennsylvania Quaker who had made a hobby of botany during the years that he was in business in Philadelphia. When his first wife's ill-health decided him to bring her West, the couple sought for a way of life that would bring health, pleasure, and enough profit to keep them alive. With her ability as an artist and his as a botanist and writer, the two issued a number of volumes, among them, *The Indians of the Terraced Houses* (1912), describing out-of-the-way places in the Southwest which had appealed to them and which they thought would appeal to others.

Saunders' interests lay in the natural beauty of Southern California, the aspect of the region which had appealed to Henry James during his visit in 1906, causing him to speak of the "charming sweetness and comfort of the spot." The wandering novelist wrote from Coronado:

> California on these terms, when all is said (Southern C. at least —which, however, the real C., I believe, much repudiates) has completely bowled me over—such a delicious difference from the rest of the U.S. do I find in it. (I speak of course all of nature and climate, fruits and flowers; for there is nothing else, and the sense of the shining social and human inane is utter). . . . I live on oranges and olives, fresh from the tree [*sic*], and I lie awake nights to listen, on purpose, to the languid list of the Pacific, which my windows overhang.

But Saunders preferred a more rugged nature than did James. He was perhaps at his best when writing about the Southern California mountains, which rose ten thousand feet from the Pacific to the great peaks of Mount Baldy and San Gorgonio. These mountains had been pretty much neglected except for some notes by John Muir in his description, in *The Mountains of California* (1894), of his trip into the Sierra Madre in the early 'seventies, although it is true that Harold Bell Wright in his best-selling novel, *The Eyes of the World* (1914), tried to capture the fascination of this country by having his characters rush from Redlands to the San Bernardino Mountains on every possible occasion, to absorb strength and morality from rugged nature; but the mountains evaded him as successfully as the desert had done in *The Winning of Barbara Worth*. The present-day reader-hiker will therefore do best to take his bedroll and coffee pot and visit that country of redolent pines, sparkling lakes, and lofty peaks in the company of Charles Francis Saunders and his *Under the Sky in California* (1913).

∽∽∽∽

Just as the Pacific Electric system stood as a link between the horse-and-buggy days and the automobile civilization that followed it, the literature of the first two decades of the twentieth century in Southern California was transitional in its ideas and methods of expression. At the very time that the members of the old school were doing the traditional thing, younger men in this area, as others were doing throughout the nation, were laying the groundwork for the postwar reorientation of American letters. Among the older school, Robert J. Burdette, famous as an Iowa humorist who had given his talk on "The Rise and Fall of the Mustache" more than five thousand times before coming to Los Angeles, found time, during his activities as the popular pastor of the Temple Baptist Church, to write poems, essays, and booster literature in which he gave genial support to the local squirearchy. The able Dr. Norman Bridge, physician and philanthropist, published small volumes of unexciting but sound advice with such titles as *The Penalties of Taste* and *The Rewards of Taste*. Jackson A. Graves, a prominent Los Angeles financier, wrote sententious articles for McGroarty's *Southwest Magazine* on the duties of the good citizen and later composed a volume of memoirs which might well have been titled "A Reactionary's Views on the Growth of Southern California." And Russell J. Waters, founder of Redlands, congressman, and banker, wrote a profusely illustrated novel called *El Estranjero* (1910), in which he mingled desert therapy, mental telepathy, and old-fashioned romance in a pastiche eulogizing God's great out-of-doors. At the same time, Henry Gaylord Wilshire was anticipating the social revolt of the 'twenties even before Upton Sinclair moved to town; Willard Huntington Wright was expressing many of the themes to be made popular by iconoclasts like H. L. Mencken in the postwar arraignment of American mores; and Robinson Jeffers, in his youthful poetry, was giving an idea of what the New Poetry movement would be like.

That Wilshire Boulevard, one of the world's most opulent shopping thoroughfares, should be named for a man who favored an immediate proletariat revolution is one of the ironies of Southern California. Henry Gaylord Wilshire, born in 1861 in Cincinnati and educated at Harvard, was involved in various commercial enterprises, principally advertising and real estate, in the Long Beach and Los Angeles areas from 1884 to 1900; it was in this period that he and William B. Wilshire opened up the Wilshire Tract and Wilshire Boulevard. Not long thereafter Gaylord Wilshire became a convert to socialism, began to deliver inflammatory speeches in the city park, for which he was jailed, and started a socialist journal called *Wilshire's Magazine.* In 1900 he moved to New York, taking the magazine with him; there the young Upton Sinclair met him as "Comrade Wilshire." During his restless career he propagandized for socialism, ran for the British and Canadian parliaments as well as for the American Congress on the Socialist ticket, edited the essays of the British Fabian socialists for American readers, operated a gold mine in the Inyo country to pay for his journal, and on the side promoted schemes for effecting perpetual motion and for curing all sorts of ailments with the use of a magnetoelectric belt. A small man with twinkling mischievous eyes, a black beard and pointed mustaches, he argued for revolution with the enthusiasm displayed by a sophomore who has just discovered the Communist Manifesto. This was the Wilshire who stated in his preface to *Fabian Essays in Socialism:* "I, as an American Socialist, put forth my patriotic plea in favor of my country's prospects of being the first to inaugurate the era of industrial emancipation. . . . The proletariat of the United States . . . should naturally and logically be the first to strike for economic freedom."

Even as Wilshire was a radical in politics, so was Willard Huntington Wright in art and literature. In the early 1900's when he was serving his apprenticeship as a writer and art critic he was the boy iconoclast of Los Angeles. After studying at St. Vincent's, the University of Southern California, and Pomona College, he went to Harvard in 1906 and from there to Europe. Returning to the West a bit heady from his cosmopolitan experiences, the twenty-one-year-old Mr. Wright wrote a series of articles for McGroarty's *West Coast Magazine* in 1909 in which he expressed for the local readers most of the tenets of the dogma which he and H. L. Mencken and George Jean Nathan were soon to publicize as editors of *The Smart Set*. Heralded as "a literary vivisectionist" who combined the iconoclasm of Ferrero and the cynicism of Shaw, he was apparently given free rein to say what he wished. What he said was that democracy was the antithesis of all art, that education was a mistake because by educating the masses we made them dangerous, that obfuscation was the mother of culture, and that civilization was not only useless, but dangerous and undesirable. Upon this prefascist doctrine were superimposed aesthetic concepts which at the time probably sounded childish to the Los Angeles readers but later were to be taken seriously by a whole school of artists and writers.

Wright insisted that the artist gave up his function if he assumed a social mission: "The artist who thinks he has a mission in life is done for." Particularly, the artist has nothing to do with moral issues, for "art has nothing to do with morals, and therefore can have no moral influence." Morals are for the youthful and unintelligent, invented to relieve people from the necessity of thinking. Art was best produced by men who cultivated sexual promiscuity because "Art is the interpretation of the sexual desire in terms of the differentiated senses. . . . Nine-tenths of all art is sex—the other one-tenth is perfume and lace." Marriage ruined the artist, convention stifled him, respectability was his death knell. It made no difference whether art was appreciated, because it was "solely a means of intoxication for the artist." With all these sweeping pronouncements went a condemnation of the mass of Americans who were later to be known as Babbitts or members of "the great American booberie." Even the vocabulary anticipated the slangy-grandiose technique to be made popular a few years later by the Mencken school. For instance, in ridiculing novels dealing with woman suffrage, Wright wrote: "The polyanthus flower of sexual equality is revealed to us in all its glory. We are permitted to share the mighty emancipation struggles of the anthropophagous fair." In later years Wright underwent a change of personality as well as of name when he became S. S. Van Dine, the mystery-story writer.

Robinson Jeffers came to Southern California with a precocious mind already stored with cultural experiences. The son of a professor of classics and Biblical literature who spent much of his time in Europe, young Jeffers had benefited from wise parental direction, supplemented by training in a number of European schools. By the time he came west in 1903, in his sixteenth year, he had not only a year of college in Pennsylvania behind him but could read Greek, Latin, Italian, French, and German with ease. In the two years he spent at Occidental College in getting his bachelor's degree, he impressed his fellow students with his ability, sincerity, and reserve and delighted them with his talents, displayed generously in writing poems for the student papers and reciting Homer and Virgil by the hour while hiking in the Sierra Madre.

The ten years that Robinson Jeffers lived in Southern California were important ones, for in them he completed his formal education, including some graduate work in medicine at the University of Southern California, he met and married Una Call Kuster, and he wrote and published his apprentice poems. These included those he wrote while at college and published in the Occidental College *Aurora* and the *Occidental* under such characteristic titles as "The Lake," "Mountain Pines," and "The Condor"; his contributions to *Out*

West, such as "The Stream" and "Death Valley"; and his first
book of poems, titled *Flagons and Apples,* printed in Los
Angeles by the Grafton Press in 1912. In addition, *Californians,* which appeared in 1916 after the Jefferses had settled
in Carmel, contained a number of poems dealing with Southern California.

Although these early poems do not use the free-flowing lines
nor contain the violent narratives of "The Roan Stallion"
and "Tamar," they are marked by choice of imagery and
theme amply suggestive of the later Jeffers. Even in his
Southern California days Jeffers drew a contrast between the
tawdry lives of his humans and the appealing beauty of nature,
particularly of the mountains—the Sierra Madre and the San
Bernardinos—and of the sea—at Manhattan Beach and Redondo, where Jeffers loved to spend his summers. And the
themes of these poems often suggest those common in Jeffers'
later poetry. In "The Quarrel," one of the bitter love poems
of *Flagons and Apples,* the poet gains relief from frustrated
passion by listening to a drunken Mexican curse his *mujer* in
the Los Angeles Plaza; in "Emelia," a beautiful girl whose
frustration has been likened to a Southern Californian
drought finds release in dancing naked in the pouring rain; in
"Stephen Brown," a consumptive tells how he has found peace
on the side of Old Grayback; and in "Maldrove," a misan-
thropic hermit living on Mount Baldy complains of the
stench of a degenerate age reaching him from the valley below. And yet there is beauty in these poems, the beauty of
yuccas upon hillsides—"tall and clear candles on the mountain's flanks"—, of eucalyptus trees standing cool and fragrant
in the summer's heat, of the sweep of the restless sea and the
moan of the thrashing wave. And it is in this feeling for nature
that Jeffers' early poems find their excellence.

〜〜〜〜

As with the rest of America, World War I proved to be the
end of an epoch for Southern California. Never again was

it to be as isolated as before that struggle, never again as nearly unique, as youthful, as forgivable in its excesses. The war fell as a curtain on the Pacific Electric era. The event which most satisfactorily crowned that era, that came as its fit climax and expressed its best qualities, was the Panama-California Exposition held in San Diego in 1915 and 1916.

In a sense, it was to the advantage of San Diego that both that city and San Francisco planned world expositions to celebrate the completion of the Panama Canal. In order to avoid too much duplication it was agreed that the San Francisco fair would be truly a world's fair, whereas the one at San Diego would specialize in Pan-American themes and would attempt to illustrate the concepts of the time concerning the Pacific Southwest. Thus the San Diego fair came to be more truly a dramatization of a regional culture, with its social and economic concomitants, than any other exposition which America had known. Other factors also combined toward producing a happy result. The dream of far-sighted citizens of San Diego, like George Marston, to develop a beautiful park on a tract reserved for that purpose in the middle of the city was aided toward materialization by the willingness of the townspeople to vote funds for the exposition and to join in the community venture in other ways. From the day that ground was broken in Balboa Park in 1911 the enthusiasm of the community remained at high pitch. Because men like Bertram Goodhue in architecture and Edgar L. Hewitt in ethnology were given free rein to develop their ideas, the exposition attained genuine dignity and influence in the arts and sciences. Because of the decision to make many of the structures permanent buildings, more care was used in developing the design.

The three themes of the exposition complemented each other and, as they were worked out, gave form and substance to the vague and sometimes bizarre search for a cultural background that had been characteristic of the region. The examination of "the social life and customs of the changing people of the Southwest" led to archaeological and ethnological displays dramatizing the shifting cultures of desert peoples, from the Aztecs to the Navajos. The emphasis on the importance of irrigation to a semiarid land resulted in scientific displays of many types of gardens, orchards, and farms and helped to earn the exposition the name "The San Diego Garden Fair." Finally, the happy choice of Spanish Renaissance architecture as the basic architectural theme of the fair, in order to symbolize Pan-American civilizations, not only resulted in producing much color and richness but made the people of the region conscious for the first time of the possibilities of a truly attractive Spanish style. Too long had they been hampered by the influence of the California mission. Bertram Goodhue boldly adapted the Spanish baroque to his purpose, giving to his buildings a beauty and variety which remain perennially intoxicating. Gem of the exposition was his tile-domed California Building, the central feature in the Spanish city which rose, with its towers and domes sparkling in the sun, at the end of the Cabrillo bridge. The richly decorated fairyland caught the best of the unbridled enthusiasm of a color-loving people; it fearlessly combined Spanish Renaissance and Spanish colonial architecture without violating taste; it stood as a reminder that Southern California was not an isolated island but the capital of a land; not the bizarre miscarriage of an expanding nation but the logical result of a long-developed culture. To visitors to the San Diego Exposition, the future of this land of the sun seemed assured.

Epilogue

SINCE WORLD WAR I Southern California has grown at a pace which has seemed miraculous, and with this growth it has lost many of the characteristics which made it unique in its youth. Just as the expansion of industry has made whole sections of the area look like bits of Detroit or Indianapolis, the standard-ization of American literature has tended to submerge the regionalism once so active. In addition, the superimposition of national—or international—literary movements, such as naturalism and symbolism, upon local themes, together with the emerging of new subjects, such as the concern with indus-trial conflict, has made it more difficult to trace a pattern in the writing, particularly without the advantage of the per-spective gained by the passing of time. Conclusions concern-ing the literary activities of the region since 1920 are, there-fore, presented in a very tentative fashion.

As in earlier days, Southern California after World War I continued to attract well-known literary figures who had nearly finished their careers and wished a pleasant place in which to pass their old age. Among these was Julian Haw-thorne, the son of Nathaniel Hawthorne, who healed some of the scars he had suffered during an unfortunate prison sentence in Georgia by living his last years quietly in Pasadena, where he contributed frequently to the *Star-News*. There was also Hamlin Garland, who lectured on the literary great and pursued the crosses of Serra under the impulse of spiritualism as he grew old in Hollywood. Gene Stratton Porter moved to Los Angeles and wrote some local fiction and composed some poems before she was killed in an automobile accident in 1924. Theodore Dreiser, in spite of feuds with the movies, found Southern California congenial, spending three years there in the early 'twenties and settling permanently in 1938, to pursue hedonism, mysticism, and social purpose until his death seven years later. There also were—and are—many foreign writers who chose the Southern California beaches or canyons as their homes late in life—men like Thomas Mann, Franz Werfel, and Aldous Huxley. Most of these have lived in the region without reflecting it in their books, although Huxley, in his *After Many a Summer Dies the Swan*, transferred the setting of his sophisticated strictures on what to him is a decadent world from London to Los Angeles. There are, of course, many books that were written about Southern California by visiting critics, particularly from Europe; their comments range from the comparatively kind remarks of J. B. Priestley in his *Midnight on the Desert* to the hilarious castigation in Evelyn Waugh's *The Loved One*. This latter satire is as severe as that of the American novelist, Myron Brinig, who disliked Southern California so much that he had an earthquake slide it into the sea at the close of his *The Flutter of an Eyelid*.

Stories for the "pulps" and "slicks" as well as best-selling novels have continued to pour out of the region that produced *Ramona* and *The Winning of Barbara Worth*. Paul Jordan Smith remarked in 1925 that the combined annual sales of Upton Sinclair, Edgar Rice Burroughs, Will Levington Comfort, Rupert Hughes, and Zane Grey, all then living in Southern California, exceeded, according to his estimate, the total production of all the novelists east of the Mississippi. Their places·have been taken by other popular writers—Earl Derr Biggers, James Tully, James Hilton, Lloyd Douglas, Frederic Wakeman, and Erle Stanley Gardner, to name just a few. Most of these write the same things here that they would have written anywhere else. More outstanding than any of these men and more important as a symbol was Will Rogers, who transferred himself wholeheartedly from Oklahoma to Beverly Hills before his death and came to represent to the world the best in American show business.

There have been a number of local writers who have turned their attention to regional themes, however. Most prominent of those concerned with social and economic problems is Upton Sinclair, who has lived in Pasadena since 1915, and Carey McWilliams, who has been much concerned with the fate of migrant workers, particularly the Mexicans, in the region. Scores of books have been written about Hollywood, ranging from Leo C. Rosten's sober sociological analysis of the moving-picture colony to stimulating and sometimes very amusing novels like Harry Leon Wilson's *Merton of the Movies,* John O'Hara's *Hope of Heaven,* Budd Schulberg's *What Makes Sammy Run?,* and Ludwig Bemelmans' *Dirty Eddie.* Of somewhat more serious intent are the works of two promising writers who died young—*The Day of the Locust,* by Nathaniel West, and *The Last Tycoon,* the unfinished chef-d'œuvre of the brilliant F. Scott Fitzgerald. Although they vary in degree of satire, humor, and shock, the novels about Hollywood nearly all agree that the life in the movie colony is artificial, the art meretricious, and the industry the graveyard of talent.

Much the mood of the Hollywood novels has been carried out in the brittle fiction of James M. Cain. His *Mildred Pierce* captures the frenzy of those who live on the fringes of Hollywood, and *The Postman Always Rings Twice,* a brutal story of murder and sordid intrigue, ends in a way particularly appropriate to the region—the heroine is killed when the protagonist strikes a culvert when he drives over the shoulder of the road to pass another car. More quietly concerned with the currents of life are the persistently probing works of Hans Otto Storm, such as *Count Ten;* the pleasant satire on the boom spirit in Mark Lee Luther's *The Boosters;* the light-spirited exposé of the follies of cult addicts in Jane Levington Comfort's *From These Beginnings;* the thoughtful social comedy found in Lee Shippey's novels, such as *The Great American Family;* the sensitive portrayal of the growth of a musician in Dorothy Baker's *Young Man with a Horn;* and the rather flamboyant basking in the sun of Frank Fenton in his *A Place in the Sun.* In this last-named novel there is more than the usual feeling for the land, a feeling which grows more attractive and pronounced as the writers get away from the city and into the country. There have been a number of able nature writers, such as William Leon Dawson and Donald Culross Peattie of Santa Barbara, but the spirit of the land and its people has been portrayed at its best by Judy Van der Veer, who presents truth as she finds it in the hills, and Max Miller, who writes graphically about the life by the shore. These people speak well, as do the local poets who write of what they know best—craftsmen like Hildegarde Flanner and John Russell McCarthy. And in perhaps the best of the regional fiction, the principal themes remain those used by Helen Hunt Jackson and Mary Austin—the mingling of races and the relationship of man to his semiarid environment. These strains are to be found in Edwin Corle's sensitive pictures of Indian life in *Mojave* and *Fig Tree John,* in Peter Viertel's account of a growing boy in a mixed community in his *The Canyon,* and in John Fante's portrayal of the wistful hopes of the Italian and Filipino in such books as *Wait Until Spring, Bandini* and *Ask the Dust.*

These books are not great books, nor are their themes new themes. They do, however, continue the effort to create a vital literary tradition, an expression of the spirit once characterized by Paul Jordan Smith as "a fevered yearning for vaster mental horizons." It is a hopeful spirit and may yet produce a literary flowering of which America will be proud.

Bibliographical Notes

THE PRINCIPAL items drawn upon for this study are listed below, with the exception of titles clearly indicated in the text and not used extensively for background material. Special lists of sources are given for the major figures whose biographies are based on materials other than the standard works of reference.

LOCAL JOURNALS

The Golden Era (San Diego, 1887–1893); *The Pacific Monthly* (Los Angeles, 1889–1891); *The Land of Sunshine* (Los Angeles, 1894–1901), continued as *Out West* (1902–1910); *The West Coast Magazine* (Los Angeles, 1906–1914); *The Pacific Electric Magazine* (Los Angeles, 1906–1932); *Touring Topics* (Los Angeles, 1909–1932), continued as *Westways* (1933—). Pertinent articles on the period and the writers were examined in: Historical Society of Southern California *Annual Publications* and *Quarterly* (since 1935), California Historical Society *Quarterly, Pacific Historical Review, California Folklore Quarterly* (now *Western Folklore*), *Grizzly Bear, California History Nugget, Overland Monthly, Californian Illustrated Magazine*, and *Sunset Magazine*.

MANUSCRIPT COLLECTIONS

The letters, manuscripts, and scrapbooks of the Jayhawker party, Horace Bell, Jeanne C. Carr, Helen Hunt Jackson, George Wharton James, Olive Percival, and Charles D. Willard, in the Huntington Library; the Charles F. Lummis papers in the Southwest Museum and the Los Angeles Public Library; the Benjamin Hayes scrapbooks in the Bancroft Library, Berkeley.

HISTORIES

In addition to the standard histories of California by Hubert Howe Bancroft, Theodore H. Hittell, Robert G. Cleland, and John W. Caughey, the following histories of Southern California were used extensively: James M. Guinn, *Historical and Biographical Record of Southern California . . .* (Chicago, 1902) and *A History of California and an Extended History of Los Angeles and Environs* (3 vols.; Los Angeles, 1915); Robert G. Cleland, *The Cattle on a Thousand Hills: Southern California, 1850–1870* (San Marino, 1941); and Glenn S. Dumke, *The Boom of the Eighties in Southern California* (San Marino, 1944). All census figures were compiled from the United States Census.

BOOKS DESCRIPTIVE OF SOUTHERN CALIFORNIA

Charles Nordhoff, *California: For Health, Pleasure, and Residence . . .* (New York, 1872); Benjamin C. Truman, *Semi-Tropical California* (San Francisco, 1874); Theodore S. Van Dyke, *Southern California . . .* (New York, 1886); Walter Lindley and J. P. Widney, *California of the South . . .* (New York, 1888); Charles Dudley Warner, *Our Italy* (New York, 1891); Peter C. Remondino, *The Mediterranean Shores of America: Southern California . . .* (Philadelphia, 1892); Robert J. Burdette, *Greater Los Angeles and Southern California* (Los Angeles, 1906); Charles Francis Saunders, *Under the Sky in California* (New York, 1913) and *The Southern Sierras of California* (Boston, 1923); Harry Carr, *The West Is Still Wild . . .* (Boston, 1932); Federal Writers' Project, *California: A Guide to the Golden State* (New York, 1939); Carey McWilliams, *Southern California Country . . .* (New York, 1946).

HISTORIES AND DESCRIPTIONS OF LOS ANGELES AND OTHER LOCALITIES

J. J. Warner, Benjamin Hayes, and J. P. Widney, *An Historical Sketch of Los Angeles County* . . . (Los Angeles, 1876; revised 1936); Yda Addis Storke, *A Memorial and Biographical History of the Counties of Santa Barbara, San Luis Obispo, and Ventura, California* (Chicago, 1891); Hiram A. Reid, *History of Pasadena* . . . (Pasadena, 1895); Charles Dwight Willard, *The Herald's History of Los Angeles City* (Los Angeles, 1901); William E. Smythe, *History of San Diego: 1542–1908* (2 vols.; San Diego, 1908); Charles Frederick Holder, *The Channel Islands of California* . . . (Chicago, 1910); Lewis R. Freeman, *The Colorado River* . . . (New York, 1923); Paul Jordan Smith, "Los Angeles: Ballyhooers in Heaven," in *The Taming of the Frontier*, ed. Duncan Aikman (New York, 1925); Laurance L. Hill, *La Reina: Los Angeles in Three Centuries* . . . (Los Angeles, 1929); Hallock F. Raup, *The German Colonization of Anaheim, California* (Berkeley, 1932) and *San Bernardino, California: Settlement and Growth of a Pass-Site City* (Berkeley and Los Angeles, 1940); J. Gregg Layne, *Annals of Los Angeles* . . . *1769–1861* (San Francisco, 1935); Boyle Workman, *The City That Grew* (Los Angeles, 1936); Margaret Gilbert Mackey, *Los Angeles Proper and Improper* (Los Angeles, 1938); George William Beattie and Helen Pruitt Beattie, *The Heritage of the Valley: San Bernardino's First Century* (Pasadena, 1939); Writers' Program, Work Projects Administration, *Los Angeles: A Guide to the City and Its Environs* (New York, 1941); Remi Nadeau, *City-Makers: The Men Who Transformed Los Angeles from Village to Metropolis* . . . *1868–76* (Garden City, 1948).

TRAVELERS' REPORTS

John Charles Frémont, *Report of the Exploring Expedition* . . . *in the Year 1842, and* . . . *in the Years 1843–44* (Washington, 1845); Bayard Taylor, *El Dorado* . . . (2 vols., New York, 1850); James Woods, "Los Angeles in 1854–5: The Diary of Rev. James Woods," *Historical Society of Southern California Quarterly,*

XXIII (1941), 65–86; J. Ross Browne, *Crusoe's Island . . . with Sketches of Adventure in California and Washoe* (New York, 1864) and *Adventures in the Apache Country . . .* (New York, 1869); William H. Brewer, *Up and Down California in 1860–1864 . . .* , ed. Francis P. Farquhar (New Haven, 1930); Stephen Powers, *Afoot and Alone: A Walk from Sea to Sea by the Southern Route . . .* (Hartford, 1872); Benjamin F. Taylor, *Between the Gates* (Chicago, 1878); Ludwig Louis Salvator, *Eine Blume aus dem goldenen Lande oder Los Angeles* (Prag, 1878), trans. by Marguerite Eyer Wilbur and published as *Los Angeles in the Sunny Seventies: A Flower from the Golden Land* (Los Angeles, 1929); William Henry Bishop, *Old Mexico and Her Lost Provinces . . .* (New York, 1883); Kate Sanborn, *A Truthful Woman in Southern California* (New York, 1893); William Ingraham Kip, *A California Pilgrimage . . .* (Fresno, 1921).

BOOKS OF REMINISCENCES

William Heath Davis, *Seventy-five Years in California . . .* (San Francisco, 1929); Harris Newmark, *Sixty Years in Southern California, 1853–1913* (New York, 1916; enlarged edition, 1930); Norman Bridge, *The Marching Years* (New York, 1920); Sarah Bixby Smith, *Adobe Days . . .* (Cedar Rapids, 1925; enlarged edition, Los Angeles, 1931); Jackson A. Graves, *California Memories, 1857–1930* (Los Angeles, 1930); David Starr Jordan, *The Days of a Man . . .* (2 vols.; Yonkers-on-Hudson, 1922); Frank M. King, *Pioneer Western Empire Builders . . .* (Pasadena, 1946).

BIOGRAPHIES AND AUTOBIOGRAPHIES

Mary A. Roe, *E. P. Roe* (New York, 1899); Zane Grey, "Breaking Through: The Story of My Life," *American Magazine* (July, 1924), 11 ff., and *Tales of Lonely Trails* (New York, 1922); Upton Sinclair, *American Outpost . . .* (New York, 1932); Harold Bell Wright, *To My Sons* (New York, 1934); Charlotte Perkins Gilman, *The Living of Charlotte Perkins Gilman . . .* (New York, 1935); Catherine Coffin Phillips, *Jessie Benton Frémont . . .* (San Francisco, 1935); Roy F. Nichols, "William Shaler: New England Apostle of Rational Liberty," *New England Quarterly*, IX (1936), 71–96; George Nidever, *The Life and Adventures of George*

Nidever (1802–1883), ed. William Henry Ellison (Berkeley, 1937); Zona Gale, *Frank Miller of Mission Inn* (New York, 1938); Susanna Bryant Dakin, *A Scotch Paisano: Hugo Reid's Life in California, 1832–1852* . . . (Berkeley, 1939); William B. Rice, *William Money, a Southern California Savant* (Los Angeles, 1943).

SOURCE BOOKS FOR BIOGRAPHICAL DATA

Who's Who in America; The Dictionary of American Biography; The National Cyclopædia of American Biography; Who's Who in the Pacific Southwest (Los Angeles, 1913); *Catholic Authors* (Newark, 1948); Zamorano Club, *The Zamorano 80: A Selection of Distinguished California Books* (Los Angeles, 1945); Ella Sterling Cummins [Mighels], *The Story of the Files* . . . (San Francisco, 1893); George Wharton James, *Heroes of California* . . . (Boston, 1910); Lee Shippey, *Folks Ushud Know* (Sierra Madre, 1930); Phil Townsend Hanna, *Libros Californianos* . . . (Los Angeles, 1931); Edwin Markham, comp., *Songs and Stories* . . . (Los Angeles, 1931); Franklin Walker, *San Francisco's Literary Frontier* (New York, 1939); Edgar Joseph Hinkel, ed., *Biographies of California Authors and Indexes of California Literature* (2 vols.; Oakland, 1942).

MISCELLANEOUS

J. H. Vincent, *The Chautauqua Movement* (New York, 1886); George Wharton James, *In and Out of the Old Missions of California* . . . (Boston, 1905); Zephyrin Engelhardt, *The Missions and Missionaries of California* (4 vols.; San Francisco, 1908–1916); Rufus Steele, "The Red Car of Empire," *Sunset Magazine,* XXXI (1913), 710–717; Edgar L. Hewitt and William Templeton Johnson, *Architecture of the Exposition,* Papers of the School of American Architecture, No. 32 (1916); Eugen Neuhaus, *The San Diego Garden Fair* . . . (San Francisco, 1916); Mary S. Gibson, *A Record of Twenty-five Years of the California Federation of Women's Clubs, 1900–1925* . . . (n.p., 1927); George Ellery Hale, "The Huntington Library and Art Gallery," *Scribner's,* LXXXII (1927), 31–43; Laurance L. Hill, *Six Collegiate Decades: The Growth of Higher Education in Southern California* (Los Angeles, 1929); Willard O. Waters, "Los Angeles Imprints, 1851–1876,"

Historical Society of Southern California *Quarterly,* XIX (1937), 63 ff.; Laura C. Cooley, "The Los Angeles Public Library," Historical Society of Southern California *Quarterly,* XXIII (1941), 5–23; Phil Townsend Hanna, *The Dictionary of California Land Names* (Los Angeles, 1946); Roderick Peattie, ed., *The Pacific Coast Ranges* (New York, 1946), particularly "Climatic Transitions and Contrasts," by Richard J. Russell, pp. 357 ff.; William B. Rice, *The Los Angeles Star, 1851–1864* . . . (Berkeley and Los Angeles, 1947); Erwin G. Gudde, *California Place Names* . . . (Berkeley and Los Angeles, 1949).

INDIVIDUAL AUTHORS *

Mary Austin: Uncollected poems and stories in *The Land of Sunshine—Out West,* VIII–XXIV (1898–1906); *The Land of Little Rain* (Boston, 1903); *The Flock* (Boston, 1906); *Earth Horizon: Autobiography* (Boston and New York, 1932); Mary Austin letters to Albert Bender, Mills College, Oakland. Henry C. Tracy, *American Naturists* (New York, 1930); Helen M. Doyle, *Mary Austin, Woman of Genius* (New York, 1939); T. M. Pearce, *The Beloved House* (Caldwell, Idaho, 1940); Dudley T. Wynn, *A Critical Study of the Writings of Mary Hunter Austin* (1868–1934) [an abridgement of a Ph.D. thesis] (New York University, 1941); *Mary Austin: A Memorial* . . . ed. William Hougland (Santa Fe, 1944).

Horace Bell: *Reminiscences of a Ranger; or, Early Times in Southern California* (Los Angeles, 1881, reprinted in Santa Barbara, 1927); *On the Old West Coast* . . . [a posthumous volume of sketches], ed. Lanier Bartlett (New York, 1930); *The Porcupine,* published weekly in Los Angeles, 1882–1895, ed. Horace Bell; Horace Bell manuscript collection, Huntington Library, consisting of manuscripts of articles, clippings, etc.; Bell manuscripts, Los Angeles Public Library. Anonymous, *Life of Horace Bell* (an 18-page pamphlet, n.p., n.d., probably printed in Los Angeles in the mid-eighties; a copy is in the Huntington Library); United

---

* Items listed previously have not been included under this heading even though they contain material about the authors listed here; and only the works of these authors that throw light on their biographies have been included.

States War Department, *The War of the Rebellion: . . . Official Records of the Union and Confederate Armies* (Washington, 1880–1901), references to Bell in Ser. I, Vols. XLI and XLVIII; C. B. Glasscock, *Lucky Baldwin . . .* (New York, 1935), pp. 225 ff.; obituary notices, Berkeley *Daily Gazette,* July 1, 1918, p. 8, and Oakland *Tribune,* July 1, 1918, sec. 2, p. 1; legal papers concerning Bell in manuscript collection, Southwest Museum.

Ina Donna Coolbrith (Josephine D. Smith): Poems in Los Angeles *Star,* listed and quoted in part in William Rice, *The Los Angeles Star* (Berkeley and Los Angeles, 1947). Ina Lillian Cook, "Ina Coolbrith," *Westward,* Vol. I, No. 4 (1928), pp. 2–5; legal records, Los Angeles County.

Richard Henry Dana, Jr.: *Two Years Before the Mast . . .* (New York, 1840) and *Two Years Before the Mast: . . . New Edition* (Boston, 1869); the latter contains Dana's account of his return to California in 1859. Charles Francis Adams, *Richard Henry Dana: A Biography* (2 vols.; Boston and New York, 1891); Samuel Eliot Morison, *The Maritime History of Massachusetts, 1753–1860* (Boston and New York, 1921); Bliss Perry, *The Praise of Folly* (Boston, 1923), pp. 53–62; Adele Ogden, "Boston Hide Droghers along the California Shores," California Historical Society *Quarterly,* VIII (1929), 289–305; James D. Hart, "The Education of Richard Henry Dana, Jr.," *New England Quarterly,* IX (1936), 3–25; *idem.,* "Melville and Dana," *American Literature,* IX (March, 1937), 49–55; *idem.,* "Richard Henry Dana, Jr.," biography in manuscript.

George Horatio Derby (John Phoenix): *Phoenixiana . . .* (New York, 1855): *The Topographical Reports of Lieutenant George H. Derby,* ed. Francis P. Farquhar (San Francisco, 1933); file of the San Diego *Herald.* George R. Stewart, Jr., *John Phoenix, Esq., the Veritable Squibob . . .* (New York, 1937). On Derby and Ames: William E. Smythe, *History of San Diego . . .* (San Diego, 1908); Millard F. Hudson, "A Pioneer Southwestern Newspaper and Its Editor," Historical Society of Southern California *Publications,* VIII (1909), 9–30.

Margaret Collier Graham: "The Angle of Reflection," monthly department in *The Land of Sunshine,* IX–XI (1898–1899); *Do They Really Respect Us?* (San Francisco, 1912). *The Land of Sun-*

shine, VIII (1897), 209; Elmer W. Holmes, *History of Riverside
County, California* . . . (Los Angeles, 1912); foreword to *Do
They Really Respect Us?*

Helen Hunt Jackson: *Bits of Travel at Home* (Boston, 1878);
Glimpses of Three Coasts (Boston, 1886); Helen Hunt Jackson
letters, Huntington Library. George Wharton James, *Through
Ramona's Country* (Boston, 1909); C. C. Davis and W. A. Alder-
son, *The True Story of "Ramona"* . . . (New York, 1914); Albert
Keiser, *The Indian in American Literature* (New York, 1933), pp.
249–252; Ruth Odell, *Helen Hunt Jackson* (New York, 1939);
Jeanne C. Carr papers, Huntington Library.

George Wharton James: *The Guiding Light* (Oakland, 1888);
How I Eliminated Fear, pamphlet (Holyoke, Mass. n.d.); *Living
the Radiant Life: A Personal Narrative* (Pasadena, 1916): *Quit
Your Worrying!* (Pasadena, 1916). Details of his dismissal from
pulpit and divorce: Los Angeles *Times,* April 24, 25, 29, 30; July
2; September 19, 21, 1889; Los Angeles County Superior Court
Records, No. 10, 453; "Divorce Complaint, Emma *vs.* G. W.
James." A. B. Ward (Alice Ward Bailey), *The Sage Brush Parson*
(Boston, 1906), based, according to data in George Wharton
James's scrapbooks (Huntington Library), on James's life; Charles
F. Lummis, "Untruthful James," *The Land of Sunshine,* XIV
(1901), 215–217; Henry M. Bland, "George Wharton James,"
Out West, May, 1912; James manuscript collection, Huntington
Library, containing notebooks, letters, scrapbooks of clippings,
photographs, etc.

Robinson Jeffers: "The Stream," *Out West,* XXIII (1904), 331;
"Death Valley," *Out West,* XXVI (1907), 443. *Robinson Jeffers:
1905–1935,* pamphlet describing exhibition commemorating thir-
tieth anniversary of his graduation from Occidental College (Los
Angeles, 1935); Melba B. Bennett, *Robinson Jeffers and the Sea*
(San Francisco, 1936); Lawrence C. Powell, *An Introduction to
Robinson Jeffers* (enlarged edition, Pasadena, 1940).

Abbot Kinney: *Tasks by Twilight* (New York, 1893). Helen
Hunt Jackson, *The Hunter Cats of Connorloa* (Boston, 1884);
Los Angeles County: Pen Pictures from the Garden of the World
(Chicago, 1889), pp. 525 ff.; see also entries under H. H. Jackson,
particularly Odell, James, and Davis and Alderson. On Venice:
Federal Writers' Projects, *Los Angeles* and *California;* Nancy

Langley, "Venice: In Beavers and Bustles," *Touring Topics,* XXVII (1935), 24–25.

Charles Fletcher Lummis: *A Tramp Across the Continent* . . . (New York, 1892); *The King of the Broncos* . . . , containing "My Friend Will" (New York, 1897); *A Bronco Pegasus,* with many autobiographical notes (Boston and New York, 1928); *The Land of Sunshine—Out West,* ed. Lummis, January, 1895–November, 1909 (with C. A. Moody, February, 1903–November, 1909). *The Works of Charles F. Lummis,* pamphlet (Los Angeles, 1928); Charles D. Willard, "Charles F. Lummis," *The Land of Sunshine,* I (1894); "Charles F. Lummis," *Out West,* XXX (1909), 366–367; George Wharton James, "The *Out West* Magazine," *Overland Monthly,* LXXXI (1923), 10–11; Perry Worden, "Agua Manse: Historical Gleanings," Pasadena *Star-News,* March 31, 1934; Edgar L. Hewitt, "Lummis the Inimitable," *El Palacio,* Vol. LI, No. 9 (1944), pp. 161–176; Francis E. Watkins, "He Said It with Music," *California Folklore Quarterly,* I (1942), 359–367, and "Collectors and Collections," *ibid.,* pp. 99–101; Sidney R. Cowell, "The Recording of Folk Music in California," *ibid.,* pp. 7–23; Henry Edmond Earle, "An Old Time Collector: Reminiscences of C. F. Lummis," *ibid.,* pp. 179–183; Farnsworth Crowder, "The Most Unforgettable Character I've Met," *The Reader's Digest* (April, 1947), pp. 121–126; C. D. Willard papers, Huntington Library; G. W. James scrapbooks, Huntington Library; Lummis manuscript collection, Los Angeles Public Library, including letters from Lummis to Maurice M. Newmark, 1923–1927; Lummis collection, Southwest Museum, Los Angeles, made up of letters, photographs, clippings, phonograph recordings, and much miscellaneous material, including a short manuscript biography of Lummis by his daughter, Turbese Lummis.

Lewis Manly: *Death Valley in '49* . . . (San Jose, 1894). Horace S. B. Foote, ed., *Pen Pictures from the Garden of the World; or, Santa Clara County* . . . (Chicago, 1888); John G. Ellenbecker, *The Jayhawkers of Death Valley* (Marysville, Kansas, 1938); Carl I. Wheat, "Trailing the Forty-niners through Death Valley," *Sierra Club Bulletin,* XXIV (1939), 74–108; Margaret Long, *The Shadow of the Arrow* (Caldwell, Idaho, 1941); "Jayhawker Papers" (14 volumes of correspondence, clippings, etc.), Huntington Library.

James Ohio Pattie: *The Personal Narrative of James O. Pattie*
. . . (Cincinnati, 1831), ed. Timothy Flint: *ibid.* (Cleveland,
1905), with notes by R. G. Thwaites; *ibid.* (Chicago, 1930), with
notes by M. M. Quaife. Stephen C. Foster, "A Sketch of Some of
the Earliest Kentucky Pioneers of Los Angeles," Historical Society of Southern California *Publications,* Vol. I, Part 3 (1887), pp.
30–35; John E. Kirkpatrick, *Timothy Flint* . . . (Cleveland,
1911); Harrison C. Dale, *The Ashley-Smith Explorations and the
Discovery of a Central Route to the Pacific, 1822–1829* (Cleveland,
1918); Charles L. Camp, "The Chronicles of George C. Yount,"
California Historical Society *Quarterly,* II (1923), 3–66; Joseph J.
Hill, "Ewing Young in the Fur Trade of the American Southwest," *Oregon Historical Quarterly,* XXIV (1923), 1–35; *idem.,*
"New Lights on Pattie and the Southwest Fur Trade," *South-
western Historical Quarterly,* XXVI (1923), 243–254; *idem., The
History of Warner's Ranch and Its Environs* (Los Angeles, 1927).

Alfred Robinson: *Life in California* . . . (New York, 1846);
ibid. (San Francisco, 1891), with additional material by Robinson;
ibid. (San Francisco, 1925), with notes by Thomas C. Russell; reprint of *Chinigchinich* (Santa Ana, 1933), with notes by John P.
Harrington; *California: An Historical Poem* (San Francisco,
1889); H. D. Barrows, "Alfred Robinson," Historical Society of
Southern California *Publications,* IV (1899), 234–236; Adele Ogden, "Alfred Robinson, New England Merchant in Mexican California," California Historical Society *Quarterly,* XXIII (1944),
193–202, 301–334.

Henryk Sienkiewicz: *Let Us Follow Him* . . . , tr. from the
Polish by Jeremiah Curtin (Boston, 1897); *Tales from Henryk
Sienkiewicz* (London, Toronto, and New York, 1931); *Orso* (San
Francisco, 1939), with biographical foreword by Carey Mc-
Williams; M. H. McCoy, "Modjeska's Mountain Home," *The
Land of Sunshine,* VI (1897), 65 ff.; William Winter, *The Wallet
of Time* . . . (New York, 1913); J. E. Pleasants, *The History of
Orange County* (Los Angeles, 1931), I, 345–354.

William Ellsworth Smythe: *The Conquest of Arid America*
(New York, 1900; enlarged, 1905); "The Twentieth Century
West," monthly department in *The Land of Sunshine—Out West*
(1901 seriatim); "The Social Significance of the Owens River Project," *Out West,* XXIII (1905), 443 ff. *The Land of Sunshine,* XIII

(1900), 416–418; George Wharton James, *Heroes of California* . . . (Boston, 1910), pp. 465–481; Clarence Alan McGrew, *City of San Diego and San Diego County* . . . (Chicago and New York, 1922), I, 198 ff.

Joseph P. Widney: *The Race Life of the Aryan Peoples* (2 vols.; New York and London, 1907); numerous books and pamphlets published in Hollywood and Los Angeles, 1909 seriatim, including *All-Fader, Ahasuerus, The Song of the Engle People, The Greater City of Los Angeles,* etc.; "The Colorado Desert," *Overland Monthly,* X (1873), 44–50. *Los Angeles County: Pen Pictures from the Garden of the World* (Chicago, 1889), pp. 200–201; J. R. McCarthy, *California History Nugget,* VII (1939), 35–39, and *Westways,* XXVII (1935), 22–23; Los Angeles *Times,* June 4, 1900, p. 7.

Index